Rough
Medicine

Rough Medicine

Surgeons at Sea in the Age of Sail

Joan Druett

ROUTLEDGE

NEW YORK

Published in 2001 by
Routledge
29 West 35th Street
New York, NY 10001

Routledge is an imprint of the Taylor & Francis Group.

Copyright © 2000 by Joan Druett

Original illustrations © 2000 by Ron Druett

Printed in the United States of America on acid-free
paper.

Design: Angela Foote

10 9 8 7 6 5 4 3 2 1

Library of Congress Cataloging-in-Publication Data

Druett, Joan.
    Rough medicine: surgeons at sea in the age of sail /
Joan Druett.
        p. cm.
    Includes bibliographical references and index.
    ISBN 0-415-92452-9
    1. Medicine, Naval—South Pacific Ocean—His-
tory—19th century. 2. Ship physicians—South Pacific
Ocean—History—19th century. 3. Whaling—South
Pacific Ocean—History. I. Title.

RC986.D78 2000
616.9'8024'09034—dc21   00-034474

CONTENTS

ACKNOWLEDGMENTS

Writing and researching *Rough Medicine* would not have been possible without the help and encouragement of many repositories and many people. I cannot even start without first registering my deep gratitude to Honore Forster, bibliographer, whaling historian, and chronicler of whaling surgeons, who so generously encouraged me to embark on this book. In particular, I thank her for permission to quote from her transcriptions and discussions of the John Wilson and John Lyell journals. In this respect, I also acknowledge the Royal Geographical Society, the holders of the John Wilson journal, and the Perth Museum and Art Gallery and the Kinross Council, holders of the Lyell collection. Thanks are due to Mark Hall of the latter repository for his help with the Lyell image. Additionally, I thank Niel Gunson for his generous permission to utilize his transcription and extensive annotation of the William Dalton journal, which is held at the National Library of Australia.

None of the microfilms and serials could have been read without the interest and assistance of staff at the Alexander Turnbull Library, National Library of New Zealand. It is a privilege to be associated with this library and its fine collection. And the microfilm collection would not be there in the first place if it were not for the Pacific Manuscripts Bureau at the Australian National University. Also on the far side of the Tasman Sea, staff members of the Dixson Library of the State Library of New South Wales have been as patient as ever in my researches into Eliza Underwood and the Sussex of her time. I thank the Hocken Library, Dunedin, New Zealand, for their help with the Hodgkinson diary, and I am particularly grateful to the medical librarians at the Philson Library, University of Auckland, New Zealand, for their assistance with the Denman memoir. In regard to the "Knyveton" journals, I am grateful to Robert Hale, publishers, and the legal firm of Taylor Vintner, Cambridge, England, the executors of the Ernest A. Gray estate, for their help and advice. In this respect, I also owe thanks to Tina Craig, Deputy Librarian at the Royal College of Surgeons of England, for her detective work with the Denman memoir and also for providing details of Dr. Fysh's career.

I am also very grateful to Betsy Lowenstein, Library Director of the Nantucket Historical Association for her invaluable advice and assistance with the Eldred Fysh journal and the John B. King collection, and I thank the association, too, for allowing the use of the Eldred E. Fysh and John B. King journals, along with the image of the Winslow family. Mr. Les Ottinger, library volunteer, was also helpful. That I have been able to flesh out Dr. Fysh's background owes much to the ready help given by Norfolk genealogists on the mailing list NORFOLK-L, available via the rootsweb.com website. I thank Judy Jones, Hazel Fuller, Sandie Slater, and most particularly John Fysh, who provided so much relevant detail.

Locating the same genealogical details for James Brown and Robert Smith Owen would not have been possible without the expert assistance of Stephen Freeth, Keeper of Manuscripts at the Guildhall Library in London. I am also grateful to the Old Dartmouth Historical Society at the New Bedford Whaling Museum for the use of the James Brown and Tom Noddy materials and the use of the image of the Roderick scrimshaw plaque. I am also very grateful indeed to Dr. Janet West for her invaluable help with this last, and thank Judith Downey for her friendly advice as well. Much gratitude is also owed to the Kendall Whaling Museum and Dr. Stuart Frank for permission to use the Robert Smith Owen journal, which came in the same generous spirit of friendly cooperation that has marked their response to my many similar requests over the years. Michelle Gait, librarian at the University of Aberdeen, has been both interested and helpful.

Searching out the history of medicine would not have been nearly so easy without the active help and encouragement of Dr. Martin Evans and Dr. Janet West. With regard to Tobias Smollett and *The Adventures of Roderick Random*, I am grateful for hints cast by Professor Paul-Gabriel Boucé. In Belgium, Patrick Marioné put aside his own very demanding researches to translate an eighteenth-century text, *Le Traité des Matières Médicales de Maistral*, and to make emplastra meaningful. In this respect, I also owe much gratitude to Dr. Mark Anderson. I am a social historian, not a physician, and the credit for medical details belongs to these two gentlemen. If there are any mistakes, they are all my own. For additional help with herbs and pharmacology, I thank Michelle Druett, Christine Markel Lampe, Gail Selinger, Tamara Eastman, John Richard Stephens, and Ken Kinkor. I am also grateful to Wes Stewart and his amanuensis and wife, Starla, who interpreted prerevolutionary medical qualifications for me. I am ever in the debt of David Meagher, who generously adapted his wonderful drafts of the Tudor warship *Mary Rose* for my purposes. I also thank Stuart Vine of the *Mary Rose* Trust for his interest.

In searching out the Sussex of the time, I am grateful first to Mr. M. J. Leppard and the East Grinstead Society, who started me on the trail that led to Jean M. Whyte and the Sussex Archaeological Society, Richard Philcox and the Sussex Record Society, and Roger Davey and the East Sussex County Council. More recently, the members of the Internet group "sussexpast" have been interested and helpful, as has Chris Whittick, archivist at the East Sussex Record Office. My thanks to all, and also to Frank Haill, who pried around in the records of West Sussex and Chichester. For the statistics of South Sea whaling, all researchers in the field owe a vast debt to A. G. E. Jones. I must also express my deep gratitude to Mr. Jones for his detailed personal correspondence with me, which proved both helpful and revealing. I thank Rhys Richards for his constant interest and informed help. Gillian Smythe has been an enthusiastic searcher, though her passion for Arctic medicine has to wait for another book before I can do it justice. For details of the Southern Fishery and the Timor ground, I am very grateful to Dale Chatwin and Nick Burningham. And of course I must thank my husband, Ron, for his patience, interest, and artwork.

Last, but not least, I must express my deep gratitude to Brendan O'Malley and Deirdre Mullane of Routledge. And it would be impossible to close this list without an acknowledgment of my debt to my dedicated and hardworking agent, Laura Langlie.

Introduction

On THE FIRST DAY OF SPRING IN THE YEAR 1829, A MARITIME MERCHANT named Captain Philip Skelton rode out from his home and office in Harden Street, off Commercial Road in the East End of London, to find a crew for the maiden voyage of his newly built ship. This was the whaleship *Kingsdown*, presently being readied for a cruise in the Indian Ocean, the East Indies, and the Pacific, a voyage that would take at least two years to complete.

Skelton's quest for men was by no means easy. For both tradesmen and laborers, life in the East End of London could be miserable, but nevertheless it was not nearly as hazardous as a trip to the far east of Asia, where tropical diseases abounded, along with pirates, savages, typhoons, and uncharted reefs. That the whaling business was generally despised had to be taken into consideration, too. Career seamen were contemptuous of the "blubber-hunters," calling them "stinkers" for the very good reason that whaleships smelled disgusting when blubber from whales was being rendered into oil in the great cauldrons that were set into their decks. Skelton, as it happens, would have been reluctant to take on ordinary merchant seamen anyway, for whalemen had to be at home in small boats, and there was not a merchant seaman alive who regarded a small boat as anything more than the last flimsy chance in a shipwreck.

It was not as if he needed just a few men, either, for whalers required a much larger crew than ordinary cargo-carrying merchantmen of similar size. While the *Kingsdown* was rated at only 346 tons, she carried four whaleboats slung out on her sides, ready for lowering the instant whales were sighted, and each one of these boats had to be crewed by an officer and five oarsmen. At least four seamen had to remain on board to steer the ship and manage the sails while the boats were away chasing whales. Additionally, there had to be a cook, a steward, a cabin boy, a carpenter, a blacksmith (often called an armourer), and a surgeon, adding up to a complement of thirty-five including the captain, Michael Underwood, who had already been appointed. Even so, the tally was not as large as for Greenland whalers, which carried a crew of fifty on their seasonal ventures into the Arctic, nor as big as the complement of a hundred or so that an East Indiaman of the same tonnage demanded, but on that fourteenth day of April, 1829, whaleship owner Philip Skelton faced quite a challenge.

Accompanied by a clerk, he headed well out of town. Up until relatively recently, whaling crews had been drawn from the maritime villages along the Thames, the building, outfitting, provisioning, and crewing of South Seamen being a hamlet affair, often resulting in whalers that were crewed almost entirely by brothers and cousins. This was no longer the case, however. Since the end of the Napoleonic Wars, the rapidly expanding industrial age had led to a flood of countryfolk into the river towns, so that the neighborly quality of the Limehouse, Ratcliff, Deptford, and Southwark villages had vanished. Slum dwellers did not make good crewmen, so the owners and masters of South Seamen were forced to go out to the provinces in search of their crews. Many owners were looking as far afield as Wales, but Captain Philip Skelton chose to ride to Heathfield in the Sussex Weald, where he hired a booth at the Cuckoo Fair.

The fair, which traditionally opened on St. Tibertius' Day—the fourteenth of April, the first day of spring—and lasted three days, must have presented a most charming picture as Philip Skelton and his clerk arrived. Booths would have rimmed the big meadow, many of them fashioned from boughs cut from nearby thickets and all of them would have been surrounded by knots of people. Hawkers and street performers surged in from as far as the City, so that shrill cries of *Hot pies hot! and Ripe speragras!* and *Goose-gogs, goose-berries, goose-gogs all an-early-oh!* mingled with the rhythmic growls of smocked and gaitered shepherds as they counted off their newly washed sheep in the ancient Sussex style—

Lewes, Sussex, 1824. COURTESY SUSSEX ARCHAEOLOGICAL SOCIETY

Quietly prosperous despite a sometimes turbulent history, this agricultural center of East Sussex also enjoyed a thriving trade by sea. The Sons of Lewes and the surrounding farmlands crewed the "hoggies" that plied the River Ouse, going out after shoals of herring—and manned the South Seamen that spanned the Indian Ocean and Pacific in the hunt for the spermaceti whale.

One-erum, two-erum, cockerum, shakerum, tarry-diddle-dee—to make a group of five. Tightrope-walkers, people on stilts, performing animals, pugilists, and Punch and Judy shows would have provided entertainment, while farmers conducted business under clumps of newly sprouting trees.

Despite the holiday nature of the occasion, a rural fair was a shrewd choice for Skelton's hunt for a whaling crew. Countryfolk had many of the necessary skills of seamen, for they were accustomed to working with tools in the fields and with nets, sculls, sails, and lines in the coastal "fares," or fisheries. Thus the crowd would have included blacksmiths, fishermen, and carpenters, all of whom customarily worked with small boats. They were used to getting along with neighbors in small hamlets, too, and a whaling ship in far-off waters was very much like a floating village. Here Skelton also found "apprentices"—young boys who looked strong and likely enough to be taught the elements of harpooning and slaughtering whales. The parish boards would have been glad to get rid of these last, for the employment and schooling of the poor was a drain on public funds, though there is evidence that the boys themselves would have much preferred to sign articles on East Indiamen and were likely to run away at the first landfall the ship would make. However, Philip Skelton could live with that, just as long as he sent off the ship with a full complement.

Oddly enough, while the hunt for a qualified ship surgeon was theoretically difficult—for Skelton had to find a man who could produce a certificate from either the Royal College of Surgeons or the Society of Apothecaries—in reality it was the easiest part of the job. Posting a notice in Batson's Coffee House in Cornhill, where all kinds of medical men gathered—or even the Rainbow Coffee House in Fleet Street, which was frequented by a more dubious set, being popularly known as "Quacks' Hall"—would bring in a dozen or more applicants. As it happened, however, Skelton found his surgeon at the Cuckoo Fair.

The name of this youthful fellow is unknown, and yet it is easy to picture him accosting Philip Skelton with one of the notices that Skelton's retainer had been handing out grasped eagerly in his fist. That we know a little about this gentleman is due to the fact that Captain Michael Underwood, commander of Skelton's whaleship *Kingsdown*, carried his wife, Eliza, on voyage. Eliza spent a great deal of time keeping a journal, in the course of which she described the ship's surgeon—invariably in terms of contempt. She did not even call him by name, simply referring to him as "doctor," without even the courtesy of a capital letter.

"Our officers enjoyed a laugh at our modest doctor," she wrote in offhand tones once, when he had the temerity to speak up at the cabin table. Bashful though he might be, however, he took over command of one of the ship's boats. Eliza was disapproving, being of the opinion that "doctor, though careful, has but lately learned to steer and cannot be so secure from accident as an officer who had steered a boat for many years." And yet there were times when he had the whole responsibility of the ship, such as the occasion on June 4, 1831, when Mrs. Underwood noted that the boats were all down, leaving "only doctor to attend the ship." This meant that the surgeon was in charge of keeping the *Kingsdown* up with the chase—no small task, because it involved not simply working the sails and the helm with just three or four men to help, but keeping the "run" of the boats and the whales, and flying signals to let the men in the chase know what was happening in the sea around them.

Eliza held a similarly low opinion of his medical skills, preferring to minister to her husband herself when Underwood was crippled with gout, dosing him with a dangerous patent nostrum called "Reynold's specific," even though she anticipated that it would lead to "several days of suffering." Sure enough, three days later (August 2, 1831), Underwood was extremely ill, "unable to move himself or bear others to lift him." His skin was so tender that he could not endure the slightest touch. "I think it must be partly the effect of the medicine," Eliza admitted, but still she did not consult with the surgeon.

It is impossible not to feel curious about this despised fellow. After all, his position on board should have commanded respect. Keeping a sailing ship's crew fit and healthy was no small challenge. Working aloft was dangerous enough, and contact with tropical shores involved contact with strange, distasteful diseases. Whaling promised additional dangers, for battling great whales was as risky as battling a man-of-war. Legs and heads were fractured when whales smashed up boats, and limbs were torn off when men got tangled in lines.

So how typical was the doctor of the *Kingsdown*? Were all surgeons on South Seamen treated in the same cavalier fashion? What were these men like? What kind of training had they received for the formidable challenges that lay before them? How useful was the medical chest they carried when a serious accident or illness struck the ship in the middle of some remote sea? What, indeed, did that chest contain? The crews of South Seas whalers were notoriously rough, hard-living, and uncultured. Why did these well-educated men ship for sea instead of hanging up a respectable shingle in some

Whaling in the Timor Straits. ENGRAVING BY T. SUTHERLAND AFTER A PAINTING BY W. J. HUGGINS, 1825

English town, where they would have been sure of compatible friends? And why choose a whaler? How did the voyage affect the surgeons themselves?

The anonymous practitioner who sailed on the *Kingsdown* in the years 1829 to 1832 left no record of his strange experiences. However, nine other doctors who sailed on South Seamen about the same time kept journals that survive:

Thomas Beale, *Kent* and *Sarah & Elizabeth*, 1830–1833
Frederick Debell Bennett, *Tuscan*, 1833–1836
James Brown, *Japan*, 1834–1837
John Coulter, *Stratford*, 1832–1836
William Dalton, *Phoenix* 1823–1825, and *Harriet*, 1826–1829
Eldred E. Fysh, *Coronet*, 1837–1839
John Lyell, *Ranger*, 1829–1832
Robert Smith Owen, *Warrens*, 1837–1840
John Wilson, *Gipsy*, 1839–1843

Additionally, the detailed journal kept by John B. King, who sailed as the surgeon of the *Aurora* of Nantucket from 1837 to 1840, and the partial diary kept in the year 1855 on the *Java* of New Bedford by a fellow with the picturesque name of Tom Noddy provide American views of the trade. In combination, these documents go a long way toward answering these intriguing questions. Indeed, the written words of these eleven men make it possible to describe the typical experience of a surgeon in those circumstances. For, taken as a group, their fascinating and revealing chronicles open a window into a dangerous, long-forgotten way of life and the rough medicine practiced in the days of sail in those most exotic seas.

I

Medicine at Sea: Woodall's The Surgions Mate

It is no small presumption
to Dismember the Image of God.

John Woodall, 1617

$\mathcal{A}$s LONG AS MEN AND WOMEN HAVE GONE TO SEA, DOCTORS HAVE accompanied them. Roman warships carried surgeons, as did vessels carrying princes and prelates in the Middle Ages. In 1588 William Clowes (1540–1604), an outstanding military surgeon of the sixteenth century, was in charge of the medical arrangements of the English fleet in their repulse of the Spanish Armada. The mighty Spanish fleet itself carried eighty-five surgeons and assistant surgeons. They were as helpless as Clowes was to stem the epidemic of dysentery and typhus that swept through the ships and decimated crews on both sides, but their presence is testament to the fact that it was standard practice to carry surgeons to sea in times of war. However, the man who can justifiably be called the father of sea surgery did not make his appearance until the early seventeenth century. This was John Woodall, a thoughtful and caring fellow who was the first surgeon-general of the East India Company.

Woodall, born about 1570, was apprenticed at about the age of sixteen to a London barber-surgeon. This indenture was supposed to last seven years, but Woodall was just nineteen when he joined Lord Willoughby's regiment as surgeon—which was not unusual, since the prime qualification for surgery was the ability to stand the sight of blood. Willoughby had been dispatched by Queen Elizabeth to assist Henry IV of France in his campaign against the Catholic League in Normandy, so going to war ensured that young Woodall was exposed to revolutionary methods of treating battle wounds that had been developed by the famous French military surgeon, Ambroise Paré. Distinguished for his practical skills, Paré promoted the use of ligatures to prevent bleeding after amputation instead of cauterizing with pitch or boiling oil, as it had always been done before—a humane attitude that, as we shall see, charac-

The Father of Sea Surgery. John Woodall (1569–1643).

ARTIST, RON DRUETT

Born in Warwick, the son of Richard and Mary Woodall, John Woodall was apprenticed to a barger-surgeon at the age of sixteen. Within three years he was serving in Europe as a military surgeon at the start of a brilliant medical career that included the publication of the first text in any language that was written specifically for surgeons at sea.

terized John Woodall too. Willoughby's troops returned to England in 1590, but Woodall stayed on, lingering eight years in Europe. Finally back in London in 1599, he gained membership of the Company of Barber-Surgeons.

The title of Freeman of the Company of Barber-Surgeons, grand though it might sound, indicates that John Woodall was a practical tradesman and not an academic. Doctors' credentials were much vaguer then than they are today, covering a whole range of medical treatment–related occupations, all of them overlapping and each with its own social status. At the top of the ladder was the physician, who was a university graduate in medicine or a Member of the Royal College of Physicians of London. Concerned with pure medical knowledge, he considered himself a gentleman and a scholar, and proved it with special dress and bearing. In the eighteenth century, for instance, he wore a distinctive wig and carried a gold-headed cane. As a physician, he prescribed medicine "physic"—but did not administer it. In fact, he might even prescribe without seeing the patient at all. A famous example of doctoring in this fashion was Queen Anne's physician, Richard Mead (1673–1754), who was available for consultation at Tom's Coffee House in Covent Garden, charging half a guinea for advice. After handing over the cash, an apothecary or surgeon would recite the symptoms he had observed in his patient. Then he would humbly wait while the lofty theorist meditated a little before writing out a prescription, the effectiveness of which went unchecked by a bedside visit.

This strange distancing of the physician from the patient dated back to Pope Innocent III and the Fourth Lateran Council of 1215. At that time, a code of behavior was drawn up which advised physicians to refrain from masturbation, intoxication, and extramarital intercourse (for any of these might endanger the soul of the patient), and prohibited them from practicing surgery even if the subject was dead, since the dismemberment of humans for study was forbidden. Physicians spent most of their time debating, writing, and preserving ancient dogma. Their role, if for instance a plague threatened, was to retire to a safe distance after writing out instructions for the guidance of the folk who were actually dealing with the sick. These caregivers were usually religious professionals such as nuns, rabbis, and monks, nursing the ill being an important part of their philanthropic and self-denying way of life. Earlier the clergy had been surgeons too, but after the 1215 Lateran Council passed an edict prohibiting priests from shedding blood, barber-surgeons performed all operations, though a priest-surgeon might shrive the patient and dress the wounds. That it was the barbers who took over the surgical role was probably due to the fact that the priests would have been used to seeing them at work when their whiskers were cut and their tonsures shaved, and, recognizing that they were clean by trade as well as accustomed to sharp tools, made use of them when it became necessary to pass on their knowledge of simple surgery along with techniques of letting blood. The earliest barber-surgeons would have worked under the supervision of priests, but as time went on, some became so adept and experienced that they took on apprentices themselves.

Today, the double role of the barber-surgeon is echoed in the red-striped pole that is still the barber's traditional sign, symbolizing blood and bandages. The name of their guild—the Company of Barber-Surgeons—also advertised this union. Chartered in 1540, the organization was formed from an uneasy marriage of two groups—the career surgeons belonging to the Fellowship of Surgeons, who had had most of their training on the jousting ground and the battlefield, and the men who had been members of the Company of Barbers and owed their elevation in status to Pope Innocent III. The barbers, who had been given the official mandate to take over the profession when the monks were no longer allowed to take a knife to the human frame, considered themselves superior. The surgeons, being specialists, thought themselves the elite. Many of these specialists became itinerant, traveling about to offer their services at fairs and building up reputations in certain operations such as cataract removal (not easy in the days before anesthesia). This led to much patient-stealing and undercutting of fees, which inspired a great deal of resentment, especially when barbers who had agreed to confine themselves to barbering had to be disciplined by the company for displaying bowls of fresh gore in their store windows, thus signifying that they were prepared to be paid to let blood.

The barber-surgeons passed on their skills through an apprentice system, also inherited from the barbers' guild. Letting blood, lancing boils, and extracting teeth were bread-and-butter skills, while amputation was the most common operation, along with sewing up abdominal wounds. They were prohibited from prescribing medicines, however, since this role belonged to the physicians. The rule was patently ridiculous, several Elizabethan surgeons pointing out the self-evident fact that as sea surgeons had to do their own prescribing (there being no physician on board to do it), it was only logical that the same should apply on land. Logical as the argument might have been, however, it did not prevail.

Barber-surgeons did not prepare medications, either (save upon the briny wave). In short, their sphere was confined to the razor, the saw, the needle, and the knife. On shore, the people who mixed the physic that the physicians prescribed were the apothecaries, who worked behind storefronts where pills, purges, and curvaceous bottles of colored fluids were displayed in bow-fronted, wavy-paned windows, usually accompanied by something mysterious and significant, such as a stuffed crocodile or a bust of Hippocrates. This, along with a large signboard that showed a pestle and mortar or apothecary's scales, served to make them seem more like arcane alchemists than simple tradesmen. They gave free advice to people who purchased medicines too, even though physicians were the only practitioners officially mandated to do so.

In the beginning, the apothecary's trade had been part of the realm of the importers and purveyors of spices and tobacco, who had been called "Pepperers" in the distant past but who, by Woodall's time, were known as "Grocers"—or, more correctly, "Grossers," because they dealt in bulk. The Grocers' Company of London received its first Charter in 1428, and for a while was extremely powerful, being in control of the cleansing and sorting of spices and the regulation of heavy weights and measures, as well as the manufacture and sale of drugs and medicines. In 1617, however, the grocers' importance in the field of medicine dwindled rapidly, for the apothecaries split away to form their own society.

As we shall see, that year of 1617 was important to John Woodall, too. Having gained his membership of the Barber-Surgeons' company, he had returned to Europe, where he spent a year or so in the Netherlands working with a Dutch apothecary-alchemist, learning the elements of practical chemistry. Then he went back to London, where he treated victims of the 1603 plague epidemic. While there is no record of it, a tropical voyage must have followed, for Woodall demonstrated practical knowledge of medicine that could have only been acquired through such an experience. Such a journey must have been taken into account when in 1613 Sir Thomas Smith, the Governor of the East India Company, appointed him Surgeon-General.

Woodall's duties as Surgeon-General of the East India Company were varied and strenuous, but at least he was given a place to live. "The Said Chirurgion and his Deputy shall have a place of lodging in the Yard," ran the wording of the contract:

> Where one of them shall give Attendance every working day from morning untill night, to cure any person or persons who may be hurt in the Service of this Company, and the like in all their Ships riding at an Anchor at Deptford and Blackwall, and at Erith, where hee shall also keepe a Deputy with his Chest furnished, to remaine there continually untill all the said ships be sayled down from thence to Gravesend.

Additionally, Woodall was in charge of "the ordering and appointing [of] fit and able Surgeons and Surgeon's Mates for their ships and services, as also the fitting and furnishing of their Surgeons' Chests with medicines instruments and other appurtenances thereto." For this he was paid the grand sum of £30 per annum, reduced to £20 as a cost-cutting measure in 1628. Meantime, he was busily shipping surgeons who met his high standards of medical skill. A few grumpy ships' captains accused him of hiring inferior characters and/or supplying defective medicines, but he easily fended off such scurrilous attacks.

Woodall held down the job for thirty years, despite other great responsibilities. In 1616 he was elected surgeon to St. Bartholomew's Hospital, thus becoming a colleague of Dr. William Harvey, the man who in 1628 first charted the circulation of the blood. He also rose through the highest echelons of the Barber-Surgeons company, attaining the status of examiner in 1626, warden in 1627, and master in 1633. Through his influence, the company was given the privilege of providing medical chests to both the navy and the army, for which they were paid by the Privy Council. This was personally supervised by Woodall. As he himself attested, he "had the whole ordering, making and appointing of His Highnesse Military provisions for Surgery, both for his Land and Sea-service," in addition to his commitment to the East India Company to provide chests for their ships. This last was a responsibility that he retained until 1643, the year of his death.

Mary Rose, 1545.
Two views, showing the *Mary Rose* under sail and a deck plan.

Named for the younger sister of Henry VIII, the flagship *Mary Rose* was one of England's first men-of-war. She carried 200 sailors, 185 soldiers, and 30 gunners. Their health and fitness were the responsibility of Master Surgeon Robert Sympson, whose mate was Henry Yonge. The surgeons' operating room—like the galley where the food was cooked—was in the nethermost regions of the hold.

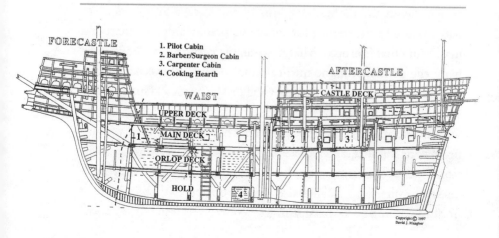

1. Pilot Cabin
2. Barber/Surgeon Cabin
3. Carpenter Cabin
4. Cooking Hearth

FORECASTLE

AFTERCASTLE

WAIST

CASTLE DECK

UPPER DECK

MAIN DECK

ORLOP DECK

HOLD

Woodall was also behind the passing of important and far-reaching bylaws, one protecting surgeons from being seized by naval press gangs without a prior permit from the company, and another requiring the company to give lectures in surgery and demonstrations in anatomy. As if this were not enough to take up all his energy and time, John Woodall also attended private patients, made speculative investments in the East India Company and Virginia, and invented the trephine, an advancement on the trepan, a tool for cutting away fractured pieces of skull and relieving pressure on the brain.

However, Woodall's greatest achievement was the publication in 1617 of *The Surgions Mate*—the first textbook ever written in any language for surgeons at sea. It is impossible to tell how many copies there were of that first edition, because it was printed to order, to accompany the medical chests, but it must been an impressive number. Woodall declared that it was "Published chiefly for the benefit of young Sea-Surgions, imployed in the *East-India* Companies affaires," but the book found its way into the cabins of hundreds of different kinds of ships. So many copies were lost at sea or in foreign ports that only eleven from the first printing are recorded in existence today. Another indication of its success is that it went on to three revisions, in 1639, 1653, and 1655, all equally popular.

WOODALL CLAIMED THAT HE PUBLISHED THE BOOK BECAUSE HE was "wearied with writing for every Shippe the same instructions a new." And that is exactly what it is—an instruction book to accompany the contents of the medical chest, "with all the particulars thereof, into an order and method." Methodical indeed, it is divided into four sections. First, there are lists of instruments and medicines, with notes about their use. Then comes a section describing wounds and other surgical emergencies, with detailed instructions for amputation, followed by a discussion of various medical problems. This includes a lengthy discourse on scurvy, the first ever published in English. The fourth section is devoted to alchemy, and contains treatises on sea salt, sulfur, and mercury. A glossary of chemical symbols and alchemist's terms completes the book, some of it, rather startlingly, in lively verse, an echo of the poet-physician fad of the previous century.

In view of the harsh social setting of the time, the tone of the book is remarkably sympathetic. When Woodall gives precise instructions for the use of dental forceps, he wryly recounts two painful occasions when his own tooth shattered while being drawn, "which maketh me the more to comiserate others in that behalfe." Where it was common practice to hack off broken or wounded limbs with merry abandon, Woodall instead advises his young surgeons to avoid amputation, "the most lamentable part of chirurgery," wherever possible, for a doctor's "over forwardnesse doth often as much hurt as good." With rare understanding of the mental state of the patient, he also counsels the surgeon's mate to spare as much emotional anguish as possible, first by consulting with the patient to make certain that the "worke bee done with his own free will," and secondly by hiding "his sharpe instruments" from "the eyes of the patient" until the last possible moment.

There were lots of these tools in Woodall's arsenal—about seventy-five stowed in special compartments in the lid of the chest and at least twenty-five more kept in what he calls the "plaster box." The former included incision knives, dismembering knives, razors, "Head-Sawes," cauterizing irons, various types of forceps, probes, and spatulas designed for drawing out splinters and shot, "One bundle of small German Instruments," enema syringes, and seven kinds of gripper for extracting teeth. In the plaster box were more homelike objects, such as scissors, probes, "Stitching quill and needles," splints, sponges, and "clouts" (soft rags), along with cupping glasses, blood porringers, chafing dishes, mortar and pestle, weights and scales, bricks for heating on the sick bay fire to warm patients' cold feet, tinderbox, lantern, ink and quills, medicine cups and glasses, and a range of plasters.

Obviously Woodall's medical chest was no small affair. While no pictures exist, it is easy to envisage a huge, ironbound object being hoisted on board by a squad of straining seamen. Yet despite this daunting armory, John Woodall was an advocate of good nursing rather than heroic measures. "Nothing cureth a fractured boane so much as rest," he declares, going on to counsel similar kind treatment for that inevitable side effect of tropical landfalls, diarrhea—dried rhubarb in wine, mixed with a small dose of laudanum, along with a gentle regimen of bed rest, and warm soft clouts applied "to the belly and fundament of the party," with which "by God's help he shall be cured."

How possible it was to maintain this kindness to "poore Seamen in fluxes" on board a plunging ship at sea, with a driving captain determined to keep every man at work, was debatable, however, something that Woodall freely admits. It is obvious throughout that he felt a strong sympathy for the sailors' lot, nowhere more eloquently illustrated than in his persuasive argument for the provision of a "close-stool," or portable toilet, in the sick bay of a ship. A "poore weake man in his extremities should not continually go to the shrouds or beake head to ease himselfe," he writes; "nor be noysome to his fellowes." With a close-stool in the sick bay, a seaman with dysentery might "finde comfort in his most pitifull distresse, whose miseries I hartily compassionate."

While "piss-tubs" were provided throughout the ship for urination (stored urine being useful for putting out fires as well as for bleaching filthy clothes), the normal place for defecation was over the bows, where the sea acted as a natural flush—and a bidet too, if the waves reached high. In smaller ships, such as whalers and traders, the seamen clambered into the nets that were strung about the bowsprit, and crouched there precariously in the full view of anyone who cared to watch. In larger vessels the situation was no more comfortable, with planks with holes—"seats of ease"—being set in the beakhead, the reason a toilet on board ship is still called the "head" or "heads."

Easing the bowels under these conditions would have been unpleasant enough in fine weather, let alone in a rugged sea. It is little wonder that constipation was a chronic shipboard complaint, or

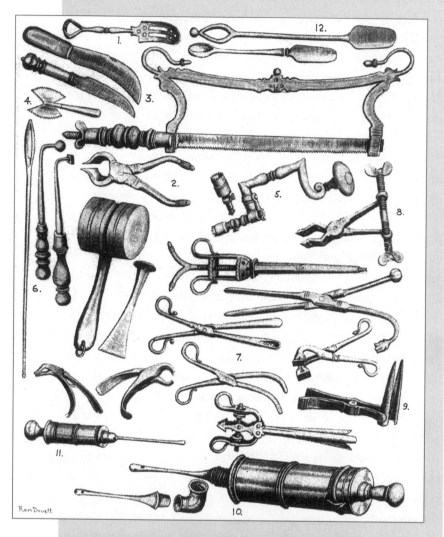

Surgical Tools from John Woodall's Chest. ARTIST, RON DRUETT

Various editions of *The Surgions Mate* are illustrated with neat, precise drawings of the tools that Woodall recommended, explained in the text with "Certaine Breife Remembrances" of their use. While this selection includes objects as homely as a tongue depressor (1), much more formidable is the array of dismembering cutters (2), knives (3), and saws, including one that Woodall's medical chests held generous supplies of laxatives, such as "Cassia fistula" (a syrup of senna, made from the pulp of cassia pods), and licorice juice ("Succus Glycyrrhizza"). The prospect of diarrhea, or worse still, the "bloody flux," must have been a nightmare. Common complications of dysentery, directly due to enforced defecation over the side of the ship, were "falling downe of the Arse-gut"—prolapse of the rectum—and stoppage of the large bowel, where the patient "desireth rather to die than to live." Recommended remedies were hot towels applied to the fundament, fumigation in the close-stool (provided with a door in the side to make this easy), or balancing the patient "on his head and hands with his legges abroad."

Woodall was moderate as well as compassionate. He often describes the dangers of overdosage of various remedies, for instance poetically cautioning those who prescribed quicksilver (mercury), that it was "a true healer, a wicked murderer, a precious medicine, and a deadly poyson" all at once—"a friend that can flatter and lie." Similarly, he was no believer in excessive bleeding, recommending that the blood taken should be precisely measured into porringers, no more than eight ounces being removed at one time. This was quite revolutionary, for at that time no one had any real idea how much blood the human body contained. Nearly two

designed for cutting the skull (4), accompanied by a trepan (5) and its bits, along with a mallet and chisel. A narrow probe (6) lies alongside cautery irons. Different kinds of forceps (7) were provided for a range of jobs, along with instruments that dilated wounds and orifices, such as the speculum oris (8), which held the mouth open while medicines were poured down the throat, and the speculum ani (9) for dilating "the fundament." Syringes ranged from large affairs that delivered enemas (10), along with their pipes, to the more slender models (11), which were used for injecting mercury up the penis. Woodall was particularly proud of the "Spatulum Mondani" (12), which he himself had designed for the removal of hard stools that "putrifieth the Arse-gut," providing "comfort and remedy" for those who suffered from extreme constipation.

hundred years after Woodall's book was first published, the physician who treated George Washington's infected throat hastened his demise by relieving him of roughly eighty fluid ounces of blood within twenty-four hours.

Despite his caution to be "sparing in the quantitie of blood to be taken away," Woodall set as much store by bloodletting—venesection or phlebotomy—as any of his forebears or contemporaries. Bleeding was part of the classical regimen of diet, purging, and sweating believed necessary to correct the physiological balance of the body. Such practice had its basis in the classical doctrine of humors—blood, phlegm, black bile, and yellow bile—all of which had to be restored to a state of equilibrium in order to return the patient to health. One side effect of this fundamental principle was that suppuration of wounds was considered a good sign, the "laudable pus" being regarded as a release of harmful humors. Another was the widely accepted practice of cupping, where the mouth of a heated glass was clapped onto the patient's thigh or shoulder, often after the skin had been pierced, or "scarified," in several places. A vacuum formed as the glass cooled, sucking up the flesh underneath, along with the excess humors.

The four humors were supposed to be associated with the four elements of fire, air, water, and earth, diagnosis being based on the temperature and sweatiness of the patient. Accordingly, Woodall describes the medical contents of his chest in terms of drying, moistening, cooling, warming, soothing, abrading, laxative, or diuretic. Clove oil, for instance:

> drieth away putrede humours, discusseth [disperses] winde, openeth the pores of the liver, digesteth colde humours, dissipateth the melancholicke humours, healeth olde and new ulcers, staieth the putrefaction of the bones, and asswageth the paine of the teeth proceeding from a colde cause.

Throughout the book, it is evident that Woodall was very aware of the inexperience of his intended readers, for he writes as a father might speak to a son who is about to hazard his life and health on a long, dangerous sea voyage, imparting the same kind of homely

CHARACTERS AND
their Interpretations.

And firſt of the ſeauen Planets.

Saturnus. ♄ • ♄ *Lead* Cold, deſiccatiue ſweet, diſcuſſing, mollificatiue, a-
Plumbum
nodine, ſanatine, laxatiue, mundificatiue, and yet full of deadlie vapors.

Iupiter. ♃ • ♃ *Tinn* Diaphoretick, la-xatiue, deſiccatiue
Stannum
ſanatiue, &c.

Mars. ♂ • ♂ *Iron or* The greateſt ſhedder of bloud
Ferrum *Steele* a ſure medicine
for fluxes of bloud, and a great opener of obſtructions.

Sol. ☉ • ☉ *Gould* A great and ſure Cordiall, for it
Aurum
comforteth the
heauy hearted, and is reputed the beſt medicine.

Venus. ♀ • ♀ *Copper* Maketh ſundry needfull medi-
Cuperum
cines for mans
health, Phyſicall and Chirurgicall, viz: *oleum, ſpiritus, & terra cum mul-tis alijs.*

Mercury

Alchemical symbols from *The Surgions Mate.*

advice. The young man must do his utmost to profit from the expe-rience, to that end keeping a detailed journal—harking back to the ancient temples of Asclepius, where records of sickness and treat-ment were left as votive tablets for later reference, and yet most revolutionary in a time when not even physicians kept medical log-books. The surgeon's mate should not only be aware at all times of his duty to God and his patients, the sailors, but of his duty to his chief surgeon too, who should in turn be expected to treat his sub-ordinate with gentleness, being "kinde in speech."

Idling, smoking, and excessive drinking were all to be avoided, and the humblest seaman should never be allowed to suffer from neglect, for the surgeon's mate must be "compassionate to the meanest creature . . . even as others should do to you in like case." The surgeon's mate must be certain to keep his instruments always sharp and in order, wrapped in oily rags to save them from rust, and the sick bay clean and tidy. As well as this, his job was to nurse the seriously ill and work as the ship's barber too. For this last he had his box of "raisers, sizers, combes," and brushes, an "eare picker," knives for cutting corns, a looking glass, aprons, shaving linen, water pot, and whetstones, which "he ought not to be [found] wanting." Whatever spare moments might remain at his disposal should be utilized to advantage in rolling pills and making up medicines—and to help him in this, Woodall translated those con-fusing Latin words.

Due to its wide-reaching advice and ease of use, the book was an instant success. Britain was undergoing a period of outward expan-sion. The great explorers Hawkins, Drake, Frobisher, Davis, Lancaster, Raleigh, Hudson, and Baffin were all Woodall's contem-poraries, and trade routes were extending ever outward. Designed for inexperienced surgeons' mates, many of whom were still apprentices, the book was just as appropriate for amateurs, and so it was eagerly taken up by a host of merchant captains who did not have a doctor on board. On most small trading vessels the master was the medic, and somehow he was expected to cope with medical emergencies by uti-lizing whatever he could find in the carpenter's chest, his wife's sewing box, or the pantry—and to him Dr. Woodall's book came as a godsend. Later editions found their way into army tents and domes-tic kitchens, where there was an equal need for a friendly guide to the use of simples, drugs, and surgical instruments. As George Dunn, another warden of the Barber-Surgeons' company, exclaimed, "this whole Globe did want your Surgeons Matchless Mate."

Never a truer word. As medical knowledge progressed and new medicines were devised and discovered, *The Surgions Mate* was supplanted by other shipboard guides. In every case, however, they took the same form as John Woodall's text, differing only in content and detail. The same applies today. John Woodall's *Surgions Mate* was a trailblazer, the forerunner of every medical guide that has ever accompanied a captain or a surgeon to sea.

2

Shipping Out

He examined the fracture and . . . resolved
to amputate the leg immediately.
This was a dreadful sentence to the patient,
who, recruiting himself with a quid of tobacco,
pronounced with a woeful countenance,
"What! is there no remedy, doctor?—
that I must be dock'd?—can't you splice it?"

Tobias Smollett,
The Adventures of Roderick Random

DESPITE THE POPULARITY OF *THE SURGIONS MATE* AND JOHN Woodall's influential stint with the Company of Barber-Surgeons, the training of surgeons and apothecaries altered surprisingly little over the next two hundred years. In an eighteenth century novel, a naval surgeon, Tobias Smollett (1721–1771), described an apprenticeship system that Woodall certainly would have recognized. Smollett himself was apprenticed to John Gordon of Glasgow, went to London in 1739, and at the age of nineteen was appointed surgeon's mate, serving in the 1730 Carthagena expedition. In January 1737 he produced *The Adventures of Roderick Random*, which recounts a somewhat similar career.

His hero, the Roderick Random of the book's title, studied surgery for three years at the University of Glasgow, merely to find that this was not enough to warrant certification. "Can you bleed and give a clyster [enema], spread a plaster and prepare a potion?" demanded one of his mentors, but though the answer was a confident yes, Random still had to work out his time as a journeyman apothecary before he could go to the Navy Office for a letter to carry to the Surgeons' Hall, "that I might be examined touching my skill in surgery." After undergoing the ordeal of a *viva voce* examination, he was presented with his "qualification sealed up," and in due course proceeded to sea.

In 1829, the indenture that the surgeon of the *Kingsdown* served would have seemed familiar to both Woodall and Smollett, and the *viva voce* examination was very similar to the one that Smollett described, too, but the time involved and the letters earned would have seemed different to the novelist. Particularly after 1815, when the passing of the Apothecaries Act meant that anyone who held a License of the Society of Apothecaries was recognized as a fully authorized practitioner, their certificate—the L.S.A.—became a very popular medical qualification. Ever since the year 1735, though, when the marriage of the surgeons and the barbers had collapsed in divorce and a separate Company of Surgeons was formed, Membership of the Royal College of Surgeons (M.R.C.S.) had been considered slightly superior. However, gaining one's M.R.C.S. meant a greater outlay in money. While it has been estimated that an indenture to an apothecary cost between £100 and £200 at the time, Eldred Fysh, who was admitted to the Membership of the Royal College of Surgeons on April 21, 1837, had to borrow £500 from his father to finance his training. Presumably, the financial rewards were commensurate, for many men with an L.S.A. went on to seek their M.R.C.S. when they could afford it, so they could call themselves a surgeon-apothecary, or "general practitioner"—a term popularized by the editor of the influential weekly magazine for medical men, *The Lancet*.

To become a Licentiate of the Society of Apothecaries, an applicant had to be over twenty-one, of good moral character, have completed a five-year apprenticeship, and then have assisted for six months at a hospital or dispensary. This was exactly the course pursued by one of our whaling surgeons, a Scot by the name of James Brown. On November 19, 1818, James signed articles with Messrs. Stewart and Jordan of Manchester for an apprenticeship of five years. Initially, his time would have been taken up with necessary but trivial tasks like rolling pills and capping bottles, keeping the books, and running errands, but as he gained experience he would have taken over some of the minor surgery, like drawing teeth and lancing boils.

Having completed his tenure to his masters' satisfaction, James hied himself to London for six months of walking the wards at St. Thomas's Hospital in Lambeth Palace Road. Founded about 1106, this was an institution with a picturesque past. One of its fourteenth-century patrons was Dick Whittington, the famous cat owner who became Lord Mayor of London. According to legend, Dick went to London as a boy and contributed his cat (which may have been a feline, or may have been a type of ship) to an outgoing maritime venture. Meeting with nothing but bad luck, he decided to go home again, but as he left, the bells of Saint Mary-le-Bow started tolling:

> Turn again, Whittington,
> Lord Mayor of London.

So he went back to work, received the proceeds of the sale of his cat, became very rich, and was appointed Lord Mayor in 1397, 1406, and 1419. When he died, Dick Whittington left most of his wealth to charity, including funds for building Newgate Prison, the establishment of a college, and the support of St. Thomas's Hospital. In the sixteenth century, the hospital was closed down for a while by Thomas Cromwell, Earl of Essex, who called it a "bawdy hospital," alleging that the master kept a concubine and sold the church plate. The cook was also the grave-digger—an ominous juxtaposition of jobs. Patients were punished for gambling, swearing, and drunkenness, and if they did not attend chapel at least once a day, they were not given any food. Nor could any person enter the wards of the opposite sex. And, most remarkably for those times, not more than one patient was allowed in each bed.

When James Brown arrived at St. Thomas's time-honored portals in June 1824, he was armed with his evidence of indenture and a testimonial of moral character penned by a Mr. W. Newton. After signing up as a Physician's Pupil, he commenced courses in chemistry, *materia medica*, anatomy and physiology, and the theory and practice of medicine, his lecturers being Messrs. Allen, Cholmeley, and Green. As well as attending lessons, James watched his mentors at work, learning to become hardened to gruesome sights in the operating theater.

The effects of ether had been familiar to scientists for over five hundred years and those of opium for much longer (as we will see in the next chapter), but their applications in surgery had not as yet been developed. Back in the thirteenth century, two monks, Hugo of Lucca and Theodoric of Cervia, had experimented with a sponge soaked in opium that was held over the patient's nose, but the effects had been unpredictable and often frightening. While the patient might be blessedly unconscious during the operation, if his or her heart were frail it was likely to stop altogether, and the fumes tended to affect the surgeon's performance, too. And so it was decided that it was best for people to undergo surgery in full (and screaming) consciousness and then be given opium (or grog, for that matter) to alleviate pain afterward.

So anesthesia lay in the future, and the lectures that accompanied the demonstrations were apt to be drowned out by the agonized shrieks of the patient. The best surgeon was a physically powerful, decisive chap who could chop off a leg in four minutes. Hospital hygiene was grim, as well. In Smollett's time, surgeons wore aprons—theoretically changed for fresh ones after becoming soaked with blood—but by the 1820s they were wearing the infamous operating room frock coat, a garment so stiff with blood and pus that it could stand up on its own. The more foul the frock coat, the prouder the owner. It was a mark of status.

James Brown studied until January 27, 1825, when he presented himself for the grueling *viva voce* examination in the grand, paneled courtroom of the Apothecaries' Hall in Blackfriars Lane. There the candidate's bearing was just as important as what he said in reply to the questions, something that even the most confident of young men found intimidating. Nonetheless James survived this. His examiner, Mr. Tegart, found his answers (and demeanor) satisfactory, and James walked out with his L.S.A.

A similar course was followed by another of our South Seas surgeons, William Dalton. Born in the Welsh port of Swansea on December 4, 1802, Dalton was not quite fourteen when he signed indenture papers with Walter Mitchell. In 1821, he repaired to London, where he lived with John Merriman (later apothecary extraordinary to Queen Victoria), and walked the wards as a Physician's Pupil at the General Dispensary for the Relief of the Sick Poor in Aldersgate. Six months later, he faced examinations in anatomy and physiology, the theory and practice of medicine, chemistry, and *materia medica*, and emerged with his L.S.A. along with a lifetime interest in the dietary diseases of seamen. Almost exactly a year later, he signed on as the surgeon of the South Seas whaler *Phoenix*, sailing in January 1823.

Much more tardy in making up his mind about what kind of career to follow was Robert Smith Owen. Born away from the sound of the sea in the Cotswolds, England, Smith Owen waited until September 7, 1824, his twenty-first birthday, before signing indenture papers with Mr. Daniel Sparks of Cirencester. Five years later, he presented himself at Middlesex Hospital in Mortimer Street, Soho, London, and embarked forthwith on an ambitious series of courses in chemistry, *materia medica*, anatomy and physiology, the theory and practice of medicine, midwifery, forensic medicine, and anatomical demonstrations.

JOHN WOODALL WOULD HAVE GREATLY APPROVED OF THE LESSONS in dissection, having overseen the passing of a bylaw that required the Company of Barber-Surgeons to give demonstrations in anatomy. For Robert Owen, however, it would have presented a financial challenge. While there were plenty of students of anatomy, there was a serious shortage of bodies to anatomize, for the very good reason that no one wanted to be dissected.

Ever since the fourth century B.C., cutting open the human corpus for scientific purposes had been a touchy subject. Occasional dissections were authorized from the Renaissance on, but the subjects were always criminals. In 1505, for instance, the surgeons of Edinburgh arranged with the baillies (town magistrates) that they should have the use of "ane condampnit man" per year, with the stipulation that they did not take over the body until "efter he be deid." Similarly, the first public dissection in America, in 1750, was performed on the body of Hermanus Carroll, who had been executed for murder in New York City. While for Carroll it could have been an interesting last thought that he was going to make medical history, this kind of practice did make it difficult to find material for future lessons, for it meant that demonstrations of anatomy became indelibly associated with criminal execution in the

Dissection of a corpse in the eighteenth century.
THE REWARD OF CRUELTY, PLATE FOUR OF *THE FOUR STAGES OF CRUELTY,* WILLIAM HOGARTH

public mind. If dissection after death was part of the punishment for some foul crime, then why should a decent citizen allow doctors to pull apart the mortal remains of himself or any of his kin?

The Anatomy Act of 1832, which authorized the use of unclaimed bodies, had not yet been passed, and so students like Robert Owen were forced to haunt the execution scaffolds, hoping to bargain for a freshly dangling corpse, or else go out grave robbing—which meant stealing out in the depths of night, muffled in cloaks and grappling a smelly sack and a spade, headed for the newly dead. It was a business that demanded strong nerves as well as strong stomachs, for a mob that caught a fellow in the process was likely to tear him to pieces. However, the only alternative was to pay as much as ten guineas per corpse to one of the grave diggers, hearse drivers, and sextons who moonlighted as body snatchers.

These unsavory characters were known to the revolted public on both sides of the Atlantic as "resurrectionists." Relatives held vigil in burying grounds, blunderbusses at the ready, until enough time had elapsed to render a corpse unsuitable for dissection. Already tense and irritated, they were likely to pull the trigger on the slightest suspicion. Wealthier families subscribed to the new fashion for erecting iron railings around graves. In Pennsylvania, emotions ran so high that Dr. William Shippen (1736–1808)—the physician who presented the first systematic course of anatomy lectures in the American Colonies and who became Professor of Anatomy of the College of Philadelphia—had to run for his life on several occasions. Despite his public assurance that his subjects were executed criminals plus a few suicides from "the Potter's Field," his carriage was fired upon and his dissecting room windows smashed.

In Robert Smith Owen's time, Shippen's counterpart was the brilliant anatomist, Dr. Robert Knox, chiefly famous for his dealings with the most notorious body snatchers of all, Burke and Hare. William Hare kept a common lodging house in Tanners Close, a dank alley at the foot of Edinburgh Castle. One of his tenants was a cobbler, William Burke, and another was an old soldier named Donald, who died owing Hare £4 in rent. As they kept watch by the coffin, Hare confided this problem to Burke, and the lodger suggested selling the corpse. Forthwith they opened the coffin, removed the body, and closed the box again after weighting it with wood. Then, with their grisly burden stuffed into a sack and hanging over Burke's powerful shoulder, they sallied out and asked directions "to the doctors."

A medical student directed them to Knox's rooms at 10 Surgeon's Square, and to their amazement and delight, they were given the

The Resurrection Men.
ADAPTED BY RON DRUETT FROM AN ILLUSTRATION
IN *THE MYSTERIES OF LONDON* SERIES,
EDITED BY GEORGE W. M. REYNOLDS (LONDON, 1844–1856)

In the late eighteenth and early nineteenth centuries, the growing fashion for demonstrations in human dissection led to some of the most macabre episodes in the history of medicine, as anatomists desperate for teaching material negotiated with so-called resurrectionists. Most of these body snatchers were people who were involved in the death trade already, such as hearse drivers and sextons. Not only did they have strong stomachs and useful connections but also the unspoken backing of a government that was reluctant to face public outrge by legalizing dissection of unclaimed cadavers.

magnificent sum of £7.10 in exchange for their burden, along with an invitation to come again whenever they had another body to sell. Eleven months and seventeen murders later, they were handed into the police. Hare turned king's evidence and testified against his accomplice, and Burke was accordingly hanged, but as it turned out, Hare suffered the most. Recognized by a mob, he was seized and thrown into a pit of lime, which burned out his eyes. He spent the rest of his miserable life begging in Oxford Street, London.

> Up the close and doun the stair,
> But and ben wi' Burke and Hare.
> Burke's the butcher, Hare's the thief,
> Knox the boy what buys the beef.
>
> "The Resurrection Men," ANON.

Despite such significant problems as finding subjects for dissection, Robert Smith Owen somehow managed to complete his courses, duly presenting himself at the Apothecaries' Hall—where Mr. Seaton and Mr. Ridout refused to examine him, instead sending him back to Middlesex Hospital for another two months "on account of deficiency in Latin." On June 16, 1831, he tried again, and Mr. Ridout failed him. It was not until a third attempt, on January 12, 1832, when Mr. Hunter was the examiner, that Robert Smith Owen finally emerged with his hard-won certificate.

Obviously, getting a medical qualification was a time for great celebration. Theoretically, all that remained was to hang up his shingle and find himself some patients, but instead Owen—like James Brown and William Dalton—ended up applying for a position at sea.

JAMES BROWN, WHO HAD QUALIFIED ON JANUARY 27, 1825, DID NOT embark on the *Japan* of London until December 15, 1834, while Owen joined the crew of the *Warrens* in the first week of April 1837. If this was the first voyage for both, it is hard to account for the long intervals between accreditation and departure—more than five years in Owen's case, and nearly ten in Brown's. It was much more common for the newly fledged doctor to sign up for sea soon after qualifying, before he married or set up in practice. Twenty-five-year-old Eldred Fysh embarked on the *Coronet* just five weeks after gaining his M.R.C.S., while another fellow whaling surgeon, Yorkshireman John Wilson, who received his L.S.A. on October 3, 1839, at the age of twenty-nine (he had begun his apprenticeship at the age of fourteen, so it must have been a real struggle), took less than three weeks to sign onto the crewlist of the whaler *Gipsy*.

From the seamanlike tone of the journal James Brown kept on the *Japan*, it seems very likely that this was his second voyage, his first probably being on the *Favorite* with Captain Ford, though he makes only a passing reference to it. Robert Smith Owen, on the other hand, was definitely a greenhand, for he made an even bigger mess of signing onto a ship than he had of passing his examinations.

Having set up in some country practice since gaining his L.S.A., Robert had become obsessed with a young woman, "my D^r. *Emma*," for whom—as he later rhapsodized—he would "sacrifice all" if only she would elevate him to "the very summit of happiness" by consenting to be his wife. Unfortunately, Emma was a flirt, and kept him dangling, and so he had the bright idea of forcing an answer out of her by the complicated ploy of signing up as a surgeon on a whaler. According to his romantic reasoning, when he announced he was about to sail for far-off seas, she would throw her arms about his neck, "begging of me not to go." At that—or so he dreamed—he would gently push her away, assuring her of "our being married in 6 mo's time." Then, with the indulgent words, "My Dear Girl—how I long for the period of my return to arrive," he would depart, leaving her to await the return of her bronzed and dashing bridegroom.

Sadly, however, it all went wrong. First, he had not done his homework. In reckoning on a six-month absence, Robert had made a gross misjudgment, one that could have been avoided simply by checking a map. There were indeed whalers that completed their voyages in about six months, but they were most certainly not South Seamen. Instead, they were the Greenland whaling ships that steered for Davis Strait and Baffin Bay to hunt the northern right whale.

The Arctic trade was extremely hazardous, and nasty too. The famous Greenland whaling master, Captain William Scoresby, recorded that there was great danger from three directions—the whales, the ice, and the climate—to which could be added the like-lihood of scurvy. The crews were huge—forty or more on ships of less than 300 tons—because once they got to the ground, there was a great deal of work. The ships were embayed, and whales slaugh-tered by the dozen, after which they were flensed on the ice. The blubber was then chopped up and headed up in casks for boiling into oil after the ship got back to London (Hull was another great Greenland whaling port), by which time the fat was quite rotten, and every man on board reeked of rancid oil. However, despite the certainty of appalling conditions, many sea surgeons undertook this strange voyage, a famous example being the creator of Sherlock Holmes, Arthur Conan Doyle, who sailed on the Peterhead whaler *Hope* in 1880 and earned the nickname "the great northern diver" because he fell overboard so often. There were two good reasons for shipping on such unwholesome craft, one being money and the other, the short duration of the voyage. The ships departed in March and were usually back in October, at which time the sur-geon could collect his pay, which was not an insignificant amount. As Robert Smith Owen himself noted in his journal, "In Greenland trade surgeon generally has from 3 to 4£ per month and 2/- [bounty] per Ton." The total might tot up to as much as £50—no mean sum for half a year's work at the time.

Instead of departing on a Greenland whaler in March, how-ever, Robert Smith Owen embarked on the South Seaman *Warrens* in April. One cannot help but wonder how he came to make such a colossal *faux pas*, for it seems so obvious that ships that hunted the sperm whale in the far-off Pacific and East Indies were very unlikely to return in less than two years. Perhaps he went to the wrong agent or even the wrong quay, for Greenland whalers had their own basin, often called "Perry's Dock," at the East India Docks. Maybe he had decided that a voyage to the South China Sea sounded a lot more romantic than a cold and smelly Arctic cruise and thus more likely to impress Dear Emma. Regardless of how Smith Owen found himself on board a South Seaman, unsurprisingly his tone was bemused when he noted in the middle of the Celebes Sea, on October 6, 1837, "This day completes the period of six months from our Sailing from London." Not only was he still half a world away from home, but the ship had taken just twenty barrels of oil—the equivalent of exactly 2.5 tuns, currently worth £205 back in London—a very poor return for six months work when divided up between more than thirty men.

It is also an illustration of the uncertainty of making money out of a South Seas voyage. Owen and his shipmates were not paid wages but a share of the profits instead. This had its roots in the ancient customs of the fishermen of the Sussex coast where ship owner Philip Skelton had gone to find his men, being the method by which the "fare,"or catch, was shared between the men who owned the boat, the men who owned the nets or lines, and each of those who got a "share for his body," having brought nothing to the venture save manual labor. In the Sussex mackerel fishery, for instance, where the fish were seined from small boats called "cocks," half the catch, or "cock-fare,"went to the owner or owners of the boat and nets, and the other half was divided into equal shares, of which one share went to the church, the rest going to the ten or so men (or women, if the men were away at war) who had crewed the cock. These were apportioned out according to rank. If the fishing boat was big enough to need a captain, he got as much as a quarter share of the catch, with his second in command being recompensed in proportion, and so on down the ranks.

It was very much the same on the South Seas whalers. Once the ship was back home and the oil in the holds had been gauged, the wholesale value of the fare was calculated, and after the cost of the original outfitting of the ship (about £4,000) was subtracted, the rest was divided between the owners and the men, according to a previously negotiated arrangement. Each man's share was called a "lay" and was styled as a fraction. While this varied from ship to ship and owner to owner, the captain usually got a sixteenth of the profits, the first mate a twenty-sixth, and an ordinary seaman, about a hundred-and-sixtieth of the net total, though he did have the advantage of having been paid a small advance to settle his debts before the ship sailed, the amount of which was subtracted from his share.

The surgeon's lay varied considerably, but was never bigger than a ninety-fifth, which was not even as large as the carpenter's share of the take. Dr. John Wilson—the man who was so eager to sail that he signed up within three weeks of gaining his L.S.A.—was awarded just a hundred-and-fortieth. This is a curious echo of the way things were in the Roman navy, where ship surgeons were lumped together with scribes, secretaries, and pay clerks, forced to take orders from all officers, no matter how petty and ignorant, and forever barred from attaining officer rank themselves. Like Roman naval doctors, too, whaling surgeons were not allowed to charge their patients for treatment, though the men did have to pay for drugs and other medications, which were all supplied by the ship. So while it was possible to do well out of a whaling voyage, there was no guarantee because it all depended on luck. All a whaling surgeon could be sure of was free board and lodging for whatever time the voyage lasted, along with the experience of strange seas and wondrous lands.

For men of romantic bent, this last was a very plausible reason for sailing, as another of our whaling surgeons, John Coulter, sunnily confessed. Coulter, an Irishman, gained his M.R.C.S. on June 15, 1827, and almost immediately sailed off to the Pacific in search of exotic sights and curious experiences. He enjoyed the voyage so much that he shipped again, leaving London in October 1832 on the whaler *Stratford*. "Altogether, [South Seamen] are very agreeable ships," he declared, "and anyone feeling a wish for adventure and variety, can be fully gratified on those vessels, as there are none others afloat that have the same endless opportunity. In cruising after whale, they frequently circumnavigate the globe, and call at every island and port at all convenient."

Sailing on a whaler offered the opportunity to study exotic wildlife, too. Another of our South Seas surgeons, Frederick Debell Bennett, born in Devon in 1806, hailed from a well-educated family with a bent for natural history. After obtaining his L.S.A. in 1828, and his M.R.C.S. in 1829, Bennett served as Assistant Surgeon on the hospital ship *Grampus*, which was moored on the Thames. Then, in 1833, he joined the London whaleship *Tuscan*. Unsurprisingly, in view of his background, he declared later that it was a decision "chiefly" inspired by a desire to study the "anatomy and habits of Southern Whales."

So, Robert Smith Owen's experience notwithstanding, a surgeon's decision to apply for a post on a South Seaman was usually a well-thought-out one based on sound personal reasons. If a young doctor wished to see the world and study nature while he saved the money to set up in a private practice, life on a South Seaman could have seemed quite inviting, despite the uncertainty of recompense and the undeniable risks. Indeed, it is very likely that every one of our South Seas surgeons from London set out in a mood of bright optimism.

THE FIRST STEP WAS TO MEET UP WITH THE MUSTERING OFFICER AT the Custom House at the foot of Lower Thames Street, where the cobbled alleys were crowded with porters shouldering their loads of dripping fish for Billingsgate Market. Then, having gone through the formalities of presenting his credentials, a surgeon was free to join his ship—which meant finding the vessel. She might still be berthed in the crowded London Docks or moored among the dense traffic on the river, or she might have dropped down the first few reaches of the Thames to the hamlet of Gravesend for the last of her fitting out and provisioning.

Dr. John Coulter joined the *Stratford* in London, where in "the month of October, in the year 1832, she was ready for sea, having all her stores, guns, &c. [etc.], on board." A steam tug towed the ship down the Thames River to Gravesend: "thence proceeded round to Spithead, the general starting port for all long and adventurous voyages." Dr. John Wilson, too, found his ship in "the East London Docks," where the riggers were hauling the *Gipsy* out of the basin into the river. With little delay, they were "towed down by the '*Dragon*',

steam Tug & anchored a little below Gravesend in 5 fathoms water."
The first officer—the "mate"—was on board, but the captain was not.
"The Pilot is *Mr. Steele*, a middle-aged man who conducts us to
Portsmouth where Capt. Gibson will join us."

It was common enough for the captain to delay joining the ship,
mainly because getting the ship down the river was not the master's
responsibility. Instead, one pilot took the ship to Gravesend, and
then another piloted the course to the port of Deal in Kent—or
Portsmouth, or Spithead, or wherever the point of departure might
be. It was all part of the duties of the Trinity House of Deptford,
which included the ancient Company of Master Mariners of England, and which had been established in 1515. In return for getting
money for ballasting all the ships that sailed out of the Port of London, the Brethren of the Fraternity surveyed the channels of the
Thames month by month, marking soundings with buoys as guides
for themselves. Not only was it was impractical to expect the com-
manders of seagoing ships to navigate the ever-changing river, but
there were hundreds of last-minute matters for them to attend to
back in the City.

Dr. James Brown found his ship in London. Accordingly, he was
on board when the *Japan* was "towed by the *Nelson*, Tug Steam-
boat to Gravesend," on December 15, 1834. In May 1837, Dr. Fysh
of the *Coronet* had the same experience, except that his ship was
towed by the *Tam O'Shanter*. "All the men or nearly all drunk," he
noted, adding, "That's nothing! It will be long before Jack [slang
for a sailor] gets another chance of being so again! So go it my Boys
make the best of your time."

On the other hand, Robert Smith Owen arrived at Gravesend
under his own steam, intending to meet his ship there. If he had
been informed that the *Warrens* had already dropped down the
Thames for her final outfitting, it would have been easy for him to
descend the steps that led down to the Thames at the foot of the
Custom House, and hire a boatman. The dank air of the river would
have echoed with cries from the multitude of watermen looking out
for custom, crying "Oars, sculls, sculls, oars, oars!" and the "long

ferries" that plied the length of the river (instead of merely crossing it) and would have taken Owen in the right direction.

At that time of the year there would have been a dense fog, probably so thick that within one punt of the oars it would have been impossible to see the steps, and the Tower of London would have been a mere gray blob in the gloom ahead. Despite the poor conditions, a crush of traffic would have plied the surface, for the river served as the City's major thoroughfare, and so Smith Owen would have heard the creak of oars in every direction, along with the curses of the men who pulled them. As they drew abreast of St. Katherine's Docks and the shipyards of Wapping, the fog would also have echoed with the eerie singing of sailors and the shouted orders of captains and mates, rolling casks, rattling chains, and ropes splashing into the water, perhaps even the bleat of shipboard goats.

Then a sudden little gust would have whisked from the west as the ferry turned into the broad, imposing reach of the Limehouse, enabling the young surgeon to study the docklands on either side— the Surrey Commercial Docks on the south bank and the West India Docks to the north, the latter cutting across the peninsula of the Isle of Dogs. Just a little below the opening of Deptford Creek he would have seen a great hulk that lay slumped against the bank, once a first-rate man-of-war, now the charitable institution *Dreadnought*, its grandness turned into a seaman's hospital. As the ferry passed about Greenwich Reach, the hulk would have disappeared from sight, the view now being claimed by the Royal Observatory and the twin domes of the Sir Christopher Wren–built Royal Naval Hospital, all set in the spring green of Greenwich Park.

Then they would come to Barking Creek at the end of Gallions Reach, where the Royal Dockyards were sited along with the Royal Arsenal. Four old, twisted trees served as a navigation mark there, and twelve feet of water was guaranteed by the men of the Trinity House of Deptford. Past Gallions Reach the river took a huge right-hand curve on the way to Long Reach, and the City was left behind. Green pastures lay to either side, where hundreds of Scotch cattle grazed. According to gossip, these same cows were used as signals by Kentish smugglers, who tethered them in patterns that spelled out a code to the incoming ships. In the distance, white gashes marked the place where chalk was quarried for the Whitbread lime-works of Purfleet. Then Owen would see Beacon Hill and the Long Reach Tavern—a notorious gathering place for those who followed the sports of cockfighting and bare-knuckle prizefighting—and the village of Greenhithe, where there was always a cluster of small craft at the wharf. After that, the river widened and flattened. The castle-like gate of Pitcher's shipyard then came into view, marking the entrance to Gravesend, with Tilbury Fort on the opposite side. Dr. Robert Smith Owen's ferry would have pulled up to Gravesend Town Pier to moor at the foot of a line of timber-framed waterside taverns—but the ship was not there!

The date—April 5, 1837—was the appointed one, even if the *Warrens*, mysteriously, had not arrived. So Robert Smith Owen booked into an inn, something he could ill afford. At dawn he was on the dock looking anxiously about, but still the whaler had not arrived. Paying a man "to give me notice when she did so," he went back to the tavern, had breakfast, "took a walk to the top of Wind-mill Hill"—no doubt for a better view—walked "across the fields to an Old Church," and then filled in more time by going to the library to write a letter to Dear Emma. Finally, at dusk, he "walked to the pier & saw the *Warrens* heaving to off Gravesend." What a relief! He promptly paid his bill at the inn, met Captain Gray, and shared a toast of hot sweetened wine and water: "had a glass of Negus, and went on board."

On October 14, 1837, on the far side of the Atlantic, another of our whaling surgeons boarded his ship—but probably not in a spirit of high adventure and lively anticipation. His feelings, by contrast, were much harder to gauge, since he had signed on to the voyage under very strange circumstances for a gentleman of his attainments.

This fellow's name was John B. King, and he hailed from the island of Nantucket. While London whalers finished their fitting out at Gravesend, Nantucket whaleships completed their preparations for voyage at Edgartown, Martha's Vineyard, where Dr. King arrived on that date. First he became acquainted with the officers and then he inspected the quarters that were to be his for the next three years, writing, "The inner stateroom on the starboard side is to be my home for the present, and I hope it may continue to be so during my stay on board [for] it is more out of the noise of the ship and dryer in rough weather than most of the others."

His room was sited forward of the captain's stateroom on the privileged side of the ship, which also indicates that he was a favored member of the crew—as was only right and proper, considering his credentials. In 1832, at the age of twenty-four, King had graduated from the New York College of Physicians and Surgeons with the very substantial degree of Doctor of Medicine and Surgery. He was immediately awarded a certificate that allowed him to practice in New York, a status which was confirmed by his appointment as Resident Surgeon of the New York Hospital and his membership of the Medical Society of the City and County of New York, both in 1833. These elaborate qualifications failed to settle him down. He moved to Nantucket—and then he signed onto the whaler.

It was a most eccentric decision. For a start, there was no legal reason for Dr. King to be on board the *Aurora*. While an English whaling master was required by law to ship a surgeon, American whaleship captains were not. Instead, they were expected to cope with medical emergencies themselves, with the aid of a medical chest and the medical guide that went with it. To help them administer drugs the little bottles in the chest had numbers on the labels, and the guide gave instructions about which bottle to use and how much to prescribe. Of course the hazards were awful, particularly when captains got desperate. Legend has it that one master, running out of number eleven, made up the deficiency by mixing equal parts of numbers five and six.

This tale does not sound quite so ridiculous when some of the well-substantiated stories are taken into account. Captain John

Whaleship *Aurora*.   ARTIST, RON DRUETT

Deblois of the famous *Ann Alexander*, which was rammed and sunk by a whale while *Moby-Dick* was in press ("I wonder if my evil art has raised the monster," exclaimed Melville when he heard of it) was renowned for his very good luck; he had the enormous good fortune of being rescued within forty-eight hours, unlike the miserable crew of the *Essex* (also sunk by a whale), who drifted about the Pacific for several months and eventually resorted to eating each other. When Deblois had gallstones, his good fortune held, for he survived his own medicating. According to his account, he "took a little of everything that was in the Medicine Chest," including "Laudanum enof [enough] to kill any well man," with the result that he was forced to head for port and a "real" doctor in a hurry.

Unsurprisingly, many skippers defied convention by shipping a surgeon in some foreign port, especially toward the end of the voyage, when the crew was run down with hard living at sea and alcoholic sprees in port. Thus, in December 1854, a surgeon by the name of Tom Noddy signed onto the crewlist of the *Java* of New Bedford. The ship was in Honolulu, provisioning for the home-

Whaleship *Nantucket*.

ARTIST, RON DRUETT

On August 20, 1851, Captain John Deblois of the *Ann Alexander* lost his ship in a famous encounter with a furious bull whale. The bull attacked two boats, bit them to kindling, and then rushed the *Ann Alexander*, going through her side like a cat through wet paper. Six months afterward, that same whale was taken by the *Rebecca Simms*, with John's marked harpoons and a lot of splintered wood still adhering to his body and head. Deblois was luckier, for he, along with all his crew, was rescued within two days by Richard Gibbs of the ship *Nantucket*. Gibbs took them all to Paita, Peru, and Deblois paid for his passage home by selling his story to the papers.

Himself completely unshaken by the incident, Gibbs carried his wife, Almira, on the next voyage of the *Nantucket*, a lengthy and protracted journey that lasted just over four years. The old ship finally sighted the shores of their home island of Nantucket on August 7, 1859—and the pilot ran the ship ashore at the southwest end of Nashawena Island. "So ends a long voyage," wrote Almira. "Saved our oil but lost the Ship after carrying us safely over thousands of miles by water we left her upon the Rocks."

ward passage, and Dr. Noddy, it seems, wanted to work his passage to the Atlantic. Perhaps he had failed to establish a practice in the islands, or maybe he had been fired from his job on an English whaleship—which often happened. Whatever his record, Captain John Lawrence was pleased to take him on, though as events proved, Tom Noddy spent more time medicating Lawrence's dogs—"a pair of Russian hounds brought from the Okhotsk Sea" that were subject to fits of madness that cleared the decks like a hail of shot—than he did in treating the men.

It was quite unheard-of for a surgeon to be shipped for the entire voyage of an American whaler. Still more amazingly, John King had signed as a seaman, to serve "before the mast." Why he had made this very strange decision is unknown, but the fact remains that he was prepared to live in the damp, noisome forecastle with the other common sailors, bunking in a narrow wooden berth with two dozen companions snoring and cursing around him, eating plain, greasy food that had been sent down in a common bucket, urinating into a barrel, and easing his bowels over the bow of the ship. And, what's more, he was not even the first American physician to make this extraordinary choice. Just two years previously, a nameless doctor shipped as a seaman on the whaler *Lucy Ann* of Wilmington, Delaware, his presence documented only when one of the men was dragged out of a whaleboat by a pugnacious whale. Noting that the poor fellow "was shockingly lacerated," a shipmate, William Gardner, went on to record that they got the injured man on board, "and committed him to the care of our physician (who although a regular graduate in his profession, was like the rest of us, before the mast)."

Captain John J. Parker of the *Lucy Ann* had ignored the unofficial presence of a doctor on his ship, but Captain John Hussey Jr. of the *Aurora* was of a different mind, for as soon as he found out that he had a physician in the forecastle, he reassigned John King to the post of surgeon. It is impossible to tell if the young doctor felt cheated of some strange ambition, for he did not confide his feelings to his journal. Instead, he immediately demonstrated that he was a conscientious and dutiful man, for one of his first actions after settling in and looking around was to check off the contents of the ship's medical chest.

3

The Medical Chest

ADVERTISEMENT—

MEDICINE CHESTS for SHIPS and FAMILIES
put up and replenished,
with approved directions.

Elisha Thornton Jr.,
Druggist and Apothecary,
New Bedford, Massachusetts, 1844

WHILE JOHN WOODALL WOULD HAVE UNDERSTOOD JOHN KING'S qualifications and, indeed, found them most impressive (for in Woodall's time the possession of a university degree would have elevated King to the lordly status of physician), the seventeenth-century barber-surgeon would have been quite flummoxed by many of the items in the medical chest of the Nantucket whaleship *Aurora*, which Dr. John B. King counted off so conscientiously in 1837.

Indeed, there is so much difference between the two chests that a comparison chart can be made (appendix A). As well as commenting on the uses of each of his medicaments, King noted the conditions he treated during the last three months of voyage (charted in appendix B), which also demonstrate the difference in resources and attitudes two centuries after Woodall.

In John King's time, the teaching in American medical schools placed great emphasis on a strenuous program of purging, bloodletting, sweating, and blistering that was designed to correct a perceived imbalance in the patient's physiological condition. It was a credo that harked all the way back to the classical canon of the four humors, which, as we have seen, was a philosophy Woodall shared—but from a stance of moderation and restraint. It was best, John Woodall believed, to leave the cure to Nature as much as possible, for he had observed that "an old wife oftentimes exceedeth a great Artist in healing, for she wrestleth not with Nature as great masters doe." John King, by contrast, would have been taught that decisive interference was best, for this was the thrust of medical thought at the time.

The man who popularized heroic therapy was Benjamin Rush (1745–1813), one of the signers of the Declaration of Independence, and onetime surgeon-general of the Continental Army. As a charismatic teacher at the University of Pennsylvania, he indoctrinated

1	Alum	*29*	Paregoric
2	Antimonial Wine	*30*	Essence of Peppermint
3	Basilicon Ointment	*31*	Rhubarb
4	Blister Plaster	*32*	Simple Ointment
5	Blue Vitriol	*33*	Spts. Hawthorn
6	Burgundy Pitch	*34*	Spts. Nitre
7	Calomel & Jalap	*35*	Sugar of Lead
8	Calomel Pills	*36*	Syrup of Squills
9	Calomel	*37*	Liquid Opodeldoc
10	Chamomile Flowers	*38*	Tinct. of Myrrh
11	Castor oil	*39*	Tinct. of Guaiac
12	Camphor Gum	*40*	White Vitriol
13	Salts of Lemon	*41*	Quinine
14	Cream of Tartar	*42*	Tinct. of Rhubarb
15	Doves Powders	*43*	Gum Arabic
16	Balsam Copaiba	*44*	Blue pill
17	Elixir Vitriol	*45*	Strengthening plaster
18	Emetic Tartar	*46*	Adhesive plaster
19	Ether	*47*	Glauber Salts (in tubs)
20	Flaxseed		Chloride of Lime (in jars)
21	Flowers of Sulphur		
22	Ipecac		
23	Kino		
24	Laudanum		
25	Mercurial Ointment		
26	Nitre		
27	Olive oil		
28	Opium pills		

Dr. King's list of medicaments in the medical chest of the *Aurora*.

hundreds of students with his single-minded conviction that just about any condition was best treated with vigorous bloodletting and a drastic purge with calomel (a form of mercury). Many of his acolytes carried this doctrine further than Rush could have ever dreamed, for this was a time when the American people were thrusting ever outward, emigrating to the West as well as pioneering new

The particulars of the Surgeons Cheſt.

The reſt that follow are not leſſe neceſſary then the former for their particular v-ſes, namely.

The *Saluatory furniſhed with ſuch Vnguents as hereafter in their pla-ces are named.*

The *Plaſter boxe furniſhed with the due inſtruments and medicines thereunto belonging.*

The *Inſtruments for the Plaſter box are as followeth.*

Sizers.
Forceps.
Spatule.
Probe.
Stitching quill and needles.
Lancet.
Burras pipe.
Leuatory.
Vuula ſpoone, &c.

Cupping glaſſes.
Braſſe Baſon.
Blood porringers.
Diſt pot.
Skillet.
Chafing-diſh.
Gliſter pot.
Funnell.
Cups to giue potions in.
One board to ſpread plaſters.
Morter and Peſtell.
Waights and ſcales.
Siues.
Searces.
Strainers.

Splints.
Iuncks.
Tape.
Towe.
Spunges.
Clouts.
Rowlers.
Gray paper.
White paper.
Empty pots.
Glaſſes.
Thred and needles.
Waxe lights.
Lanthorne.
Tinder-boxe furniſhed.
Inke and Quilles.
1 Cloſeſtoole.
1 Bedſtoole and a braſſe paile.
Brick:s to heat vpon occaſion.
Pipkins.
Empty bags.
Skins of Lether.

The particulars of ſuch Emplai-ſters as are moſt common in vſe by Sea Surgeons.

Emplaſtrum.

Stipt: paracelſ.
Diachilum cum gummis.
Diachilum ſimplex.
Diachalcitheos.
Oxicrotium.
Melilotum pro ſplene.
Melilotum ſimplex.
De Lapide Calaminari.
de Minio.
Callidum or ſpiced plaſter.

Vnguents

Woodall's list of "The particulars of the Surgions Chest."

trading routes at sea. Rush's theories went with them—not just because they were easy to follow, but also because his pharma-copoeia was so largely based on inorganic substances, which, when carried long distances, kept much better than herbs.

In direct contrast, of the 281 remedies listed in Woodall's book (more evidence of the massive size of his chest), 145 are herbal, while a total of 204 have significant biotic content. This, of course, created problems over long voyages. Woodall himself admitted the difficulty of keeping herbs viable, listing fourteen herbs and roots—rosemary, mint, melilot clover, sage, thyme, absinthe, blessed

The particulars of the Surgeons Chest.

Vnguents most in vse in the Surgeons Chest.

Vnguentum
- Bazillicon.
- Apostolorum.
- Aureum.
- Ægyptiacum.
- Albū Camphoratū.
- Diapompholigos.
- Pettorale.
- Rosarum.
- Nutritum.
- Populeon.
- De Melle & Sapo.
- Contra Ignem.
- Contra Scorbutum.
- Dialthea composita.
- Dialthea simplex.
- Potabile.
- Mercurij.
- Linamentum arcei.
- Aragon.
- Martiatum.
- Axungiæ porcinæ.
- Axungiæ Cerui.
- Mel simplex.

- Annisced.
- Absinthij.
- Melissa.
- Angelica.
- Minthe.
- Cardui sancti.
- Theriacalis.

Rosæ Damaski.
Rosa Rub.
Odorifera.
Plantaginis.
Falopij.
Viridis.
Aqua fortis.
Uerinice.
Lotion.
Luinum forte.
& Commune.
Acetum Rosarum.
Acetum Vini.

Spiritus
- Vini.
- Vitrioli.
- Terebinthinæ.

Causticke liquid.

Sal
- Absinthij.
- Gemmæ.
- Nitræ.

Waters or liquors fitting the Surgeons Chest.

Aqua
- Cælestis.
- D. Stevens.
- Rosa solis.
- Cinamon.
- Limoniorum.
- Rosemary.
- Sassafras.

Oleum
- Rosarum.
- Anethinum.
- Chamomeli.
- Lumbricorum.
- Liliorum.
- Hipericonis simplex.
- Hipericonis cum gummis.
- Balmi Artificialis.
- Sambucorum.

A 2

thistle, melissa (balm mint), sabina (juniper), althea (hollyhock), *Raphana silvestris* (horseradish), pellitory (pyrethrum), angelica, and comfrey—as the "herbes most fit to be carried." John King did not have that problem, for he carried just seven herbal remedies—dried chamomile flowers, castor oil, flaxseed, olive oil, peppermint essence, and rhubarb, plus myrrh, the aromatic resin of the desert tree *Commiphora abyssinica*. Valued since the dawn of history as an ingredient in perfume, incense, and ointments, myrrh is still used in mouthwashes for spongy and ulcerated gums. However, in the continuous medical record that he kept in his journal over a three-month

The Particulars of the Surgeon: Chest.

period (August 17 to November 22, 1840), King made no mention of using myrrh—though he did note two instances of prescribing absinthe ("wormwood"), once in a regime for easing the mate's foul stomach, and again in the treatment of a head wound. He must have obtained the tincture on shore, for it was not in his original inventory. A hint of absinthe in vermouth imparts the bitterness that flavors martinis, and wormwood leaves provided the flavoring ingredient in "absinthe," a popular nineteenth-century aperitif that was enjoyed by many French Impressionist artists. Now recognized as a poison, it was probably one of the most dangerous alcoholic drinks ever devised: Van Gogh was most probably

The particulars of the Surgions Cheſt.

Pils
- Agaricum.
- Aurea.
- Chochie.
- De Euphorbio.
- De Cambogia.
- Ruſſy.

Puluis laxatus.
- Bendict Laxatiue.
- Arthreticus.

Trochiſcus
- Abſinthia.
- Alhandall.
- De Spodio.
- De Minio.

Simples.

- Foliorum ſena.
- Rhabarbare.
- Agaricum.
- Scamonia.
- Aloes.
- Hermodactilis.
- Polipodium.
- Dens Elephantis.
- Cornu cerui.
- Euphorbij.
- Turbith.
- Mirabulanorum.
- Cambogia.
- Caſſia fiſtule.

Certaine other Simples.

- Crocus.
- Opium.
- Chine.
- Sarſſaparilla.
- Saſſafras.
- Guaiacum.
- Cortex guaiaca.

- Cortex granatorum.
- Licorice.
- Hordia com:
- Hordia gallice.
- Semen aniſa.
- Feuiculi.
- Carraway.
- Cumini.
- Petrocelini.
- Lini.
- Fenigrece.
- Anetha.
- Papaueris.
- Plantaginis.
- Sem: quatuor frigide.
- Maioris.
- Minoris.
- Saccacum.
- Amigdalarum.
- Vna paſſa.
- Annuum.

Spices, viz.

- Sinamone.
- Macis.
- Piper.
- Cloues.
- Nuces Muſcati.

Gummes.

- Guiace.
- Opoponax.
- Bdelium.
- Amoniacum.
- Sagapenum.
- Galbanum.
- Myrrhe.

A 3   Maſticke.

deranged with absinthe poisoning when he hacked off his ear and sent it to a friend. One item notably omitted from Woodall's list but found in the *Aurora*'s medical box is syrup of squills (a distillation from the dried bulb of the sea onion *Scilla maritima* that is sweetened with honey), a vegetable remedy that had been used as an expectorant and diuretic since earliest classical times. Homer wrote about it, and it was described in detail by Dioscorides, a Greek army surgeon of the first century B.C. who wrote the first superstition-free pharmacopoeia, *De Materia Medica*. However, if Dr. King dosed any of the seamen of the *Aurora* with syrup of squills, he failed to make any note of it in his journal.

The particulars of the Surgions Chest.

Masticke.
Laudannm.
Storax calaminthe.
Liquida.
Beniamen.
Tragagantum.
Pix naualis.
Resina.
Succinum.

Cerusa venetia.
Lithargum aureum.
Viride aes.
Tutia.

Baccæ { Iuniperi.
       { Lauri.

Ferni { Tritici.
      { Fabarum.
      { Hordei.
      { Furfuris.
      { Volatilis.

Other needfull Simples of diuers kindes.

Cera citrina.
Mummia.
Sparmaceti.
Sanguis Draconis.
Lupines.
Cantharides.
Camphora.
Spodium.
Sumach.
Galls.
Bolus vere.
Bolus comunis.

Herbes most fit to be carried.

Herbæ. { Rosmarinus.
        { Mentha.
        { Melilotum.
        { Saluia.
        { Thimum.
        { Absinthium.
        { Carduus benedictus.
        { Melliffa.
        { Sabina.

Mineralls.

Antimonium or Stibium.
Sulphur.
Alumen roche.
Vitriolum commune.
Vitriolum album.

Radices { Althea.
        { Raphana siluestres.
        { Peratrum.
        { Angelica.
        { Confolida.

Calx viua.
Album grecum.

And

Instead of relying on herbs, John King depended on chemicals, like copper sulfate ("blue vitriol," for burning ulcers and chancres), zinc sulfate ("white vitriol"), and lead acetate ("Sugar of Lead," mixed with white vitriol and water to make a bath for inflamed eyes). He considered magnesium sulfate (Epsom salts, a strong laxative) so essential that he went to the trouble of procuring an ample stock of it himself, for it was not supplied with the chest. Mercury, copper, sulfur, and lead were the foundation stones of his pharmacopoeia. Of the twenty-three medicaments noted with any frequency in his journal, only eight had any herbal origin. Interestingly, this difference is reflected in a controversy of King's own time. While surgeons were carrying Benjamin Rush's theories to the far boundaries of America and the sea, back home on the Eastern Seaboard an "anti-calomel" movement had sprung up as the dangers of mercury poisoning were recognized by an alarmed public. Increasingly, common people were turning away from the physicians and resorting to herb doctors, many of them Indian. Given the choice of Woodall's therapy and Benjamin Rush's, back East the popular vote would have been overwhelmingly for Woodall.

Nonetheless, the medical chest of the *Aurora* had definitely been made up by a disciple of the Rush line of thought. John King listed no less than five manifestations of mercury, one of which, calomel, Benjamin Rush promoted as a heroic purge. Otherwise, mercury was the standard remedy for syphilis, a disease traditionally associated with seamen.

SYPHILIS WAS PROBABLY CARRIED TO EUROPE BY THE CREWS OF Christopher Columbus's ships. In November 1493, during the second voyage, the expedition's physician, Dr. Chanca, noted that the Carib Indians of Guadeloupe captured many women in the course of their tribal wars, "especially those who are young and handsome, and keep them as body servants and concubines; and so great a number do they carry off that in fifty houses we entered no man was found but all were women." These unfortunate females were used as brood stock; Chanca remarked earlier that the Caribs "eat the children which they bear them, only bringing up those whom they have by their native wives," so it is very understandable that "more than twenty handsome women came away voluntarily with us." The consequences were dire. The following year, a new disease was described by such experts as Nicolo Leoniceno, Professor of Physic at Ferrara, Italy, that was characterized by painful pustules on the infected part, spreading to the rest of the body and the face, and leading to ulcers, sore and swollen joints, fever, blindness, and death.

A much more severe condition than it is now after five centuries of exposure, it was officially called "syphilis," but was known to thousands of seamen by the name of any country that did not happen to be their own. Thus, the Spanish called it "the French Pox," and the French called it "the Spanish Disease," and each blamed the other for spreading it. In fact, just about all of Europe was responsible, for it was also very much more infectious than it is now, and could be passed on by kissing or even drinking from the same tumbler.

Primary, secondary, and tertiary stages were quickly recognized in the progress of the disease. First, infection was indicated by a hard sore, or "chancre," on the site of contact. Dr. King, like John Woodall, burned this away with the application of some caustic substance, but in fact this made no difference, for whether it was treated or not, the sore would heal of itself, leaving a small scar. Six to eight weeks later, the patient would develop a fever and a rash. This was when he was at his most infectious, and consequently it was the stage treated most drastically. A standby was mercurial ointment (King's number 25), which was made up of equal parts of mercury and lard with a small addition of prepared suet. A walnut-sized lump of this was rubbed into the inside of the thighs night and morning until so much mercury was absorbed through the skin that the inside of the mouth became sore and the patient drooled. This was known as "salivation," and was a sign that the desired effect was being achieved.

And then there was blue pill (King's number 44), more usually known as a "mercury pill," made up of two parts of mercury to three of confection of roses, with one part of powdered licorice root being added last. If this did not seem to work, then the next recourse was the calomel pill (number 8), made up of one part of mercurous chloride, one part of sulfurated antimony, and two parts of guaiacum resin, combined with castor oil and ninety-percent-proof alcohol. This, as Dr. King went on to note, was guaranteed to produce "the action of mercury on the system"—something considered laudable despite the dreadful hazards.

Woodall was familiar with calomel, for mercurous chloride was a form of mercury that had been widely used since the sixteenth century. He called it *Mercurius Sublimatus*: "let none attempt to make this medicine without good direction or experience, for there is no

MERCVRIVS. ☿

My shape and habit strange you see,
    my actions best can witnesse me:
About the world I take my way,
    with Sol in circuit once a day.

From earth to skie with oft returnes,
    from skie once to a blast:
From good to bad and good againe,
    hence winged, I flie in haste.
                    N ıı 2

OF

small danger in the working thereof," he nervously wrote. Even King regarded it with some caution. "This is often used as a purge mixed with other medicines," he wrote. "Ten grains is a full dose." A level teaspoon measured "about four times that quantity," he noted, presumably to avoid overdosing. The symptoms of mercury poisoning include loss of weight, constant drooling, foul breath, blurred vision, slurred speech, and impaired balance; if treatment is continued, kidney collapse is inevitable, resulting in death. It is certain that doctors were aware of this, but, because the symptoms of syphilis went away and the patient seemed cured (if he did not die of mercury poisoning first), it seemed as if the regime was worth the risk. What the surgeons did not realize is that the symptoms would disappear just as rapidly—within six months of infection—without any treatment at all. It certainly did not signify a cure. Years later—in some patients, but not all—the syphilis would resurface in its tertiary stage, leading inevitably to madness and death.

It is horrifying now to think that hiccups, infant diarrhea, and morning sickness were also treated with calomel, but it was quite routine in the mid-nineteenth century. In fact, mercury was considered a cure for a wide range of complaints. "Calomel & Jalap," wrote Dr. King, was prescribed "where there is costiveness with indications of foul stomach or furred tongue, bad taste in the mouth, feverishness &c." Jalap, the powdered root of *Ipomoea purga*, a Mexican twining plant related to the convolvulus, was unknown to Woodall, for it had not been imported to England in his time. It is a mild, safe cathartic that is still used today. When combined with calomel, however, its effect was painfully brisk. Nonetheless, Dr. King prescribed it without restraint, once for sciatica!

Jalap was not the only plant derivative in the medical chest of the *Aurora* that would have been unfamiliar to Woodall. Another was kino (*Pterocarpus marsupium)* the dried sap of a tree native to the Indian subcontinent, noted by Dr. King as a "powerful astringent" and used in cases of severe dysentery. A third was Peruvian bark, refined as quinine, which—as John King noted—is "the active ingredient of Peruvian Bark from which it is obtained."

Harvested from *Cinchona* trees native to South America, Peruvian bark was introduced to Europe from Peru by Jesuit missionaries in about 1640 as a cure for "intermittent fever" (malaria). The medicine was first advertised for sale in England in 1658 by James Thompson, and twenty years later it was made official in the London pharmacopoeia, but the plant producing it was not known to botanists till 1737. There was some confusion, as certain *Cinchona* trees have much more of the active ingredient, quinine, than others, but nonetheless the bark was hailed with such enthusiasm that there was a race to introduce the tree to other parts of the world. The Netherlands East India Company was the winner, successfully establishing plantations of *Cinchona succiruba* in the islands and archipelagoes of the South China Sea and then settling back to enjoy huge profits. The greatest blessing, however, was that thousands of sailors' lives were saved from the ravages of malaria.

Quinine "is preferable to bark," Dr. King went on, "as being less bulky and less likely to nauseate or disturb the bowels":

> It is the principal remedy in the cure of intermittent fevers. It should be taken in the intermissions between the hot stages, in the dose of a grain every hour, an emetic at the commencement of the chill, and a purge of Calomel & Jalap afterwards having been given before commencing with the quinine. Quinine is also serviceable in many other fevers and diseases attended with debility. In the latter stages of small pox, in Typhus Fever, and generally, where the system is greatly prostrated, this medicine will be found highly serviceable. Attention should be paid to the bowels. If the medicine produces much looseness a few drops of laudanum may be added to each dose.

And then there was ipecac, an emetic made from the root of *Cephaelis ipecacuanha* that is still a standard means of inducing vomiting. In Woodall's time, the same effect was achieved with euphorbia, for ipecac was unavailable to him. Although commonly used in Brazil, where it is native, the plant derivative did not arrive in Europe until 1672, when an explorer by the name of Legros carried samples of the root to Paris. Eight years later, the physician Helvetius began prescribing it for dysentery after making it up into a patent medicine that he had acquired the sole right to dispense. Finally, the French government bought the secret formula, handing over the generous sum of one thousand louis d'or. At last, in 1688, it was made public. John King prescribed ipecac with an enthusiasm that is in marked contrast to his disinterest in the old herbal remedies, it being his standard remedy for gastrodynia ("foul stomach") and even occasionally his recourse for treating a headache. Additionally, it was a feature of Dover's powder, a patent medicine that John King also prescribed freely, sometimes in combination with calomel.

The originator of this medicine was the famous "Quicksilver Doctor," Thomas Dover, who for many years had a private practice in Bristol. In 1708, at the age of forty-eight, Dover suddenly decided that life was boring, and went to sea with the famous privateer captain, Woodes Rogers, on a voyage that proved very successful indeed. First, on Woodes Rogers's ship *Duke*, he took part in the rescue of Robinson Crusoe (a.k.a. Alexander Selkirk) from his self-imposed exile on the island of Juan Fernandez, and then, in 1709, in command of a captured Spanish ship, he sacked the port of Guayaquil, sailing off with a fortune in plunder. When plague struck his ship after his men had looted churches that were full of dead Spanish bodies, Dover (no advocate of Woodall's doctrine of moderation) cured all but eight of 180 of his crew by bleeding them from both arms until they fainted. After that, much enriched by the money his adventure had earned him—a salary of £422, £100 "storm money," £24 "plunder money," and a share of the booty that totaled £2,755—he set up in private practice in London and proceeded to augment this vast income by inventing his patent medicine. Prescribed for colds, coughs, insomnia, rheumatism, pleurisy, and dysentery, Dover's powder became a standard feature of the medical chest, circling the globe until the mid-twentieth century, when it was supplanted by antibiotics. One of the major ingredients was ipecac. The other was the processed resin of the capsule of the poppy *Papaver somniferum*, otherwise known as opium.

POPPY RESIN HAS BEEN FAMOUS AS A SOPORIFIC AND APHRODISIAC since very ancient times. In the third century B.C. the Greek botanist Theophrastus referred to the gummy sap extracted from poppy-seed capsules as "opion," while the juice obtained by crushing the entire plant was known as "meconion." Thebaic opium—collected from the poppy fields of Thebes—was particularly cherished. The method of harvesting was carefully noted by Dioscorides. "Those who wish to obtain the sap," he wrote, "must go after the dew has dried and draw their knife around the star in such a manner as not to penetrate the inside of the capsule, and also make straight incisions down the sides. Then with your finger wipe the extruding tear into a shell. When you return to it not long after, you will find the sap thickened and the next day you will find it much the same. Pound the sap in your mortar and roll the mass into pills."

However, opium did not become the ingredient of choice for every huckster's miraculous elixir until after the second century A.D., when a man by the name of Galen rose from the humble status of a surgeon in a school for gladiators to become the medical paragon of the era. This was partly because Galen summarized what had gone before, making classical medical science accessible to all; and partly because he offered a complete system of understanding and therapy based on physiology. It was he who classified herbs into "degrees" of hot, cold, moist, and dry, thus cataloguing their affinity to the four humors. Because of Galen, the section of Woodall's book labeled "Of the Medicines, and their uses," makes such statements as, "Opium is colde and drie in the fourth degree," and "blacke pepper is hot and dry in the third degree." Benjamin Rush was not uninfluenced, either, because bleeding, purging, and blistering were basic Galen-style therapy. However, the major reason Galen's theories dominated medical practice for the next fourteen hundred years is that his view of scientific medicine was consonant with Christian dogma. A gifted anatomist, Galen believed that God's purposes could be divined by examining nature—which certainly helped make his theories the universally accepted yardstick throughout the Middle Ages.

Opium was turned into a mythic cure-all when Galen popularized mithridate, an antidote for poison that had been invented by Mithridates VI, who ruled Pontus (in modern Turkey) during the second century B.C. Obsessed with the prospect of assassination (he eventually died by his own hand), this scientific monarch had reached his medical conclusions by experimenting on hapless criminals. No simple concoction, mithridate contained about fifty ingredients, dried follicles from the sex organs of male beavers being one of them and lizards' bellies another. Though relatively weak in opium content compared to some of its successors, it had lasting powers as a patent medicine, for Woodall listed it in *The Surgions Mate* as "Methridatum," extolling its virtues for those who might be "fearefull of waters" (quite a disadvantage for a seaman), as well as those who were afflicted with the bites of serpents, mad dogs, wild beasts, and creeping things. According to him, it was also supposed to be effective against the falling sickness, pain in the bowels, ulcers of the mouth, spitting of blood, flux of the stomach, obstruction of the guts, and ringworm—just about everything, in fact; it was a universal comfort for "any griefes within the body."

The acceptance of mithridate as a medicine led to a movement that can aptly be called polypharmacy, which catered to the fashion for complicated potions. One of the most interesting and popular products was a concoction called "theriac" by the common populace, and "Theriacha Andromachi" by Woodall, who declared that it had all the virtues of mithridate and was good for hoarseness as well. Originally devised by Andromachus, court physician to Emperor Nero, theriac was a witches' brew of more than seventy ingredients, including gentian, valerian, aloe, rhubarb, cassia, various minerals, vipers' flesh, and honey, which were ceremoniously combined with the gum of *Papaver somniferum* in a ritualistic procedure. In Venice, on March 24 , 1645, John Evelyn (who was to become one of the founders of the Royal Society in London, as well as a Commissioner for Sick and Wounded Seamen), noted in his diary that he had been fortunate enough to witness its manufacture, the "extraordinary ceremony whereof I had been curious to observe, for it is extremely pompous and worth seeing." Because this version was so widely sought after, theriac was also known as "Venice Treacle."

A century before Woodall's time, the Swiss physician, Theophrastus Paracelsus (1492–1541), adapted the formula for theriac to produce laudanum, an opiate that Woodall, in a neat play of words, dubbed "This Laudable medicine. If were upon my life tomorrow to undertake a voyage to the East Indies in any great shippe," he went on to declare, "I would renounce all other compositions of that kinde whatsoever, rather than misse it." Forthwith, he produced a recipe "for the true preparation thereof," which included powdered coral, musk, crushed pearls, hartshorn, bezoar, "Succi Hyoscyami," oils of aniseed, cloves, cinnamon, and amber, and, of course, the all-important opium, which amounted to 25 percent of the mixture.

Many of these ingredients have histories that are as fascinating as the story of opium itself. Hartshorn—carbonated ammonia—was called "hartshorn" because it was produced by heating the horns of oxen and deer. Dr. King carried it as number 33, spirits of hartshorn. This was the "smelling salts" beloved by the writers of Regency romances. (The crew of the *Aurora* must have been a stalwart lot, for Dr. King never seems to have used it.) Bezoar, an ambergrislike concretion found in the intestines of grazing animals, was considered yet another specific against poison, the name itself being Arabic for "antidote." A nervous Spanish noble would drink out of a goblet with a little cage holding a goat's bezoar in the hollow stem, designed to neutralize any toxin an assassin might have slipped into the drink. Ironically, another ingredient in this mixture—"Succi Hyoscyami"—was a deadly poison in itself. This was the juice of henbane leaves, its active principles being hyoscyamine, atropine, and hyoscine (known today as scopolamine). Henbane has been regarded with respectful caution throughout history. A member of the order Solanaceae, and therefore a relative of belladonna (deadly nightshade), it is supposed to be the poison that killed Hamlet's father when it was dripped into his ear. In 1578 Lyte's *Herball* warned people about sleeping "under the shadow" of the plant, for fear that they "thereof become sicke and sometimes they die"—and then went on to recommend henbane drops for earache!

DR. KING CERTAINLY DID NOT HAVE THE FLAMBOYANT ARRAY OF opium-based cure-alls that Woodall boasted, the death-knell of polypharmacy having been struck in 1745 when William Heberden, physician to King George III, published his *Essay on Mithridatium and Theriaka*, so thoroughly debunking these so-called antidotes that they were struck from the pharmacopoeia. However, King did have his laudanum (number 24), albeit a more modern version, the Paracelsian formula having been adapted by Thomas Sydenham (1624–1689), the great English physician. Apart from opium, Sydenham's laudanum contained saffron, cinnamon, and cloves macerated in Spanish wine, a pleasant and efficacious remedy that was often a direct route to opium addiction, especially in ships that carried a medical chest with plenty of laudanum and no surgeon to supervise its use. Opium came as pills as well, and King prescribed them freely for pain relief, dysentery, and diarrhea. And then there was paregoric (number 29), a camphorated tincture of opium that was recommended for "slight cases of pain in the bowels or stomach, and in coughs & colds."

Another recourse that Dr. King had in common with Woodall was camphor gum, a product of the camphor tree, *Cinnamomum camphora*. This was—and is—useful as an antiseptic and a mild local anesthetic, and for sniffing up the nostrils to ease a cold. Dr. King noted that it worked best when combined with opium. They also shared "flowers of sulphur," which was, as Woodall poetically described:

'gainst itches tri'd
In country and in town

And to kill wormes in man and beast
Is us'd of every clowne.

In short, mixed with hog's lard, sulfur was a certain cure for the itch, and a good vermifuge as well. Combined "with the same quantity of cream of tartar," remarked John King, it "forms a good purge in piles." Dr. King was just as preoccupied with the bowels of the seamen under his care as Woodall had been. As well as rhubarb root in both powdered and tincture form (not, by the way, your usual kitchen rhubarb, but another species, *Rheum officinale*), and the Epsom salts that he procured and prescribed so freely, the choices on the *Aurora* for whalemen whose guts were out of order were castor oil, cream of tartar, and Glauber salts—hydrated sodium sulfate, number 47. Episodes of diarrhea were as common as in Woodall's time too, and Dr. King's recourse for this was opium and Dover's powder. Unsurprisingly, he had to treat a persistent case of hemorrhoids, that proved so intractable he finally resorted to Woodall's ancient remedy of fumigation in the close stool.

And then, of course, there was the drastic, Rush-inspired, calomel and jalap purge, for those who needed their humors balanced. Dr. King, to do him justice, delivered it only once in that three-month period on board the whaler *Aurora*, and he blistered only once as well.

BLISTERING WAS ANOTHER IMPORTANT ELEMENT IN THE heroic regime that had been popularized by Benjamin Rush—accompanied, of course, by bleeding and purging. Further, John King noted:

> In all cases before applying a blister the part should be washed with warm vinegar and wiped dry. The plaster should be spread as thick as a wafer, on soft leather. When laid aside it soon becomes mouldy in the dampness of a ship, but if rubbed over with a knife, the same one will draw [a blister] two or three times. When very old, it loses its strength. From eight to twelve hours is the time usually required for drawing a blister. Then remove it and dress with basilicon or simple ointment.

Plasters had been part of the medical armory for many centuries. To make a plaster, an apothecary took two parts each of powdered lead monoxide (white lead, or "litharge"), pork lard ("axungia porcine"), and olive oil, placed them in a large pot, and heated the mixture until boiling. Then he added water gradually, so that the mixture did not go off the simmer. Watching it narrowly as he stirred, the practitioner added more water as needed, until the mass had acquired a uniform white color, and the bubbles at the surface were large and elastic. When a small quantity dropped into cold water made a firm ball, he knew it was cooked (rather like making toffee), and set it aside. Once cooled, it was ready for shaping into bullets—"magdaléons"—on a wetted slab. These were stored until needed, when they were softened with heat, mixed with medicine if required, and then spread onto a piece of soft cloth or thin leather and slapped onto the patient. Thus it can be seen that the "plaster" is the substance "plastered" onto the fabric, and not the fabric itself—a common misconception.

Always used externally, plasters were (and are) adhesive, being sticky enough to cling to the skin of the patient. One of the advantages of this is that the area is kept moist, something that Woodall lauded because perspiration was retained while humors were drawn out and corns and other callosities softened. Adhesive plasters were also used to protect skin conditions like ulcers or to join the edges of a wound where stitches would not be desirable, such as in the face. (This, of course, is still the way that sticking plaster is used.) They were also very useful as a means of applying some kind of medication and then preventing it from evaporating or being rubbed off. In King's list there is a "strengthening" plaster—number 45—which would have incorporated something stimulating such as turpentine to warm and invigorate a particular area of the skin and "strengthen" the muscle underneath. And plasters are still used to apply medicine in that way, such as in the prevention of seasickness.

Thankfully, however, blister plasters are no longer standard medical practice. To prepare a blister or "epispastic" plaster, a surgeon mixed in a blistering agent, cantharides—powdered "Spanish fly" (though it is a beetle, not a fly, and quite rare in Spain)—being the popular choice. Lacking that, he could make do with burgundy pitch (King's number 6, spruce tree resin), though household mustard would do the job at a pinch. This plaster was applied to the skin and left until the epidermis separated from the flesh, forming a blister full of serous fluid. In severe cases the blisters were then opened with a lancet, the skin removed, and suppuration maintained with basilicon ointment or burgundy pitch.

The best that could be said for this treatment is that it was most surely a counter-irritant to whatever aches and agues the patient was suffering at the time. Theoretically, it drew foul humors to the surface, stimulated the system, and thus repaired an imbalance in the body. As late as 1884, a blister laid over the bowels was a recommended treatment for diphtheria—something that would have horrified Woodall. "It is a shamefull error of many foolish Artists still to be too busie with Causticke medicines," he wrote. There are eleven different plasters ("emplastra") listed in Woodall's chest, but not one of them was for blistering, and while he included cantharides in his list of "needful simples," he cautioned that "they are most dangerous," and should never be administered internally—"I once knew it given, but it killed the party the third day." King, by contrast, listed only two emplastra—the blister plaster and the adhesive plaster. However, in his journal he mentions prescribing a tonic, antispasmodic plaster for a man with palpitations, which he called "Empl. Rob. & Asef." (Emplastrum Roborans & Asafetida). For this, the aromatic resins frankincense and asafetida were mixed into the usual lard, oil, and litharge base. As neither frankincense or asafetida are mentioned in King's list, it seems probable that he obtained the plaster in ready-made form.

Such items mark one of the essential differences between the two medical inventories. Not only was the nineteenth-century practitioner much more reliant on inorganic substances, but many of the medicaments in the medical chest of the Nantucket whaler *Aurora*—Dover's powder, blue pill, blister plaster, adhesive plaster, mercurial ointment—were pre-prepared. Obviously, at least part of the reason for this was that whaling skippers, while expected to do the general medicating, did not have the knowledge necessary to make up pills and unguents themselves. However, it was a general trend, for John Wilson, the surgeon of the London whaler *Gipsy*, mentioned previously prepared items—adhesive plaster, blistering ointment, blue pill—in his journal, too. Woodall's surgeon's mate, on the other hand, had to make up just about everything himself, in single doses according to need. That is one reason the huge array of ingredients—twenty-three organic oils, twelve syrups of honey or herbs, six conserves (jellylike concoctions made of fruit and sugar), fifteen herbal "simples," eighteen different types of seeds, six spices, eight kinds of dried flowers, along with various berries, herbs, and roots—was necessary for him, while a surgeon like John King could manage with so few.

Because sores, cuts, and bruises were a constant hazard of work in the rigging and on a wildly pitching deck, Woodall's surgeon's mate would have spent a lot of his time making up ointments ("unguents"), lotions, and liniments. He would have had to learn quite a number of recipes, for Woodall listed twenty-one different ointments, ranging from "Ægyptiacum"—an oil-free mixture of copper acetate (verdigris), vinegar, and honey that was used to treat poisonous bites—to "Unguentum Album Camphoratum," an emollient of camphor, white wax, lard, and almond oil that was applied to skin sores "in any place, but chiefly in the yard [penis] betwixt glans and preputium." An unguent with the daunting name of "diapompholigos," made up of litharge, red lead, and the powdered root of deadly nightshade, was also applied to the penis for ulcers. Populeon, or "poplar" ointment, was a mixture of herbs and lard used for scurvy sores, while henna and attar of roses were mixed with wax and lard for inflammations.

In his original inventory, John King listed just three ointments and one liniment. One of them, basilicon (number 3), an unguent made up of resin, oil, and lard, was such an ancient standby that it is in Woodall's list as well. In his journal, King called it "Ung. Res."—Unguentum Resinæ. "This is the proper ointment to dress blisters with when it is desirable to keep them running for a few days," he wrote. "It is often the best application for ulcers following burns. For foul ulcers and sores, its stimulating properties render it preferable to simple ointment." As uncomplicated as its name suggests, simple ointment (number 32) was a mixture of yellow wax and lard, or wax and some vegetable oil. "This is used to dress blisters when it is wished to heal them up," wrote King, and forthwith supplied a recipe for making up the unguent if the original supply should go hard and rancid: "One part of melted beeswax and two of sweet oil mixed together and stirred till cold make an ointment similar to this." Opodeldoc (number 37) was a liniment made of soft soap, ammonia, and the essential oils of rosemary and thyme. A Victorian standby, it was something else that would have been made up by an apothecary onshore. Another liniment, which is not in the list but mentioned in King's journal, is "Lini. Ammon. Fte."—Linimentum Ammoniatum Forte—a compound liniment of camphor, alcohol, and lavender oil that he prescribed for a man with a contracted spermatic cord. Again, he would have obtained this ready-made.

In his diary, King also cited Turner's cerate, which was a patent ointment of calamine mixed into a base of wax, olive oil, and butter, and which he applied to an ulcerous wound. Likewise, he went to an apothecary for two medicaments for gonorrhea—Mistura Adamsi and Piperine—which he prescribed very freely indeed. Piperine is an extract of black pepper ash, drunk in water and useful in urethritis. What Dr. Adams's mysterious mixture might have been, however, is very hard to tell.

Strangely, unlike John Woodall's surgeons, John King did not have official recourse to brandy (Woodall's "spiritus vini"), though one suspects that he lifted some from the pantry when needed, for according to his diary he treated his skipper's intractable headache with hot punch. Similarly, while he did not include vinegar in his original list, he must have procured some from the ship's stores, for he used it in warm fomentations for bruises. An interesting tincture that he obtained on shore and he prescribed quite freely (once in combination with opium for palpitations), was Tinctura Lavandulæ Composita, a bracing mixture of lavender and rosemary oils, cinnamon, nutmeg, and ninety-proof alcohol. Another he procured on his own account was one of the few spirits that he did have in common with Woodall—Elixir Ad Longam Vitam, a sweetened alcoholic extract of aloes, gentian, rhubarb, and saffron. It was noted in his journal once when he prescribed it for the mate's sore stomach and at another time as part of a complicated regimen for a seaman's sciatica. However, the official inventory did include Elixir Vitriol (number 17), a sweetened alcoholic mixture of sulfuric acid, tincture of ginger, and spirit of cinnamon, though there is no record of him ever prescribing it. Similarly, he did not seem interested in dosing anyone with guaiac (number 39), the gum of a West Indian plant, *Guaiacum officinale,* usually prescribed for rheumatism. Ancient enough to be in Woodall's armory, it is still used today as an emulsifier in commercial foodstuffs.

Otherwise, the substances that King had in common with Woodall were inorganic, for instance the metallic element antimony. In King's case, it was carried in the form of a wine, the recipe for this being 40 grains of tartarated antimony dissolved in a fluid ounce of boiling water and then made up to a pint with alcohol or sherry. "It is good in cases of severe cough, in doses of a teaspoonful, mixed with the same quantity of paregoric, to be taken at bed time, and oftener, if necessary," he noted, and he prescribed it quite freely, often in combination with absinthe. Like Woodall, he included alum (potassium aluminum sulfate) in his armory—"A powerful astringent," wrote Dr. King. It was also a good gargle for mouths made sore with mercury. A very odd substance they had in common was what King called British Oil (it was not in the inventory, but was mentioned in his journal when he prescribed it to two men with running ears), and what Woodall called "Oleum Philosophorum: Oyle of Philosophers, or of tile-stones or brickebats." It was obtained by crushing hot bricks that had been soaked in various oils, sometimes a fossil oil, which would have resulted in some kind of petroleum extract.

Sweet spirits of nitrous ether—Dr. King's "Spts. Nitre" (number 34)—was a "useful medicine in affections of the urinary organs, in sickness of the stomach; in dropsies and bloatedness; in flatulency; and in many fevers." Number 19, ether—ethyl oxide—was "sometimes serviceable in sea-sickness in the dose of a teaspoonful taken in a glass of wine." Dr. King made no note of prescribing either of these. Employment of ether as a painkiller still lay in the future—though only barely so, for in 1842, just two years after John King's return to Nantucket, American surgeon Crawford Long successfully used it as a general anesthetic during surgery.

"Chloride of Lime is chiefly used for destroying infection and for removing foul smells," concluded Dr. King. "It should be placed in different parts of the vessel in buckets, pans, or anything else and moistened two or three times a day with water or what is better water made slightly acid with oil of vitriol, or Elixir vitriol, or vinegar." And so he came to the end of his official inventory—forty-seven items packed into a single wooden box. King might have stocked the chest differently if he had been given the option, for not only did he neglect to prescribe a significant number of the original items, but he supplemented the supplies whenever he had a chance. On August 19, 1838, for instance, he was pleased when the *Aurora* gammed with an English South Seaman, "the ship *Harpooner* Capt. Locke." Not only did it give him the opportunity to "make some acquaintance with Mr. Hill Doctor of the English Ship," but he was able to beg "a few articles of Medicine."

Short though the *Aurora*'s list may be, it was probably not atypical. A survey of apothecary bills in Cold Spring Harbor—which sent out a small whaling fleet from Long Island, New York—reveals that the average ship's medical chest contained just seventeen ingredients:

Adhesive plaster
Blue vitriol
Castor oil
Ceratum resinae

Elixir of vitriol
Epsom salts
Essence of peppermint
Flax seed
Purging powder
Laudanum
Sugar of lead
Paregoric
Peruvian bark
Stick caustic
Flowers of sulfur
Sweet oil
and something mysterious called "Turlington's Balsam of Life."

Obviously, this list indicated that this was a chest that had been stocked with economy in mind—an attitude of thrift that was certainly not confined to Cold Spring Harbor. "Having put up some thousands of ships' medical chests," runs an advertisement placed by Thomas Ritter, M.D., of "104 Cherry Street, New York, four doors above Oliver," in 1849:

> he ventures to say that for neatness of style, the excellent quality of the medicines, and for the care taken for the preservation of perishable articles, he is exceeded by no one in this country. In the replenishing of Medicine Chests, he is strictly careful to put up only such quantities as may be needed, never crowding the chest in order to enhance the amount of the bill.

And yet, with this scant stock of medicaments, plus a few lancets, a key for extracting teeth, and a simple medical guide, an American whaling skipper was supposed to treat successfully any of the large range of diseases and accidents that might befall his crew of more than thirty men. Accordingly, the crew of the Nantucket whaler *Aurora*—like the crews of English South Seamen—could be considered uncommonly fortunate, despite the possibility of Rush-style purging, bleeding, and blistering.

The *Aurora* sailed from Edgartown on November 5, 1837, in rugged weather, but not before Dr. King had performed his first operation. While the ship waited out a gale outside the harbor, he extracted two teeth for the small daughter of the lighthouse keeper. Then they took their departure, heading for the Pacific, and, like his fellow surgeons in the same situation, John King settled down to take stock of his surroundings and the folk with whom he would share the long journey.

4

The First Leg: Day-to-Day Life

I have leisure from morning to night
and from night to morning—
to employ myself in what?

Dr. John B. King,
onboard the Aurora

"I WAS THIS DAY ASK'D TO PRESCRIBE FOR A COMPLAINT I NEVER heard of before," mused Eldred Fysh, surgeon of the London whaler *Coronet*. It was June 15, 1837, and the ship had been at sea for two weeks.

"What is the matter with you?" Dr. Fysh asked this first shipboard patient, John Packham.

"Don't know, sir."

"What do you complain of?"

"The all-overs, sir."

"The all-overs?" Fysh echoed in astonishment. "Tell me what they are—in all my practice I have never heard of this before."

"Oh! Sir, it is pain in the head, pain in the belly, pain in the legs, pain all over."

"Ah, now I understand," quoth Dr. Fysh with a secret grin. "And, having the added information, I will endeavour to drive the all-overs all out of you. Which I succeeded in doing," he concluded, "by giving him two or 3 doses of salts."

On the *Japan*, the first call on James Brown's professional skills came on January 9, 1835, three weeks after departure. An outbreak of vomiting and diarrhea had affected all the crew "except those belonging to the Cabin." The cause was easily ascribed to polluted water in the scuttlebutt, from which the seamen drank, but the cure was more of a puzzle. In the end he gave them all a glass of rum, suggested that the water in the butt should be changed, and left the rest to nature.

This was an indication of the class system that ruled whalers, where "those belonging to the Cabin" had better quarters, drink, and provender than the people in the rest of the ship. The captain was at the head of a pyramid of authority. Below him were three officers in ranking order of first, second, and third mates, each of whom headed the six-strong crew of one of the four whaleboats. Next, came four harpooners—called "boatsteerers" on American vessels—who pulled the foremost oar and, as the name "harpooner" suggests, pitched the harpoons at the whale. Allied with these petty officers were the tradesmen of the ship—the cooper, the carpenter, the cook, the steward, the sailmaker, and the blacksmith. Next ranking down were the seamen, and lowest of all were the "boys."

Within this shipboard social ladder, the surgeon's place was an uneasy one. While John Packham might call Dr. Eldred Fysh "sir" and obey his directions in the matter of medicine, he would not take ordinary seagoing orders from a doctor, even though he himself was only a lowly apprentice. As we have seen, the surgeon's lay—or share of the profits of the voyage—was not even as big as the carpenter's, another indication of his humble status. However, as we have also seen from John King's arrival on the *Aurora* in Edgartown, the surgeon did have a stateroom (the name for a shipboard bedroom) of his own—quite a privilege, for the only other man to be so favored was the first officer.

This does not mean that either Eldred Fysh or James Brown would have felt particularly thrilled when he first clapped eyes on his accommodations for the next three years. On whalers the cabins were all below decks, the open deck being kept as clear as possible to allow room for tackling whales. Accordingly, the surgeon's cabin would have measured no more than six feet by five, much of it taken up by his wooden berth. To appreciate his luck, the doctor would have had to remember that the second and third mates shared a room of the same size as his, with one bunk above the other, while the harpooners and other petty officers lived in a room in the steerage (the area amidships), and the two dozen men who worked before the mast bedded down in the dark, damp, noisome forecastle, inside the bows.

Looking around his stateroom, the new surgeon must have wondered how he could possibly carry out his duties in such a restricted space. There was scarcely floor enough to stand on, and so his bag, his trunk, and his boxes of surgical instruments would have been stowed beneath his berth. It was common for a chair to be set by the head of the bed, placed facing a broad shelf that was hung on the wall. This would have served as his desk, and would have had another, narrower, shelf above it to hold a few books. Here was the place where he would keep his journal by the light of a lantern. Though the surgeon's stateroom usually had a sidelight or porthole, it was only just big enough to let in a glimpse of sky and a reflected ripple of water. Holding consultations here was not going to be easy.

Surgery promised to present an even greater problem. While his berth could serve as an examination couch, there was simply not enough elbowroom to carry out an operation, and so an alternative would have to be found. On early men-of-war, surgery was carried out in the hold. There, the great Tudor military surgeon, William Clowes, working in the dank bowels of the *Aide* in 1570, managed to open a man's chest and remove a rib that was puncturing a lung. The hold of a whaleship, however, was already crammed with casks, which held water as ballast until the day they would be filled with oil. Later, on men-of-war, a special place for emergency surgery called the "cockpit" was set aside between decks, usually on the orlop deck, which was one level above the holds. The between decks space in whalers—the "blubber room"—was reserved for chopping up blubber, however. Obviously, any necessary surgery would have to be carried out on the mess table—in the mess room, on the other side of his louvered door.

The mess cabin did have the advantage of being very much lighter than the surgeon's stateroom, the "ceiling" being fitted with a skylight that extended up into a kind of caged glasshouse in the deck above. The mizzen—or aftermost—mast extended up through the floor of this cabin, and a big table was built around the foot of this. Here all the "after gang"—the captain, the three officers, and the surgeon—ate their meals, often in two shifts. Sometimes the boatsteerers ate there, too. And here the officers and the surgeon spent their free time, unless they were on deck or in their respective staterooms. Accordingly, this room was usually called the "saloon." Forward of this was a small pantry, which was next to a door that led to the steerage, which in its turn led through the blubber room to the forward part of the ship, the domain of the common men.

This pantry was furnished with a dry sink and bins and lockers where any fancy edibles were stowed. Here, the dough for soft bread was mixed, coffee was made, and finishing touches were given to meals before they were placed on the table. Compared to merchant ships about the same size, whaleships were traditionally well provisioned. While waiting for the *Gipsy* to finish readying for sea, Dr. John Wilson counted "115 casks of salt provisions," and thirty-two more of hard ship's bread, along with "pale Ale, Stout, Hollands [gin], Rum, & Brandy: pickled cabbage, vinegar, molasses, sugar, Tea, coffee &c., also, some salted fish, & tripes in small casks: and a few Hams." He also observed fresh vegetables coming on board, and a quarter of beef hanging from the skids on deck. Once the fresh provender ran out, however, the shipboard menu was firmly based on preserved meat and fish, ship's bread, and dried peas and beans.

The ship's bread was a kind of thick, round biscuit, measuring about 8 inches in diameter, and so hard that more than one seaman had the same nasty experience as a crewman on the whaler *Baltic*, who recorded "while eating some hard bread the other day I broke off both of my front teeth close to the gum. I now try and keep my mouth closed as much as possible," he added. Baked to last for years, this bread came on board in barrels, was nicknamed "hard tack," and was commonly full of weevils. In *Roderick Random*, Tobias Smollett described bread where "every biscuit whereof, like a piece of clock-work, moved by its own internal impulse, occasioned by the myriads of insects that dwelt within it."

The dried peas and beans, on the other hand, were usually full of maggots. The first time Smollett's hero encountered peas, they were borne to the surgeon's mess on a large wooden platter by their mess boy, who cried "Scaldings!" as he rushed along, to warn anyone who might bump into him that what he was carrying was hot.

Random took one look at the dish and lost his appetite, though his messmates ate heartily, advising him that "it was banyan-day," meaning that this was one of the two days of the week when no meat was served.

This did not happen on whalers, where meat was a daily staple. On the *Gipsy*, Dr. Wilson observed that they had "beef for breakfast, for dinner, & for supper: South-seamen only partake of three meals a day:—it is either a feast or a famine." The meat was salted, unless a hog or a sheep had been sacrificed or the cook had been lucky with his fishing. Known as "salt horse," or "salt junk," it was soaked in seawater for a few hours before boiling, because it had gone so hard and mahoganylike in the cask that it was possible to carve it into useful little curios like snuffboxes.

This basic fare was baked or stewed by the cook, who was also known as "the doctor," possibly because one of his original duties had been to cut the hair of the crew. He often lacked a limb, the loss of which had disqualified him from ordinary sea duties and meant he had to be found another job. In Tudor times the ship cook's kitchen, like the surgeon's operating theater, was down in the hold, just above the bilges. Fires were kept burning in brick-lined hearths, and there the ship's cooks labored away in the smoky dark, while rank fluids from the filth accumulated on all the decks above dripped down into the cauldrons as they bubbled. Add the stench from the wet ballast (where, on French men-of-war, dead bodies and even amputated limbs were stored), and it is little wonder that ships were swept with mysterious epidemics.

The galley was a distinct improvement on this. On a typical merchant ship this was a small room set on the deck, usually sited forward so the smoke from the chimney would not get in the helmsman's eyes. This meant that the cook was given yet another job; Dr. John Wilson of the *Gipsy* recorded that "the Cook has to haul on the fore sheet and jib downhaul, and to look out for the clue-garnet, in maneuvering ship, least the funnel of his caboose be capsized." This was because the leads to the foresheet were usually outside the galley doors. When the vessel went round in stays the cook would let go of one sheet, dash through the galley, and clap onto the other sheet as the foreyards came round. This led to an old saying: "Shipshape and Bristol fashion, the captain on the poop and the cook to the foresheet."

The galley was furnished with a big iron range, and the wall above this was hung with the tools of the sea cook's trade—a couple of big boilers and a huge frying pan, along with coffeepots and teapots and two or three big oven pans. There were knives, including the knife used for slaughtering livestock, a hatchet for chopping kindling, huge spoons, a ladle, and a long fork called a "tormentor." And that was all that was considered necessary for providing three meals a day for more than thirty hungry whalemen.

The results of the cook's labors, as in Smollett's novel, were carried to the sailors in a common wooden trencher called a "kid." On the foredeck if the weather was good, or otherwise in the forecastle and steerage, it was shared out onto the men's own tin plates, often with a certain amount of dissension and strife. Then they attacked it with their jackknives while seated on their chests. At the beginning of the voyage a few of them might have had the foresight to carry along a few choice victuals to spice up the provisions. Mr. Morgan, the chief surgeon's mate on Random's ship, converted his share of beef into a "salmagundy" by adding pepper, salt, oil, vinegar, and raw onions from the store he kept in his chest, and similarly improved his ration of beer by sweetening it, heating it, adding a good dollop of spirits, and calling it "flip." However, once the extra ingredients had run out, he was condemned to the same monotonous fare as the others.

This fancying up of the food happened much more commonly in the cabin, where the after gang's share of the fare was taken to the pantry to be garnished with sauces and spices. Then it was served up nicely, accompanied by the "extras" the members had brought on board, which usually included brandy and wine. Thus on the *Coronet* in June 1837, Dr. Eldred Fysh was able to write, "This eve at 8 we met round the Cabin table, & for the first time took a Glass of Grog to the health of sweethearts & wives—God bless them."

For the surgeon, it was one of the advantages of being one of the "after gang" that lived in the after quarters, and some compensation for an unexpected downside to daily life on a whaler.

ON DECEMBER 9, 1854, TEN DAYS AFTER DEPARTING FROM HONOLULU, Dr. Tom Noddy had no sooner eaten breakfast than he was "called upon for the first time since leaving Port to act in my Profession, viz. that of Physician." His patient was one of the foremast men, "who came aft and complained of a severe pain in his Breast." Noddy put it down to overeating, and "administered an emetic from No. 1, which set him right immediately:

> In about half an hour another one came to me; he was affected with loss of appetite, indigestion, sour stomach, headache &c. &c. &c. and to him I gave an extraordinary dose of Jalap from No 2 and I think he is out of danger.
>
> Last of all came Don Antonio Quixote (as the sailors call him). He was affected with a disease which perhaps better be nameless; to him I administered external applications of Red Precipitate [of mercury], and dress with simple cerate [ointment]; A mild purgative in the form of Glauber's Salts, to be taken twice per day, and a mercurial plaster, to be placed in the Groin, with that I think he'll do!

And so, for a little while, Dr. Tom Noddy was quite busy. This, however, was unusual, for on the whole it is remarkable how seldom whalemen reported ill in the first few weeks of voyage. Dr. Eldred Fysh's encounter with the "all-overs" and the spate of food poisoning on the *Japan* were quite uncommon, for most whaling crews were healthy at the time of embarkation. What made the difference in Noddy's case was that while he might have been new to the ship, the voyage was two years old—two years in which the health of the whalemen of the *Java* had become eroded with hard living at sea and riotous sprees in port.

This initial lack of patients meant that once the novelty of being at sea had worn off, novice South Seaman surgeons made the unexpected discovery that life on passage was extremely boring. No whales had been raised, scurvy had not made its appearance, no landfall had been made as yet, so all the doctor had to do was watch and wait until someone got sick or hurt.

That experienced seafarer, Dr. John Coulter, passed the first two or three weeks of voyage watching the crew test the paces of the ship. It was a rewarding experience, he said, for the men were so delighted with the way the *Stratford* breasted her first storm "that they danced and waved their clear arm (for one held on), and appeared like madmen." Without a doubt, as Coulter heartily agreed, she was a "jewel of a ship." However, he did admit that otherwise he "had little to do but look about" at the sea, the sky, the birds, and the fish, and kill time "talking over shore scenes" with the others in the cabin. Similarly, Robert Smith Owen recorded confiding his romantic dreams to Captain George Gray. "The Capt. & myself amused by talking over the pleasing moments passed in the Company of those we love & my dearest E.," he wrote, adding that the subjects of their chat would have been "highly gratified by the encomiums pass'd on them." Such conversations probably provided little lasting comfort, however.

This was very different from the lot of the naval surgeon and his mates, who were kept at constant work according to naval regulations, those of 1804 being a very good example. First, the naval surgeon was reminded that he had "the entire charge of the sick," and was directly responsible for the cleanliness of the sick berth. "The surgeon, or first [surgeon's] mate, is to be always on board," the written ruling continued, while patients who were sent ashore to the hospital were escorted by the junior surgeon's mate. "When in a foreign port, the surgeon is to visit the hospital, or sick-quarters, every second day," and on his return he should "make a written report to the captain of the state of the sick people's health, and the probable time when they will be able to return on board." Furthermore:

> The surgeon is to visit the between-decks every morning, and to make his report to the captain, at the time he delivers the sick

list, of its state; pointing out any improvement which may con-
duce to render it more salubrious or wholesome.

When punishment takes place on board, the surgeon is to
attend, to be ready to answer any questions respecting the pris-
oner's health, or ability to receive the punishment.

On board a man-of-war the surgeon's day began early, as Tobias
Smollett testified: "At a certain hour in the morning, the boy of the
mess [the "loblolly boy"] went round all the decks, ringing a small
hand-bell, and, in rhymes composed for the occasion, invited all
those who had sores to repair before the mast, where one of the
doctor's mates attended, with applications to dress them." Other
boys summoned their customers by beating upon a mortar with a
pestle—and even at the beginning of the voyage there were plenty
of those clients, for many of the men who had been dragged on
board by the press gangs were sick or hurt already. Those who had
been seized from incoming ships might even be very ill with
scurvy.

Men who could not drag themselves around were certified off
duty and were sent to the sick bay. This was a damp recess in the
lower decks where the hammocks were hung so closely together
that the sick men swung as a mass—presenting quite a problem to
Smollett's hero when he was directed to administer an enema.
Completely puzzled, Roderick Random watched another surgeon's mate, Thomson, prepare for the same operation by thrusting
his wig in his pocket before creeping on all fours under the massed
hammocks until he reached his quarry. On arrival, he forced his
head between the patient's hammock and the one next to it, and
kept them "asunder with one shoulder, until he had done his duty."
This might have been an exaggeration, the book being an exercise in
satire, but it was not too far removed from reality.

On whalers there was no sick bay for the surgeon to organize.
He did have the responsibility of the lime juice, wines, brandy, and
other spirits that had been shipped under the heading of "medical
stores," but that task was scarcely onerous. A conscientious man

may have gone through the ship to check the state of the between-decks, forecastle, holds, and bilges, but this was only likely to happen if there was any infectious disease, when the doctor was in charge of fumigating procedures. This usually involved burning some pungent material such as sulfur on a shovel as it was carried about the lower quarters of the ship, though—as we have seen—Dr. John B. King's preferred alternative was chloride of lime.

Fumigation was often necessary on a man-of-war during the early days of voyage, for recruits pressed from the slums brought disease-bearing lice on board—a good reason for surgeons to wear wigs. Smollett recorded that his hero was forced to shave his head within days of first embarking, "a ferocious colony" of lice having made their home in his hair. This was not usually necessary in the early part of a whaling voyage, however, and so a South Seas surgeon was fated to spend the first few weeks of his adventure idling about the decks and smoking a pipe at the rail, with nothing much to do save gaze about at sea and sky and hope for the sight of another ship, if only to prove they were not alone upon the deep.

If a merchantman was sighted, then the contact was likely to be brief, with a mere exchange of signals as the two ships passed. Merchant vessels had a destination to reach, and their captains wished to get there as quickly as possible. The sight of another whaler, however, promised a much more leisurely treat. Because the whaling voyages were so long and the ships were either heading to a whaling ground or had arrived on the ground and were quartering the sea in the endless hunt for whales, there was time to spare for socializing, and other whaleships were hailed with delight.

First the two ships exchanged signals in a flurry of flags. This was known as "speaking." Then the downwind ship would haul aback so that she stilled on the water, waiting while the windward ship swept down on her, a dramatic process that required nerves of steel and a firm hand on the helm. "At 2 hove the M^{n}Yard to the Mast for the *Venelia*," wrote Dr. James Brown on the *Japan* in June 1835. It

Whaleships Gamming.

ARTIST, RON DRUETT

Gamming, or mid-sea visiting, was a process that involved a time span of hours or even days, as whaleships lay hauled aback and whaleboats were pulled from ship to ship so that everyone either visited or received visitors, and was a practice peculiar to the whalemen. While merchant ships did speak to each other, it was done hurriedly, for they had tight schedules to keep and were intent on reaching port with the minimum of interruption. The whalemen, by contrast, were cruising back and forth in their endless hunt for their quarry and going into port as infrequently as possible. Hungry for company and conversation, they visited each other often and at length, so that clusters of several ships all a-gamming were not infrequently recorded.

must have been a sight well worth watching; the lovely full-rigged ship bearing down on them, then catching the light on her sails as she braced up to sheer past their stern. Captain Hill, standing on the quarterdeck, would have been gripping his speaking trumpet in his mahogany fist, set to share a shouted conversation with the other ship's skipper, Captain Miner, during which he would invite him on board for some liquid refreshment in the course of an exchange of visits that the whalemen called a "gam."

Well, this is what usually happened. In this instance, however, some misjudgment occurred, for instead of sheering off, the *Venelia* sailed right into them. First, her bowsprit snagged their spanker boom, and then, in a long, ominous, splintering commotion, the mizzen mast's gear was torn away. It gave them quite a surprise, as Dr. James Brown commented, and it was quite a little miracle "that he did not strike us on our starboard quarter" and send the *Japan* to the bottom. As soon as the dust and splinters had settled, Captain Hill lowered a boat and went over to the other ship, no doubt in a towering rage, and did not make his reappearance for another six hours. "Mr. Johnston, Chief Mate of the *Venelia* came on board us," wrote Dr. Brown; "he was at the Masthead when the accident happened and had to call to the boy at the Helm to put it down, otherwise I suppose our ship would very soon have gone down." Alcohol had something to do with it, no doubt. Both Hill and Miner were openhanded with grog. All-night gams were common, with boats in constant motion between the ships, and dancing, singing, and drinking on the respective decks. Surgeons got together and spent pleasant hours comparing experiences, enjoying the chance of compatible companionship.

However, the moment when the skippers recollected the reason they were at sea was inevitable. As Dr. James Brown recorded during another gam, this time with the *Favorite*, "The Captains came on board *Japan* in the evening, also Dr. Johnston," because they had decided it was time "for a parting glass; the Dr. and I had the same." The farewells were protracted, the party going on "till an early hour this morning"—five A.M., to be precise, at which hour Dr. Johnston of the *Favorite* proposed they "make a day of it, but the Captn said, Na, na, so off they went to the *Favorite*, and I to bed." And so the ships parted, and the sea became empty again.

"NO ONE CAN CONCEIVE THE DREARY MONOTONY & UTTER SOLITUDE of a South Seaman's life," mused Dr. John Wilson; "& particularly that of yᵉ Doctor, who has no routine of duty, no fixed or regular employment to divert his mind." While overabundance of leisure was disconcerting enough for the novice sea surgeon, the captain was likely to take it even more badly, finding the sight of a doctor idling about his decks irritating in the extreme. "The devil's delight this morning in the Cabin at breakfast," recorded Dr. James Brown in pained surprise less than three weeks after sailing, in January 1835. Captain Hill had attacked him verbally "for some supposed misconduct last night or this morning."

The plain fact of the matter was that shipping a surgeon was considered by British whaling captains and whaleship owners as nothing more than a legally required gesture, and watching the doctor devour expensive rations was an exasperating reminder of that much resented requirement. Naval vessels, like East Indiamen, carried a surgeon to supervise the health and well-being of huge crews, while on immigrant and convict ships doctors cared for large human freights. The masters of these ships might be annoyed when seamen were put sick off duty, but they could easily see the reason for having a surgeon on board. On slavers, too, the presence of a doctor was perceived as necessary to keep the cargo in marketable condition. Various Ship Passenger acts legislated between 1803 and 1855 also required the presence of a doctor on board passenger ships in certain circumstances, to care for those who had paid fares to travel. Otherwise the owners of most merchant vessels were left to make their own decisions, which meant that doctors were hired only for unusually long voyages.

In the eyes of the law, however, the whaling business was different. Whether in the Arctic areas of Greenland and the Davis Straits or in the tropical seas of the Asian archipelagoes, the pursuit of whales was recognized as being particularly dangerous. And so, in legislation dating as far back as 1733, the British Parliament required the presence of a surgeon on board all whaleships, which on South Seamen meant that they had only about thirty-five people to treat. Many masters were not at all backward in making their surgeons aware that they were only there on sufferance and should do something to earn their rations.

Just one of that sort was Captain William Edmund Hill, a hard man who had been more or less constantly at sea since his early teen. He first shows up in the records for in June 1796 on the way to South Seas as a harpooner on the *Nimble* under Captain James Richardson, Admiralty Protection papers in his hand. In 1824, he took command of the *Sarah* at the start of three successful voyages, bringing her home for the last time in October 1831. In March 1832, Captain Hill took over the *Pacific*, returning with a full fare of oil just twenty-nine months later, and then, not content to rest on his laurels, he almost immediately took command of the *Japan*, leaving London four months afterward with Dr. James Brown on board.

With such a tough, seasoned, and resourceful man for a boss, Brown should not have been at all surprised to find that he was suddenly handed the job of captain's unofficial amanuensis, which meant keeping the ship's books and accounts. He might even have mused that he was lucky to not find himself fired—something that Hill had done not once but twice to his surgeons in the past, seizing the flimsiest of excuses to cast them off on some foreign shore. Other skippers were not averse to this practice, either. When Dr. Robert Smith Owen's ship, *Warrens*, was gamming with the *Samuel Enderby* in October 1837, Captain Lisle of the *Enderby* boasted that he had discharged his surgeon within the first two months of voyage on the grounds that he had "conducted himself very improperly—making free with Sailors." Shortly after that pronouncement, Dr. Owen found out why Lisle had invited him on board: the chief mate, Mr. Nore, was very ill indeed, and the captain did not know what to do for him. Without comment, Dr. Owen "prescribed and made up medicine for him," and then returned to his ship.

Like James Brown, Robert Smith Owen also found himself set unexpected tasks. Captain Gray gave him a handful of fishhooks with a broad hint that he could be stocking the larder while lounging at the rail. On the *Coronet* in 1837, Captain William Bond set Dr. Eldred Fysh the job of handing out the Bibles that the owners had put on board. After all, they had no need of a surgeon, not yet, and so he may as well take on the duties of a chaplain—or so went the reasoning. This had a certain strange logic, for on men-of-war it was traditional that the chaplain should assist the surgeons in the cockpit during battle.

Dr. Fysh felt no stirring of the missionary spirit, however, instead expressing strong doubts about the value of the gesture, prophesying that they would not be "looked into a dozen times during the voyage." He was right. As Dr. John Wilson of the *Gipsy* noted in October 1839, "Sunday is a perfect *dies non* with the sailors, their religion is that of the elements, against which they have to contend, for it is only when danger threatens or became imminent that he remembers his God, & then mayhap as I once heard an old tar say: he prays bloody hard." But nonetheless, Eldred Fysh did as the captain wished, understanding that it was a good idea to keep the skipper happy.

Captain Bond, highly gratified, promptly proposed that his surgeon should become the ship's clerk and purser, which meant writing up the accounts and supervising the handing out of rations to the cook. Again, Eldred Fysh complied—so he should not have been surprised to find himself keeping the captain's logbook as well. "This day owing to the irregular manner in which Mr. Brandon [second mate] kept the ship's log book, the Captain appointed me to keep it," he wrote. He had a piece of bad luck, for while he was writing up a day's entry, a cask of beef bumped on the quarterdeck above his head, the jolt knocking over his lamp and spilling oil all over the book, but Captain Bond merely counseled him to write out the whole log again. It is little wonder that on the beautifully cursive title page of his journal, Dr. Fysh described himself as "Surgeon &c."

The captains felt as if they had logic and justice on their side. As Dr. John Wilson observed, whaling was "a joint-stock concern, a

Scrimshaw Plaque by Dr. William Lewis Roderick.

The tedium of whaling voyages meant that all hands on board were forced to find some means to fill the lagging time, leading to the folk art called "scrimshaw," in which pictures were engraved on whale teeth or flat pieces of whalebone. Some of the most spectacular examples of this were created by William Lewis Roderick, surgeon of the South Seaman *Adventure*. The son of David and Susanna Roderick, William was christened on October 15, 1826, in St. Martin in the Fields in the parish of Westminster. After gaining his L.S.A., he almost immediately signed up for a voyage (giving his age as twenty-three), and in October 1847 departed from England on the first of three voyages in the same vessel, finally returning home in 1856. His subsequent career is unknown, but his name lives on in beautiful artwork like the intricately wrought whaling scene pictured here, which was inscribed with a fine blade (possibly a lancet), and enhanced with black, blue, brown, and red pigment.

speculation in the success of which every one is interested, and all without exception are expected to lend a hand in accomplishing the voyage, else it is argued that those who toil and strive while others lay idle, are unfairly dealt with, inasmuch as only a part [of the crew] obtain the cargo, while the rest reap equal benefit." However, the surgeon could legitimately reason that he had been shipped to look after the health of the men and not for fishing, sermonizing, or secretarial duties, and he could take measures to avoid this shameless exploitation.

Scribbling in a book was a good way to look busy and preoccupied, and this was probably a good reason for keeping a journal. Dr. John Wilson wrote at voluminous length, decorating the result with delicate watercolors. Equally artistic was Dr. Fysh, who embellished his diary with outlines of land sighted and lively little sketches of whales. Dr. John B. King of the *Aurora*, by contrast, turned up his cuffs, dipped pen in ink, and made a list of the surgical "instruments, dressings &c." available on the ship:

One Amputating knife
One Tourniquet
One saw
One Tenaculum
One Tooth Key and hooks
Two Bleeding lancets
Surgeons needles for sewing wounds
One Large injection Syringe
Two penis syringes
Sticking plaster spread on cloth
Patent Lint
Soft leather for plasters
Spare vials and corks

That done, King set to writing out surgical memoranda. "When an arm or leg has been injured to such a degree that the loss of it is inevitable," he wrote, "amputation should be performed thus making a healthy wound in the place of a mashed or torn mass that would certainly mortify and in all probability destroy the sufferer. Some plain directions for performing such operations in cases of necessity, may not be unacceptable." And with that short preamble, he launched himself on a series of detailed descriptions of the lopping of various limbs, ranging from whole legs and arms to mere toes.

"For the thigh," he wrote:

> The tourniquet must be trapped around the upper part of the thigh with the screw about an inch inwards from the middle of the front part. A small roller or pad is to be put under the screw, which is directly over the course of the main artery. The tourniquet is then to be screwed up tight to stop the circulation of blood The operator passes the knife under the thigh and reaches under so as to bring that part of the edge nearest the handle to the front of the thigh. He then draws the knife completely round the thigh cutting through the skin and fat down to the red flesh. The depth of this cut will be half an inch or more. It should be made about six inches above the knee pan. The assistant should then grasp the thigh above the cut and draw the skin back while the operator clears it from the flesh underneath for about an inch and a half above the first cut.

Perhaps he did this because he did not have his medical texts with him, having been so unexpectedly propelled into the position of ship's surgeon, or perhaps he was doing it because even the most hardened skipper was unlikely to read much further before recognizing that this was serious literature. Just as impressive were observations of wildlife and natural phenomena, something for which the sea surgeon was particularly qualified, being literate, of scientific bent, usually an eager observer, and capable of writing precise and meaningful descriptions of unfamiliar objects and scenes.

"On those who have not the inclination to resort to intellectual pursuits to beguile their time," pronounced Dr. Frederick Debell Bennett, the tedium of voyage "falls with greater force." He proceeded forthwith to compose long descriptions of all the wildlife he saw—plant, animal, and human—both on and off the ship. Bennett, who, as we have seen, had pursued and gained both his L.S.A. and

M.R.C.S. before embarking on the *Tuscan* of London in 1833, was a most dedicated naturalist. Even the humble domestic fowl was not immune to his pen. He approved of hens highly, for they were very cheap. "The only food they require on board ship is the scraped kernel of the cocoa-nut, and on this," along with a little raw meat, "they thrive and improve rapidly." The natives of the Society Islands had a novel method of dispatching them, he further noted, by plucking one of the bird's own primary feathers, and then using it to "pith" the fowl to death by "piercing the spinal marrow near the head."

"On [Gough's] Island, which is uninhabited, are a great many Penguins," wrote Dr. James Brown on February 28, 1835, off Timor. "We have 6 on board, they are of a small size. Yellow bill— long yellow feathers hanging down from behind & above their eyes forward, blue on head and back—neck, breast, and belly white, their wings or fins are blue—they cannot fly—these are only useful in the water in which they go very quick." The crew often exhibited a spirit of friendly cooperation when they noticed the surgeon's interest in strange fauna, catching birds or butterflies that had swarmed out from shore, and giving them to the doctor for his collection. On the *Phoenix* of London in September 1823, the men caught a female shark and gave it to Dr. William Dalton to dissect. "On opening it I found eight young, four on either side, separated from each other by a thick membrane. They were about twenty inches long, full of animation and very eager to get in the water." All this was intriguing and valuable stuff, well worth noting. In fact, it was not at all uncommon for prominent naturalists to pay sea surgeons to bring back prized specimens.

And then there was the awesome power of the elements. Waterspouts fascinated them all, being both enigmatic and unpredictable. Robert Smith Owen recorded that he saw one broken by a squall, "the upper half being visible—and hanging like a Curtain in the air—the atmosphere from the Wind & Rain was quite hazy—and misty—it lasted for better than ½ an hour—then continued to thunder & Lighten." He was soaked to the skin as he stood and watched, but it was worth it. Storms, too, provided excellent fodder for the quill, and Thomas Beale (writing on the *Kent* during the first part of his voyage) was particularly evocative when conveying the might and terror of a gale. He was unlucky enough to endure a hurricane, during the second night of which the wind suddenly ceased, "the ship being left entirely to the mercy of the waves, which caused her to roll most frightfully, her chain-plates striking the water occasionally with terrific force, and the waves striking against the stern." Some of the sailors thought that the storm was over, but the good doctor knew better. Not at all to his surprise, the "wind again suddenly arose, and in about half an hour blew a complete gale," which lasted from mid-afternoon till two in the morning, "when a sudden howling blast of wind of extreme violence laid the ship entirely on her beam ends," he recorded.

> The uproar which was set up at this time from the howling of the wind, the beating and dashing of the waves, the working of the ship, the creaking of the masts and clashing of the backstays, intermixed with the hoarse calling of the sailors, made "night hideous," and rendered the scene altogether indescribable. That was a dreadful night to me, and to all on board; we met each other with melancholy looks, at the same time clinging to anything which was within reach, to prevent ourselves from being thrown down.

A humanitarian and pious man himself, Beale took special note of the men who shared this terrifying experience. "Blustering bullies" were pale with fear and "in pitiable plight," while the quiet, gentle ones "were now seen facing the danger with unaverted heads, quiet—yet bold, unassuming—yet proud; they feared not the raging of the elements, because, knowing their own hearts, they trusted to Him who 'rides in the whirlwind and governs the storm.'"

Much of the writing, however, was frivolous, ranging from doggerel to spur-of-the-moment comedy. Dr. Tom Noddy whiled away idle hours on the *Java* of New Bedford by writing a play (or perhaps the libretto to an opera) which he called *The Father Outwitted*. The cast numbers five—Guadarrama, his beautiful daughter

Isabella, her lover Leander, a saucy servant named Lorenzo, and "A Neighboring Merchant"—and is supported by a troupe of musicians and dancers. The dialogue is rousing, if not very original:

Scene—the street before the house of Guadarrama. Enter Guadarrama from the house with his sword drawn and dragging out Lorenzo.

Gua.—Come along rascal! Tell me the truth, infamous villain.

Lor.—Famous! Famous yourself sir. Take care what you say. Don't call me famous.

Gua.—Tell me directly, scoundrel, whom you took that letter to from my daughter.

Lor.—Took it to—who I took it to—now, listen—I took it to— you have a confounded deal of curiosity.

Gua.—Have you a mind to be strangled? *(Collars him.)*

Lor.—No, truly—take care what you do—Hold a little—My young mistress gave me the letter—mind—she gave it to me—and I took it.

Gua.—Who the devil doubts that? But where?

Lor.—She said to me, said she, Lorenzo, says she, there—there's a rial for thee—and do take that letter thou knowest where.

Gua.—Oh ho! What. She paid you beforehand then—and you like a good-for-nothing knave, are plotting with my daughter to dishonor me.

Lor.—Do you think so? Lord, sir, we can't dishonor you.

Gua.—How so?

Lor.—Because, sir, you have no honor.

Unfortunately (or maybe not!), the muse failed Noddy just a few pages further on, and the play was never finished. One would like to think that he had been inspired by Dr. Charles Fletcher, a naval surgeon in the forty-four-gun *Roebuck* during the American Revolution, who wrote a book with the charming title, *A Maritime State Considered as to the Health of Seamen with Efficient Means of Rendering the Situation of That Valuable Class of People*

More Comfortable, that recommended regular bathing and ship-board theatricals as a means of keeping up morale. It is more probable, however, that Noddy was following a current fashion for writing plays.

Sometimes, however, intensive journal-writing failed in its aim (perhaps because the captain had caught sight of this kind of composition), and the surgeon was given something more seamanlike to write. On the *Warrens* in 1837, Dr. Robert Smith Owen laboriously penned:

> When taking in sail always take first the *lee sheet* of the Top Gallant Sail—when the Topsail the Weather Sheet. When a ship pitches very heavy in a heavy sea & blowing hard more effect will be produced on the action of the ship by taking in a reef in the Fore Top Sail—if not sufficient, 2 reefs & 1 to the main—then if she pitches take in F.T. Gallant Sail—next the main, then another reef of M. Sail.

One cannot help but wonder about Captain Gray's motives in ordering Dr. Owen to take note of this. Was he training his surgeon to take over the job of one of the mates, just in case one of them died or deserted? James Brown recorded that Captain Pockley of the whaleship *Eleanor* fired his first officer and "promoted" his surgeon to the fourth mate's position. Or did Captain Gray simply object to having an ignorant lubber on board? He was certainly determined to turn his surgeon into a seaman, for Dr. Owen also found himself learning how to pull an oar in the captain's boat.

Gray was not the only skipper to pursue such a course. As we have seen, Captain Michael Underwood of the *Kingsdown* put his surgeon in charge of one of the boats. Dr. Eldred Fysh, who hailed from a village near Lynn, Norfolk, was obviously accustomed to the sea, for he took the "youngsters" down in the captain's boat to teach them how to row. John Packham (the same boy who had complained of the "all-overs") made such a poor job of it that "After coming on board [he] had to practice dry pulling for a few hours which brought him to a sad 'Dirty State' but he was obliged to pull on 'til he could pull no longer."

After the ship reached the "blue waters" about the Azores, a constant daytime masthead lookout was kept for whales. This was another chance for the captain to order his doctor to make himself useful, and so the bemused surgeon was apt to find himself included in the lookout roster. One such was Dr. James Brown, who recorded on January 19, 1835: "I went to the masthead today—the first time I ever did so." Evidently, William Edmund Hill was a tougher proposition than the captain of the ship on Dr. Brown's prior voyage. However, he soon became accustomed to mounting the rigging, being scheduled for two two-hour tricks at the masthead each day.

Not satisfied with this, Captain Hill gave him a quadrant and yet another job: "to take an observation at noon every day it is practicable." This was no small responsibility, even if the surgeon's calculations were checked. As Dr. John Wilson observed in 1843, "The navigation of a South Seaman is no light task, for they traverse seas but rarely frequented by any other vessels, they run into bays & roadsteads, creeks & channels in search of their prey, such as no other ships would venture in." It also meant that James Brown had to change his routine: "in consequence have altered my watch at the masthead to morning and evening."

However, Brown seemed quite happy about his new duty, perhaps because Captain Hill had put up a bounty for the man who should raise, or sight, the first whale, the promise of clothes, tobacco, or money being a common incentive to keep a sharp lookout. "Offer'd a fresh bounty for Mast Heads," Robert Smith Owen recorded as the *Warrens* arrived on the whaling ground in December 1837. The man who raised a forty-barrel whale would get two sovereigns, while two sovereigns, a "monkey jacket," a dozen plugs of tobacco, and a dozen pipes would be awarded for the raising of a whale that rendered eighty barrels of oil. A bottle of grog was an even more common reward.

Robert Owen was eligible for the bounty himself, for he was another surgeon who did regular lookout duty—a testament to Captain George Gray's obstinacy and sure knowledge of the nature of his fellow men, for (as we have seen) Owen was the greenest of seafarers when he shipped on the *Warrens* in April 1837. Six months out, fortified by the grog issued during the celebration of the captain's birthday, and urged on by Captain Gray himself, he went "for the 1st time to the mast—& got as far as the Maintop." This was no great mountaineering from the sailor's point of view, the maintop being only about a third of the way to the masthead. For Robert Smith Owen it was quite an accomplishment, however. The ring of futtock shrouds (which braced the upper mast) had to be negotiated to get there, which meant clambering outward at a precarious angle beneath the platform at the top of the lower mast, and then throwing himself up and over the edge, timing his movements to the roll of the ship.

Within three days Owen was spending more time on the maintop than he was on deck, partly to escape the plague of mosquitoes that was afflicting the ship, and was very soon confident enough to chase butterflies in the rigging and to be put on regular lookout duty. Yet the lookout perched on the lofty topgallant crosstrees, where the slender mast swayed like a pendulum sixty feet above the pitching deck and even further from the tossing sea; it is easy to empathize with Dr. John Wilson when he wryly noted that while he understood that everyone on board should pull their weight, "It is not everyone who can manage to gain ye masthead, nor steadiness of nerve to make ye attempt." And as for pulling an oar in a boat, "it is far beneath the dignity of the office which he professes to fill," he pronounced—which goes to prove that while he might have been too timid to climb the mast, in standing up to the captain, Dr. Wilson displayed more courage than most.

But he did not have the satisfaction that Dr. James Brown enjoyed (as we shall see) of being able to say: "I raised a whale." Nor—unlike Dr. Robert Smith Owen—did he ever have the right to claim the bounty.

5

The Whale Hunt

Killing whales is sometimes
attended with bad accidents.

Dr. William Dalton

$\mathcal{A}$RMCHAIR TRAVELERS OF THE TIME FOUND WHALE-CATCHING SO fascinating that it is little wonder that the surgeons paid so much attention to the process or that they described it in such detail in their journals and—some of them—in very popular books later. Not only was it exciting to watch, but the taking of whales improved the morale of the crew.

From the moment the ship arrived on blue water, everything was in readiness for the first whale, with the blubber tackle rove to the mainmast, and four or five whaleboats slung on davits outside the ship, poised for a quick lowering if the prey was raised. "Ships lower from three to five boats according to their tonnage, and generally carry two or more spare boats in case of an accident," wrote Dr. William Dalton. "The boats are from twenty-five to thirty feet in length and about five or six feet in breadth and sharp at both ends, they are made of light fir or cedar of half an inch in thickness and are clinker built; they pull five oars, each being from sixteen to eighteen feet long, and are steered by an oar of twenty-two feet in length." Equipped with a mast that could be stepped when needed, and a sail to set to it, they were like graceful greyhounds compared to the generally tubby shape of the ship.

Dr. John Wilson's first whale made its appearance on January 16, 1840, a full two months after departure from England. It is little wonder, then, that when the cry was heard from the lookout— "*There she blows!*"—he recorded that everybody rushed up on deck, "tumbling up the hatchways like mad things." Arriving on deck at the head of the horde, the skipper instantly commenced a lively conversation with the lookout. One such exchange, between Captain Stavers of the *Tuscan* and the man at the masthead who had raised the whale, was described so dramatically by Dr. Frederick Debell Bennett that it can be told like a play:

Lookout—There she blow-o-os!

Capt. Stavers—Where away?

Lookout—Two points on the lee bow, sir, a school of whales.

Capt. (to the steward)—Bring up the spyglass, boy! *(To the lookout)*—How far off do you see them?

Lookout—About four miles, sir.

Capt.—Back the main-yard, brail up the trysail.

Lookout—There she blo-owos!—There again!—Flukes!

(An expectant pause ensues, and all are intent to discover the next rising.)

Lookout—There she breaches!—There she blow-o-s! Th-e-r-e a-gain!—on the lee quarter.

Capt.—Get your boats ready for lowering!

Lookout—Th-e-r-e a-gain!

Capt.—Lower away! *(And, conversationally to the surgeon)*—I see there is a large whale amongst them that wants a passage to London.

On the *Gipsy*, the procedure was just the same, the lookout somehow managing the feat of singing out "*She blows!*" and answering the captain's urgent queries all at once and at the same time. "Now is heard the voice of the Captain, roaring above the noise and tumult, 'where away,'" related Wilson, "to which question they reply either that the whales are on the lee bow or beam so many points, or to windward, whichever direction they may be as regards the ship."

The ship was steered accordingly, chasing the whales for as long as the spouts could be seen, like dandelions misting against the horizon as the gigantic mammals filled their lungs with air, but then, inevitably, the whales would finish their business, "peak flukes," and sound, or dive down suddenly, slipping under the surface with an arch of the back and a flick of the great horizontal tail.

Now it was anyone's guess which way they would swim and where they would next appear. While the captain watched tensely through his spyglass, having mounted the mast meanwhile, the

Whaling Scenes   FROM *HARPER'S MAGAZINE*
1. Raising the Whale.
While inaccurate in much of the detail, engravings such as these, which were
widely reproduced in popular magazines such as *The Illustrated London News* and
Harper's Magazine, illustrate the public perception of the danger and glamour of
whaling in the South Seas.

mates were busy pushing their crews into getting ready for lowering the instant the whales rose again, by fetching all the craft and
gear necessary for the chase and the capture—harpoons, lances,
small kegs with bread and water and a lantern in case the boats
were drawn a long way from the ship, knives and balers and
round wooden tubs filled with many fathoms of neatly coiled
whaleline. All of these were stacked ready to be stowed into the
boats once they were safely down on the water. That done, Wilson went on:

> all await in breathless suspense for the joyful sound of "there
> she spouts" . . . "a whale close-to by God" sing out several
> voices—all is hurry-skerry to get away, and the bawl of the
> Skipper is heard for less noise—"haul aback the main-yard"—
> presently, "lower away," and almost before the words are out of

2. Lowering Boats. FROM *HARPER'S MAGAZINE*

his mouth, round go the yards, and then down go the boats amid a shower of oaths.

It was no different on American whalers. In his excitement, Dr. John King of the *Aurora* completely abandoned the scientific tone that characterized his descriptions of amputations, lapsing like Dr. Wilson into the present tense as he watched "the crisped locks" of the steward "emerge from the stairway" in response to Captain Hussey's cry for his telescope:

> He presents the spyglass, an unequivocal smile separating his lips, and his eyes rolling with joy, though trying to preserve his dignity and imitate the coolness of the captain. With the spyglass on his shoulder, the captain goes aloft, and looks through his tube to determine whether it is a sperm whale, or some other kind. . . . The boatsteerers look to the boats to see that everything is in its place. Superfluous clothing is thrown aside. Belts are buckled on and suspenders thrown off. The cooper must stop working . . . lest the noise should reach the whales and alarm them. The boys are strung out on the lower yards and

have just caught sight of the spouts. "There she Blows—blows—blows" becomes more frequent and less loud. Now they are seen from the deck. A few minutes have elapsed and the captain is coming down. He passes aft to the quarterdeck. . . . The mate is standing by the captain. "Let the mainyard come aback, Mr. A." "Haul the mainyard aback," says the mate. It is done and the ship is stationary. "Stand by the boats." . . ."Lower away gently." The boats are in the water and the crews tumble in as they may.

"Away they go, as though old Nick were in their wake," as John Wilson put it, tensely watched by those left behind on the ship. It was an eager chase. As Dr. John Coulter (a man whose passion for slaughtering innocent wildlife was equaled only by his lust for adventure) exclaimed, "No huntsmen ever followed a pack of hounds with greater glee than the boats' crews of those ships pull after their game."

Coulter wanted to experience the thrill of this novel chase himself—so much so that he "begged" Captain Abijah Lock for permission to lower a boat. Receiving consent, he rushed for the rail hollering: "Volunteer boat's crew to chase whales!" He was pursued by a crowd of keen recruits who wished to join in the fun. Taking off his jacket and shoes (stockinged feet were safer, being less likely to slip, and waterlogged boots or shoes could drown a man if he fell into the water), Coulter jumped into the boat with five companions, and off they went.

"I believe no boat's crew ever shoved off from a ship's side in so much haste and confusion," he declared. His spur-of-the-moment crew was a rowdy lot, "and on this occasion they exerted their liberty of speech so much, that I was obliged frequently to sit down and finish my laugh." At last, however, "after a short pithy speech from me, they all agreed that get a fish we must, for the honour and glory of it, and that they would do as I should tell them." Sorting themselves out, they got a grip on their respective oars and lustily pulled for the whales, "which were amusing themselves on the surface of the water."

3. Going on to the Whales.   FROM *HARPER'S MAGAZINE*

Usually the chase was a lot more serious than this. In each boat five of the six-strong crew, including the harpooner in the bow, earnestly heaved at their oars while the mate, or boatheader, stood at the steering oar in the stern, watching tensely for spouts and breeches ahead. Then—a snort, and the plume of a spout. "Now you will see the headsman," described John Wilson, "pushing at the after oar, and animating his crew, his arm flying about like the leg of a telegraph"—a toylike figure from Wilson's distant vantage on deck. Five long sculls dig into the water and are mightily hauled, while the officer leans powerfully on the steering oar, turning the boat in the direction of the breaching whale.

"It is his duty," Wilson explained, "to place the Boatsteerer, who is foremost in the Boat, alongside the whale to enable him to 'fasten' to it, or in other words [put him] within reach of the whale; now this is not done without a good deal of management & caution." When the whale is clearly in sight, the headsman raises his hand and the oarsmen obediently lift their oars, while the boat swishes quietly onward by momentum. Overrunning the submerged flukes, would be very dangerous, and would "gally" (frighten off) the "fish" as well.

"Now is the critical time," as Wilson goes on to describe, for "the Boat is not far from a whale which is going leisurely through the water & spouting very regularly." The oars are peaked, and the men take up paddles and stealthily prowl toward the prey. "Gently my lads, no noise," the headsman whispers, and not a word is spoken. And then they are upon their quarry. A cry rings over the water—"often a shriek, so earnest & excited they become by the chase"—as the officer orders the harpooner in the bow to stand up and face the whale. "The Boatsteerer jumps up (already in expectance), seizes the harpoon and darts into the body of the whale, following it up with a second one if he can, all this is the work of an instant."

"I DARTED BOTH IRONS WITH ALL MY FORCE," RECORDED DR. JOHN Coulter. These "irons" were the harpoons. The barbed head of each was attached by a warp to a whaleline coiled in a tub, so that once the weapon was securely "planted" in the whale's side, the prey was "fast" to the boat. Then the good doctor lost not a second in crying out to his men: "Stern all!"—a command to push hard with their oars so that the boat skipped backward out of the whale's way.

This was because the whale, quite naturally, made violent objection to the stinging indignity. "Then, the whale is seen dashing its ponderous flukes about, fanning the air and raising a mighty mass of spray & foam," exclaimed Wilson, "rolling over and over & tumbling about in sheer agony, & woe betide the boat and crew, who fall within the circuit of the flukes, it will be a smash to a certainty and likely enough a death, for a whale has no mercy."

Some of the great mammals tried to get rid of the harpoons by rolling over and over, a tactic that could entangle men in the rope, tearing off their limbs or dragging them down to a watery grave. Others turned about and attacked the boat. "Now you will behold the rage and agony of the big monster," described Wilson, "as it lashes its ponderous flukes about, creating a vast surface of foam, and rolling over and over."

Somehow, more by luck than good management, Dr. John Coulter's men managed to dance the boat out of the way as "the fish breached high out of the water, causing such a tremendous splash, that the boat was nearly half filled." Then, instead of sounding, it rushed off, dragging the boat behind, so Coulter and his men boarded their oars, baled out, and settled down for the ride. "I took a turn of the line round the loggerhead, to hold on, and off we flew through the bay, towed away at a rapid rate." This was what was known in the American trade as a "Nantucket sleigh ride." While the whale was using up its strength in towing its heavy burden, the boatsteerer and the officer in charge of the boat were changing ends, so that the harpooner now steered the boat (the origin of "boatsteerer," the American version of the name), and the mate stood in the bow facing the whale, ready to lance and kill their prey.

Well, that was what normally happened. John Coulter, though he had been the one who had harpooned the whale, was determined to be the one to lance it, too. This was pretty foolhardy, for both harpooning and lancing were exhausting procedures that required a lot of courage and strength. As it turned out however, it was easily done. Four hours after fastening, the whale tired and slowed, the men brought the boat up to its flank by hauling on the line, Coulter "got two fortunate darts of the lance into it," and the great mammal quietly settled and died.

It was much more usual for the whales to thresh about in a frenzy in the last moments before death. "Just before the whale is dead, its death struggles are fearful indeed!" exclaimed Dr. John Wilson:

> its immense bulk begins to quiver & shake, which augment and merge into the most stupendous convulsions, lashing its flukes, rolling over and over, darting about in rapid circles, and exhibiting mighty power, and the most poignant anguish, and at last becomes quite exhausted and turns over on its side—dead!

This last paroxysm was known as the "death flurry," and wise whalemen gave it a wide berth. As with everything else, though, Coulter had been lucky. His men delivered "three hearty cheers" and then took the dead whale in tow by passing the line about its flukes.

Getting the carcass to the ship was usually a tedious struggle, but Coulter was fortunate in this as well. Being to windward of the ship, they were able to step the mast, set the canvas, and sail. And as they brought their huge trophy to the side of the ship, there was another round of "tremendous cheers," this time "from the lads on board, which we of course politely answered." Such good-humored camaraderie was not always the rule, for whaling officers were highly competitive, strongly resenting the very notion of any-one stealing "their" whales. John Wilson recorded that the first and second officers of the *Gipsy* got into an argument, for one of them accused the other of forcing him away from a fastened whale. "The 2nd Mate when he came aboard, absolutely foamed at the mouth, & was more like a madman than any thing reasonable: he accused the Mate of cutting his line wantonly."

If ships were whaling in company—which often happened, for they all followed the migrations of the whales—the skipper of one ship was likely to have an apoplexy if a boat from another ship filched what he considered to be his rightful whale. In December 1838, the *Coronet* and the *Folkstone* were both cruising the same part of the Sea of Japan, and "The *Folkstone* Captain came on board and before he left there was a row between the skippers— and Mr. James [third officer] got his foot dreadfully cut," recorded Dr. Eldred Fysh. Presumably, the third mate had been hurt while working on the whale, and not on account of the fight, but it must have been a scene of some excitement. Dr. Fysh, who had a dry sense of humor, noted a couple of months later, "Spoke the *Folkstone*. The Captain went on board and I believe no row occurred." This time, both ships were anchored off Honolulu and there were no contentious whales.

Coulter's *Stratford* was a remarkably happy vessel in comparison. Captain Lock merely breathed a sigh of relief that his surgeon had been fortunate enough to kill a whale. As he told Coulter afterward, they had been so often in range of the whale's flukes that he had expected at any moment "to see the boat, crew, and all sent to Davy's locker." However, he managed to resist giving his surgeon a well-deserved scolding, congratulating him instead.

While whaling was very like the naval service, in that it was an existence made up of long months of boredom occasionally interrupted by hours of excitement, violence, and terror, the lot of the whaling surgeon during whaling was rather different from the circumstances of a naval surgeon during battle. Instead of having a chance to view proceedings safely from deck—or even take part in the struggle—the naval surgeon was trapped on the orlop deck, far below the waterline, at the ready in the cockpit for the inevitable stream of gravely hurt men. The midshipmen's sea chests were shoved together for an operating table, the floor was strewn with sand to prevent them all sliding about in the blood, and the only light was a flickering lantern. The ship around them jumped and rolled with every broadside, and from above came a constant rumble and roar as the guns were run in and out. Add the vibration of frantically running feet, distant panicked shouting from the officers and the gun-crew captains, and the terrified screams of the wounded as "arms and legs were hewed down without mercy," as Smollett described it, and it must have seemed like a nightmare.

On the plus side, the commencement of a battle would give a naval surgeon the reassuring feeling of being an important and appreciated part of the scene. During whaling, by contrast, most whaling surgeons felt more superfluous than ever. Because of this, they were usually cooperative about making themselves useful— something for which there was plenty of opportunity. Dr. Frederick Debell Bennett noted that when the boats were off, the ship was left "almost tenantless and deserted."

Some of the doctors even took over the quarterdeck, especially if the captain was down in one of the boats or was ill. As we have seen, one of those who did so was the surgeon of the *Kingsdown*.

4. The Flurry.   FROM *HARPER'S MAGAZINE*

Dr. Robert Smith Owen of the *Warrens* was another to find himself in this taxing situation. Over the early part of the voyage,
Captain Gray had prepared the way well. First, Dr. Owen had
been instructed to learn how to pull an oar, and after that, his
skipper had craftily incited him to clamber the mast. Then, when
they raised their first whale, Gray sent the poor downtrodden
doctor into the chase, so that Owen could find out what it was
like to be a real whaleman. No sooner was the whale harpooned
than Leviathan put "his nose under the bow of the Boat, lifting it
up—& opening his mouth & cutting her on her gunwale as she
turned." As terrifying as it must have been, Robert Owen had
enough spirit to see some humor in it. One of the whale's teeth
snagged on the captain's trousers, he wrote, with the result that
the boat's crew did not merely see the whale breach, but saw the
captain's "Breech also."

After this it was as if the surgeon had been "blooded," for Owen
took an increasingly active interest in the chase, with the result that

by the time the ship had been out six months, he was in control of the deck when the boats were off. On October 11, 1837, in the middle of the afternoon, a school of whales was sighted: "3 Boats were lowered—1st, 2nd, & 3d. Mates—and about an hour after all fast to Sperm Whales," Owen recorded with palpable excitement. "2d. Mate kil'd 2, & 3rd M 1, Chief Mate loosing his, the Whale biting his line off." Then "the Captns Boat was lowered," and Owen was in charge of the ship. It was a nerve-wracking time. Not only was the *Warrens* in "the narrowest part" of the Timor Straits, but dark was descending with tropical abruptness. So Dr. Owen ordered the shipkeepers to "put lights to the side of the ship that they might see," and was soon rewarded by seeing the "lights of the Boats" in the distance.

On November 2, 1837, two weeks from the time he first climbed all the way to the topgallant crosstrees, Robert Smith Owen took on yet another responsibility. When whales were raised and the four boats were lowered, he clambered up the mast (or, as John Coulter put it, "took a walk upstairs") to keep the run of the chase and let the boatheaders know where the whales were rising and where the boats were needed.

This new duty entailed a lot of hair-raising scrambling about to fly signal flags in different parts of the rigging, according to a pre-arranged code. First Owen "saw a large whale close on the lee no more than ¼ mile off the 3. Mate's bow," and flew a signal to warn him of that, with the result that within fifteen minutes the third mate's boat was fast. However, the iron drew out, so Owen hastily signaled the first mate to come up to the whale and take over the attack—which he did. However, the first officer had the same bad luck in fastening. Another signal, this time to the second mate—and he "got fast—& held till sunset—at one time coming athwart the Head of the Ship."

It was an exciting contest, with the gratifying result that the boats brought "a fine Bull" whale to the ship. And Captain Gray was so delighted with his surgeon's prowess that he gave him a present of six bottles of grog.

JOHN WILSON RECORDED HELPING THE COOK, CARPENTER, SAILMAKER, and cooper "keep" the ship while the boats were away, which for him meant helping to prepare for "cutting in" by assembling all the gear such as fluke ropes and blubber tackle, along with the implements used for cutting the blubber, and the cooper's grindstone, which would be busy keeping the tools sharp. "The Whale being killed, the next step is to secure it to the Ship," William Dalton wrote; "this is done by making a small cable fast round the tail or flooks, by means of a running eye, and is secured to the ship by the other end." This was accomplished in such a manner that the carcass could revolve in the water, with the head to the stern of the ship and the tail to the bow:

> The blubber or fat of a Sperm Whale with its coverings or skins is the external part of the whale and varies in thickness on different parts of the body being in a large male whale from eight to sixteen inches, and on the head or as it approaches the tail it terminates in a hard ligamentous substance containing very little oil. In shoal or cow whales the blubber is from 4 to 10 inches thick.

Getting this blubber off the whale and onto the ship was accomplished by the process of "cutting in," a highly skilled operation that had to be left to men who knew exactly what they were doing. Years of experience went into knowing how to cut and where. This was strictly the business of the captain and mates, while the brute labor was provided by the sailors. Two narrow "stages" on legs were lowered from the starboard gangway, between them encompassing the whale, and the captain and first and second mates clambered out onto these, while "the third Mate has charge of the deck," as John Wilson described:

> The Skipper with a long handled spade cuts the "rising piece" into which a hook is placed, then he begins to separate the head from the body . . . when . . . the body is peeled of blubber going round and round, the same as peeling an apple, and the several portions cut off in the process of hoisting in, are called "blanket pieces."

5. Cutting In.   FROM *HARPER'S MAGAZINE*

"They commence by cutting a hole in the blubber about twelve or eighteen inches behind the eye, into which is dropped a large iron hook, previously secured to the strop of the purchase block," wrote Dr. William Dalton:

> The mates who are standing each on one of the stages have sharp tools called spades which are fixed on poles 18 or 20 feet long. They cut the blubber in a semicircular direction about 20 inches outside the hook and continue cutting in parallel lines towards the ship's side rising by means of the fall which is now heaving at the windlass a piece of blubber of four or five feet in breadth. The first piece being raised which keeps the whale on the surface of the water, they next proceed to cut its head off . . . the whale is turned by heaving the blubber up at the windlass. A hook is fixed in the head by means of the other fall and it is hove upon deck.

"For my part," said Dr. John Coulter, "generally the way I occupied my time on such occasions of cutting in, was sitting in

6. Trying Out.   FROM *HARPER'S MAGAZINE*

one of the quarter boats, and murdering the sharks with a lance, which I had fitted and expressly sharpened for those gentry." This meant that he clambered into the starboard quarter boat—the one hanging in the davits near the stern, on the right-hand side looking forward—and stood there with a lance poised, ready to kill the sharks that swarmed about this great feast, so eager to get at the blubber that they plunged right up onto the whale. As he remarked, this voracious horde made it very unsafe for men to jump down onto the slippery carcass—as often happened when the blubber hook had to be inserted into the start of a new blubber strip or when it was necessary to free up jammed tackle. A rope was tied around the waist of whatever brave seaman had been assigned the task, and the men at the other end of the rope "were frequently obliged to jerk him up off the whale." Actually, the man dangling about on this "monkey rope" had more reason to be worried about Coulter's marksmanship (luckily he had a very sure eye), for the sharks were much more interested in scavenging whale blubber than in adding some variety to the feast with human flesh. However, they did rip off huge jawfuls of the fat, tearing it so that the hard job of flensing was made even more difficult.

"The head is divided into parts by a longitudinal cut," wrote Dalton; "that part next to the lower jaw is called the junk and the part in which is the spout hole is called the case and contains a quantity of sperm[aceti oil] in a fluid state. The junk and case of a sperm whale constitutes about one third of its produce and is the most valuable." Dealing with this most profitable part of the whale was no small task, the head being so massive and unwieldy. "It requires all hands at the windlass to heave the junk in, when on deck it stands from six to eight feet high and is nearly all solid fat." All of it involved a lot of backbreaking work. Dr. Thomas Beale recorded a whale that measured eighty-four feet, which would have rendered in total more than four thousand gallons of oil after boiling out in the try-pots used for this purpose.

Meanwhile, "The blubber is then rolled off the whale," Dalton continued. Once hauled up, these huge blanket pieces—the size and weight of great slabs of granite—were lowered into the blubber room to be chopped into smaller "horse pieces," which were reduced further by mincing, slicing, or crimping to make the extraction of oil as easy as possible. "It is then fit for the Trypots," wrote Dr. John Wilson. These were two or three great cauldrons set into a brick furnace just aft of the foremast. The furnace was initially lit with wood, and the first pieces of blubber were rendered in fresh water. Then, as the oil accumulated, bundles of connective tissue—the "scraps"—bobbed to the seething surface. Skimmed and shaken before being poked into the fire, these made excellent fuel which burned up brilliantly, shed great billows of black and orange smoke—and stank like a charnel house. It has been said that a whaler trying out could be seen for five miles and scented downwind, for fifteen.

Altogether, the task of cutting in and trying out was long, arduous, and filthy, as dangerous in its way as the whale chase had been.

As Dr. John Wilson noted, there were "sharp tools flying about in abundance, & from the motion of the ship attended with no little danger." In 1853, for instance, the captain of the American ship *Ontario* was crushed to death when a slab of blubber collapsed. Obviously, accidents could easily occur "from the people's carelessness" as well as because of the slippery rigging and decks.

6

Accidents, Injuries, and Ailments

A strip of cotton cloth about two feet long
and eight inches wide torn up the centre from one end for
half the length is then to be drawn over the flesh
close around the bone. The ends are brought together
and the whole serves to draw the skin & flesh up
while the bone is sawed off.
Very little pain is felt from sawing a bone—
If there is any splinter or corner left
it should be pinched off with nippers.

Dr. John B. King,
instructions for amputating a leg

On A SAILING SHIP, ORDINARY WORK WAS DANGEROUS ENOUGH without counting the extra hazards of whaling. Falling from aloft was common. One man who pitched from the rigging of the American ship *Lancaster* was rather gruesomely fortunate, because he fell on top of his skipper instead of hitting hard planks. The captain was killed, but the seaman emerged unscathed.

Many of the men must have been as agile as cats, for they managed to survive even when there was nothing to cushion the fall. On the American ship *Zone*, the log recorded in matter-of-fact tones that a man named Dett had fallen from aloft and fractured his thigh—"he is subject to fits & while painting the head of the mizen mast took a fit & down he came." The captain did his best to put the leg right, but two weeks later, "Bill's leg got out of place & set it again this forenoon." Mercifully for the reader, Bill's screaming went undescribed.

At other times the medical treatment was even less successful. On the Edgartown ship *Perry*, the mate noted in the log that when a man named Francisco slipped while furling the main topsail, he was brought into the "Cabbin senseless with a large bunch on his left temple and left eye closed up & badly swollen." Captain Nickerson bathed the contusion with cold water and camphor, detailed a man to keep an eye on him, and left it at that, being unable to think of anything more. Four days later, Francisco passed away without anyone expressing surprise. But then again, the skipper was having no better success in treating himself, the mate observing six months later that Captain Nickerson was "badly off with swollen testicles brought on by stopage of water and to frequent and careless use of the Bougie"—the bougie being a thin flexible instrument used for probing the passage up the penis.

However, it is surprising how seldom South Seas surgeons had to patch up the victims of accidents. Dr. Tom Noddy had a few nasty moments when "a man named Santa Anna fell from the mizzen futtock shrouds, striking on the companionway and then to the deck and injured him some," for he found it impossible to get any blood from him, bleeding being the usual remedy for this kind of drastic situation. However, the wounds and bruises were bathed in "New Rum," which did the trick, for the hardy fellow recovered.

Dr. John Wilson had a more harrowing experience. In August 1841, the second mate, Mr. Smith, was standing on the fore hatch, looking down into the hold where men were restowing the oil, when the tackle that was hoisting casks slipped. It knocked him through the hole and into the hold, where he fell headfirst, "pitching first upon the right promontary of the occipital bone (indicated by a puffy swelling), and upon the right shoulder, which was dislocated." Brought up onto deck, the unfortunate man briefly regained consciousness, "when he writhed & seemed in much pain about the head." Dr. Wilson tried to bleed him by opening the jugular vein, but to no avail—"no blood flowed—or but little," and within five hours of the fall the patient was dead.

Dr. Thomas Beale's book makes passing reference to a bad case of sunburn and a hip fracture, though he had more to say about the amputation of the second mate's arm. This was caused by a stupid, needless accident which occurred "while discharging a cannon by the captain's orders, for the purpose of foolishly saluting an American ship, which was about leaving the harbour," as Dr. Beale described it:

> The poor fellow had discharged it several times, but the reports were not sufficiently loud to please the captain, who ordered it to be again loaded and fired, which the mate thought he would do this time with effect, and therefore not only did he cram into its mouth a seaman's capful of powder, but commenced ramming down the wadding with a handspike, which as he was doing, a spark that had remained in the breech of the gun from the previous firing ignited the charge, and the explosion which took place shattered his right arm to atoms.

Naturally everyone was very upset, particularly the captain, who "wrung his hands, and shed tears like a child" at the tragic result of this pointless piece of patriotism. "It was my painful duty to amputate the wounded member," Dr. Beale announced; "which I am proud to have to state was accomplished with celerity, and without giving unnecessary pangs to my unfortunate shipmate, who soon recovered, and still lives [in 1839] to tell the melancholy tale." Unfortunately, the good doctor neglected to describe what kind of anesthetic procedure was used, if any. Instead, his mind was firmly focused on the ship's business of whaling. "By this unfortunate catastrophe our mate lost his best friend, his right arm, and we lost a valuable officer in a distant part of the world, at which his equal was not to be found." And it was the beginning of the busy whaling season in the Sea of Japan ground, too.

Such accidents were even more inconvenient when there was no surgeon on board—a category of ship that, as we have seen, included just about every American whaler—and boded to be more difficult still if the patient was the captain himself. In 1822, Captain George Clark of the New Bedford ship *Parnasso* was hit by the flukes of a fighting whale that he was trying to lance. He instantly collapsed and "hung across the gunwale of the boat without sense or motion," apparently quite dead, according to the shocked boat-steerer, John Sampson.

Then, to make matters even worse, the damaged boat filled with water and sank. As the sea began to close over his head, the captain gasped "and gave signs of returning life," so the men towed him to the nearest boat and took him on board the ship:

> We hoisted the Captain up in the boat and carried him below. It appears that the whale struck him on the right side of his face and across the nose, which is at present even with his cheeks. His lips are also cut very bad and he bled copiously from his mouth and nose, but the extent of the injury done him cannot be ascertained as it is so much swelled as to scarcely retain the appearance of anything human.

At this point, an objective observer could well have considered that Captain Clark had lost enough blood already. However, his officers bled him, apparently because they could think of nothing else to do. Indeed, it "seemed to revive him" somewhat, but instead of trying anything more ambitious, they held a general meeting: "all hands were called aft by the mate who requested the opinion whether to stay and take in the whale which lay dead near us, or to tack the ship and stand for Payta [Paita, Peru] to obtain needed medical aid for the captain."

The decision was unanimous. They set sail and fled for port and a doctor. Incredibly, George Clark recovered, though he did not seem quite the same man that he was before. After a few weeks on shore he returned to the ship but behaved somewhat irrationally, for instance when he exchanged a new whaleboat for an old one.

"I told the second mate to moove a cask of water acrost deck," wrote Captain Josiah Chase of the New Bedford ship *Hunter;* "in hauling it over Gilbert R. Jenney got jamed between the cask and rail badly I took him aft and bled him in great pain, thus ends." The fact that he solemnly gave the whole of Jenney's name indicates that the situation looked hopeless, and it is with no note of surprise that he recorded next day: "poor Jenney in great pain—at 12.00 a.m. Jenney died from the internal injury received, thus ends, all hands mourning the death of a good shipmate and boatsteerer."

If there were any other ships in speaking distance, the standard procedure in this kind of situation was to send boats to beg for help. An English ship would be hailed with gratitude, for everyone knew that English whalers were supposed to carry surgeons. On October 29, 1840, Dr. John B. King noted that they were spoken by "the *Francis*, Capt. Hussey of N. Bedford," who requested the favor of a visit from the doctor "to see a man sick with dysentery." The captain of the *Francis* might have been surprised to find a physician on board a Nantucket whaler, and certainly would have felt relieved.

Usually, the only ships nearby were other American whalers, and so the men who responded to the call could be expected to be

Mary Stickney— Unofficial Ship's Surgeon.

Mary, wife of Captain Almon Stickney, sailed on the *Cicero* of New Bedford in the years 1880 and 1881, keeping a diary that is replete with lists—lists of sewing done, and of seamen she helped to medicate.

"Names of persons I have doctored at sea," she wrote in June 1880:

W. Haren (the cook) burned arm
Charles Kanaka (seaman) felon [inflammation of a fingernail cuticle]
John Cornell breeding [bleeding] sore on his head
Manuel Silva boil on his arm
Mr Blancenship sore on hand
Almon sore on his hand
Alexander Gifford Cabin Boy cut his finger
John Cornell cut finger
Mr Gomez a cask rolled against his leg
Almon leg where he fell over the grindstone
King's hand cut with a boarding knife
Mr Gomez poultice his foot
Dick soar throat
Cornell cut his leg with a gaff hook
John Kanaka for cough & spitting blood
Philip jambed [h]is finger
Manuel Sylvia soar thumb
Will Winslow for pain in his stomach
Cornell cut his foot with the ax

Captain Almon Stickney attended to most of the emergencies that demanded internal medicine, though how successfully is doubtful, for when he himself was the patient he merely "wrapped himself up in the jib and laid in the bottom of the boat nearly all day." Shipboard accidents were left to Mary, who had carried "1 Paper box of Medacine" in readiness.

no more expert than the skipper himself. However, though he might finish up with an assortment of brother captains without a single medical qualification between them, at least it was moral support. Thus, when a seaman belonging to the *Vesper* of New London, Connecticut, got his leg entangled in the line, tearing off most of his foot, the ship's logbook records that Captain John Hempstead "sent for the Captin of the Minerva Smith of New Bedford & the Captin of Columbia of Sag Harbor & the Captin of the Maury of New Bedford."

The four old salts pulled their whiskers and consulted, and then rolled up their cuffs "& took of the leg above where the line had cut it of & left the Steward of the Bark Columbia witch was a doctor. So Ends," concludes the entry in seamanlike fashion, completely omitting to tell us what we would like to know about that intriguing steward. Was he truly a doctor? It is possible. Dr. John B. Troy, the steward of a Sydney whaler, was immortalized as "Doctor Long Ghost" in Herman Melville's book, *Omoo*. Or perhaps the steward of the *Columbia* was simply a young physician who

While she did not describe the contents, or how they were administered, there are occasional mentions in the body of her diary of the causes of the accidents, imparting an eloquent hint of just how rough life was on a whaler. Unsurprisingly, many of the mishaps happened when a man lost his balance on the decks or in the rigging, but other wounds were due to more than simple clumsiness. King's hand was cut during a fight with the cook, while Cornell's "breeding" sore on the head was the result of being hammered with a handspike by a mate who had found him asleep when he should have been on duty.

Mary Stickney was as phlegmatic about that as she was about John Winslow's ailment. He was very sick indeed, being both feverish and delirious, but was back on lookout at the masthead before the week was out. "I doctored five different men tonight," she penned in matter-of-fact fashion on June 4. Somehow, it is no surprise to find that she kept a talking parrot, who rode about on her shoulder.

wanted to experience adventure, like Dr. John King. Whatever the answer, it is lost to history.

For a desperate skipper, it was best of all if there was a friendly man-of-war within reach. In 1824, one of the boats belonging to the Nantucket whaleship *Lima* was dashed to pieces by an infuriated whale, injuring several men. George, the son of Captain Abraham Swain, was the most seriously hurt, for his right foot had been crushed and his left arm badly broken. Captain Swain immediately steered for Callao, Peru, where the frigate *United States* was lying at anchor. George was carried on board, and was operated on by two surgeons, Doctors Tinslow and Fitzhugh. Fortune was certainly on the lad's side, for Commodore Isaac Hull was carrying both his wife and his sister-in-law. Mrs. Hull's presence was against regulations, let alone that of her sister (at one time the commodore's officers complained that Mrs. Hull "has in fact assumed command of the ship"), but the two women took on the role of ministering angels and nursed young George back to health.

At other times, a ship would be alone on the boundless ocean, and so the skipper had to find someone on board who could cope if he himself, for some reason, felt unequal to the task. "By some means or other," wrote the cook of the American whaler *S. R. Sopler*, the whaleline "took a round turn around each of the boat-steerer's legs, taking him from the boat as quick as a flash." The poor fellow shouted: "Cut the line!"—but no one responded, simply because the whale had capsized the boat. While the boatsteerer was dragged along by the whale at "engine speed," the rest of the boat's crewmen were struggling for their lives in the water.

Twenty minutes later, they had sorted themselves out, were back in the righted boat, and set to hauling in the line. Eventually the body swam up into view. "A shudder passed through everyone's frame at the sight, it was a sad spectacle, the legs were nearly cut off just above the knee." At that stage, the captain and the mate arrived in another boat and took the body on board the ship, where it was handed to the cook with instructions to revive the corpse and repair the damage as best he could. The choice was more logical than it sounds, for while the cook (a whimsical fellow by the name of Caleb Hunt) could read, and thus make use of the medical book, the captain could not. In this case, literacy did the "doctor" no good, however. More than a little flummoxed, he commenced working on his patient by "rubbing him and bathing his feet" in warm water, but (possibly to Caleb's secret relief) it was to no avail—the harpooner was definitely dead.

This is in great contrast to a number of flamboyant stories told of American whaling skippers and their resourcefulness. One such yarn relates the amazing feat accomplished by Captain Charles Ray, who commanded the ship *Norman* on the voyage of 1855–1860. His third mate, Mr. King, was taken out of a boat by a whale, his right foot entangled in the line. After cutting him free, Ray took the poor fellow on board, cut off the grossly damaged foot above the ankle, sewed the flap, and then went back and killed the whale.

In similar spirit, when a man was brought on board who had had his leg cut when his boat was stove, or smashed in, by a whale, Captain Bill Hegarty gave the fellow half a pint of rum, washed the wound in seawater, and then sat on the fore-topgallant deck with the man's leg on his lap and sewed it up with a sail needle and waxed twine. He made the same stitches that he used when mending sails, so that the patient ended up with a distinctive scar in a neat herringbone pattern. This, incidentally, is one of the very few descriptions of grog being administered as an anesthetic. The quantity of ardent spirits supplied as "general stores" could be quite generous (particularly when compared to the miserly contents of most New England medical chests)—one whaleship out of New Bedford was provided with seven assorted gallons of rum, wine, and whiskey, plus two bottles of brandy and three of Hollands gin. However, the fact that "pain killer" (probably laudanum) also featured in the provision list of the same ship indicates that liquor was used as a pick-me-up when the operation was over.

Captain Jim Huntting of Southampton, Long Island, a giant of a man six feet six inches tall, weighing 250 pounds, and with a leather-throated voice that boomed from one end of the deck to the other, did not deign to use grog—or laudanum, for that matter. According to a tale told by seaman William M. Davis in *Nimrod of the Sea*, when a man who had been tangled up in a whaleline was brought on board more dead than alive:

> it was found that a portion of the hand including four fingers had been torn away, and the foot sawed through at the ankle, leaving only the great tendon and the heel suspended to the lacerated stump. . . . Saved from drowning, the man seemed likely to meet a more cruel death, unless some one had the nerve to perform the necessary amputation. . . . But Captain Jim was not the man to let any one perish on [such] slight provocation. He had his carving knife, carpenter's saw and a fish-hook. The injury was so frightful and the poor fellow's groans and cries so touching, that several of the crew fainted in their endeavors to aid the captain in the operation, and others sickened and turned away from the sight. Unaided, the captain then lashed his screaming patient to the carpenter's bench, amputated the leg and dressed the hand.

Another stirring tale told is of a Captain Coffin, who was hurt so badly in a whaling accident that it was obvious his leg would have to go. Being the master, the medic, and the patient all at once, he knew the situation was complicated, but he was more than equal to the task. He sent for his pistol and a knife, saying to his mate, "Now, sir, you gotta lop off this here leg, and if you flinch—well, sir, you get shot in the head." Then he sat as steady as a rock while the mate went at it with the knife, holding the pistol unwaveringly until the operation was completed. No sooner was the stump wrapped up and the leg cast overboard than both men fainted.

PERHAPS IT IS A PITY THAT NOTHING SO DRAMATIC OCCURRED ON our surgeons' ships, for surely such heroic deeds would have improved their social standing on board. Dr. John King, despite his careful notations of surgical procedure, did not have to carry out a single amputation. Dr. Robert Smith Owen did remark that the whalemen under his care seemed to suffer badly from boils while

Captain James R. Huntting.
Stove Boat.

FROM *NIMROD OF THE SEA*,
WILLIAM M. DAVIS (NEW YORK, 1874)

Captain Jim Huntting (1825–1882) was a well-known figure in his home town of Bridgehampton, Long Island, New York—partly because of his commanding height (six feet, six inches), partly because of his full-lunged voice (he could be heard from one end of the main street to the other), but mostly because of the flamboyant stories told of his dash, strength, and courage. He first went out in command of the *Nimrod*, sailing in September 1848 and returning exactly two years later, and then took out the *Jefferson* on two voyages, the first in November 1850, and the second in October 1853. After returning home in March 1857, he took over the *General Scott* of Fairhaven, Massachusetts, sailing in October 1858, and returning in May 1862. His last command was the *Fanny* of New Bedford, which he took out in September 1864, returning home to retire in April 1869.

cutting in and trying out: "the *black skin* of the whale with the green oil i.e. before boiling appears to act as a powerful poison & yet acts as a powerful cleanser of the skin with sea water," he noted. These painful boils are caused by microorganisms that live naturally on the skin of the whale and may have a protective function, but Dr. Owen could do little more than issue an unguent of flowers of sulfur in lard. In truth, Dr. Owen was more interested in his own troubles—"got terribly scorched by the sun today on the fore part of my feet owing to my going without shoes & stockings on deck," he complained after trying out.

Typically, accidents were not the greatest or most common challenge faced by whaling surgeons. "I stand by a table in the door of the largest ward," wrote the Reverend Sereno Bishop in a letter that was quoted in the Honolulu paper *The Seamen's Friend* in February 1860. He was describing taking a service in the Seamen's Hospital at Lahaina, Maui, where he served as chaplain from 1853 to 1862:

> Around are the patients, seated upon the beds or on seats brought in for the purpose. One has lost his right leg above the knee; another is nearly blind, an elderly man one who always sits in the rocker is recovering from papalysis [paralysis]; two of those mild looking Portuguese, from the Western Islands, recline on their beds low in the latter stages of consumption: and yonder is a fine looking young man, full of attention, whose legs are shackled with heavy irons to prevent his sudden escapades. He was struck on the head by a whale last winter and is deranged. . . . The number now in the hospital is small, but in a few weeks they will be thronging in, a forlorn crew, with all shapes of scurvy, rheumatism, dysentery and consumption . . . most of them will recover, and some will leave in a short time, while others will remain until Spring.

According to a list that was published in Honolulu in 1844 by Mr. R. C. Wyllie, secretary to the British Consul, seamen were most commonly hospitalized for "mercurial rheumatism," common rheumatism, secondary syphilis, "phthisis pulmonalis" (tuberculosis), chronic dysentery, stricture (narrowing of the ure-thra), fistula (funneling, usually of the anus), bronchitis, chronic gastritis, hepatitis, pericarditis (inflammation of the membranes around the heart), scrofula (tuberculosis of the lymphatic glands), scurvy, chronic enteritis, hemiplegia (paralysis of one side of the body), nephritis (inflammation of the kidneys), dropsy, epilepsy, lumbar abscess, cystitis, and insanity. This last ailment was surprisingly common, so much so that the Sick and Hurt Board in London theorized that its high rate on men-of-war was due to seamen banging their heads on low beams while drunk. Dr. Eldred Fysh noted that when the *Coronet* spoke the *Rochester*, he heard of the loss of several ships, including the *John Calvin*, where the ship was set afire by the cook, who had gone mad and cut his throat soon thereafter.

Overcrowding, as pointed out by Sir Gilbert Blane (1749–1834), led to many seamen contracting diseases such as tuberculosis from each other—and yet whaleships, like men-of-war, were over-crowded by necessity. Battle fatalities on navy ships, like accidents on whalers, counted for only a fraction of the mortality rate, particularly on tropical stations, and many of those who did die as a result of enemy action succumbed not because their wounds were mortal, but because they became infected. Catarrh and pneumonia were commonplace, along with liver disease. Because of the harsh life and constant exposure to the elements, rheumatism was an occupational disease of seamen—as also was erysipelas, a very painful and infectious skin condition that was with good reason known as "Saint Anthony's fire." Typically, seafarers' teeth were bad, and their guts clogged and flatulent. The coarse diet that was directly responsible for these woes was sometimes contaminated, too, leading to outbreaks of botulism, salmonella, and typhoid.

Infestation with worms and lice—often typhus-bearing lice—was general. On the *Coronet*, while on deck talking with the cooper and the cooper's mate (a Scot laid up with a broken leg), Dr. Eldred Fysh noticed that one of the men was "picking & killing something from his hair. I asked what he was about," he went on. "Killing fleas," guessed the cooper, "in true London accent." At that the cooper's mate laughed, saying in his broad Scots, "Na! Na! That w'll nae do! Fla's are not likely to stop & b'catch'd." And, "Sandy was right," Dr. Fysh concluded in disgust. "For they were lice."

The challenge faced by the surgeons became even more taxing when the ships dropped anchor in tropical ports. Men swarmed ashore to eat local food, quaff local liquor, drink local water, and sleep with local women. The medical logbooks of South Seamen typically record outbreaks of "fever & ague," "fever & dysentery," "intermittent fever attended by fits," "dysentery attended by typhoid fever," "venereal ulcers," "dysentery caused by intemperance and excess of fruit," and "diarrhea attended with violent spasms," during or after such visits. On the verge of entering the Timor Straits for the first time, Dr. John Wilson recorded that they had spoken an American ship, the whaler *Clifford Wayne* of Fairhaven, Massachusetts. While in Java, the captain informed him, "he had nine of his crew taken with sickness, of whom two died, both boatsteerers & the most useful men aboard, & lamented their loss: reported another ship at anchor at the same time, had fourteen men sick, of whom several died."

Timor was just as dangerous. Dr. James Brown noted that in just one fever season "there was upwards of 300 carried off by Dysentery or Diarrhea," while "intermittent fever" (malaria) was common at all times. There, as Dr. Wilson wrote:

> ships have lost as many as eight or ten men in Port, & the voyage in consequence has been seriously impeded: many & many is the English-man who has fallen a victim to the proverbial "Timor Fever," & lies buried in that fatal soil.

"At 3 P.M. Robert Gutteridge, alias Lovell, died, after an illness of 12 days," recorded Dr. Eldred Fysh on December 5, 1837. However, he did not blame the notorious miasmas of the region. In his considered opinion, Gutteridge's collapse and death was directly due to Gutteridge (alias Lovell) himself. His decline had been "brought on by his excessive intemperance on shore at Batta-gady"—the

Timorese port of Batu Gadeh. Even though the sailor had been warned how "injurious the climate was to Englishmen and also, of what a Poisonous nature the native spirit was," this sage advice had been "of no use—where drink of any sort was to be had he would have it. At one time he drank 1½ pts. of the spirit in one hour, the consequence was he brought on an inflamation of the lungs & heart—And although he had every attendance he sank under it.

"I have seen many people die," Dr. Fysh (who had just celebrated his twenty-sixth birthday) added on a ghoulish note, "but not one the horrible death this man had." Then he drew a neat gravestone at the bottom of the page, filling it in with the epitaph:

To

Memory of

Robt Gutteridge alias

Lovell, Seaman

Who departed this life

On Board

The Barque Coronet

Dec^{br}. 5th 1837

His Body was com-

mitted to the deep

In Lat 00.22S

Long. 129.00E

"Take heed ye swinish

among the people. O ye

Fools, when will ye

Understand?"

PSALM XCIV, VERSE VIII

Alas, there were many "fools" aboard South Seamen, men who died in agony of chronic dysentery, inflammation of the bowels, or "tertian ague" after a run on shore. Many of these were buried on land, in the "fatal soil" of some exotic island. Interment was what people of the time preferred. However, it is a rare South Seaman log that does not record a burial at sea—an example being the funeral of the second mate of the *Gipsy*, Henry Smith, the man who had been unfortunate enough to pitch headfirst into the hold. Smith's corpse was sewed into his hammock and bed linen, though it was more usual for the body to be sewn into a canvas shroud, often with the last stitch being taken through the nose to make sure the subject was dead. In all cases, weights of some kind were included so that the corpse would sink when cast overboard. Then the dead man was laid on a hatch on the main deck, with "the emblem of his Country," in this case a Union Jack, spread over him. Dr. John Wilson read the service while all hands stood around with bowed heads, and then the body "was committed to the deep" by the simple process of upending the hatch and tipping the corpse over the amidships starboard rail. "He was about 30 years of age," Wilson added, "& had married but a few months before he left England."

That done, Captain Gibson busily set about reallocating boat-headers and boatsteerers to make up for the second mate's loss. And forthwith, "in half an hour, after the Funeral Service, the four Boats were lowered after whales, when after a long chase . . . the 1st. Boat fastened to a large whale, and soon after the 2 & 3 Boats, so that it was speedily dead." By nine in the evening the dead whale was alongside, and to all appearances the deceased had been totally forgotten. "Death in any shape makes but a transient impression on a sailor," Dr. Wilson concluded, but at least some properly solemn respect had been paid, as simple as the burial had been.

It is probably an axiom of the sea that even the most simple arrangements must at some time go wrong. During a fearful storm in the South Pacific, one of Dr. John Coulter's patients died of overindulgence in something or other. He was an unpopular man, gross in habits and appearance, probably rather like Dr. Eldred Fysh's "Robert Gutteridge, alias Lovell." However, the captain was determined to bury him in the proper manner, though the sea was still very rugged. The ship was hove to, the shrouded corpse was placed on a plank (because all the hatches were in use), and the ser-vice commenced.

At first, everything went as usual. But then, at the words, "We commit his body to the deep," a huge wave arrived, and the heavy lee-lurch that followed threw down most of the men, with the corpse crashing about amongst them. "As soon as they could stand on the slippery deck, they did," Dr. Coulter related, "each casting strange looks at the other, whilst some gave audible vent to sundry marine maledictions."

Worse still, the captain was overtaken with the "drollery" of the scene, and "had to turn his face away and close the book for a moment." However, when he recovered, the order came out firmly enough: "Right him again."

"Aye, aye, sir"—and the plank was put back in position.

"Again the book was opened," Coulter went on; but before the captain could utter a word, "another heavy swell burst in upon us amidship, and washed both the living and the dead across the deck to the other side."

Water foamed while the men struggled madly to get away from their dead but all too lively companion. After they had scrambled to their feet and shaken themselves down, the boatswain approached the captain. "Beg pardon, sir," said he, "but there is something not right. He won't start off from the gangway; suppose we drop him over the stern?"

His skipper, albeit with a twinkle in his eye, merely bid him not to be such an old fool and to rig the plank again. Then, having got through the service a second time, he cried out: "Launch!"

"The board was elevated," Coulter related, "yet the body remained without sliding off." The captain hollered, "Higher!" But even when it was upright, the body refused to budge. "Several of the men now got superstitiously impatient, and shouted to those who supported the board to heave; and heave they did; for the body was jerked some distance away from the ship's side, performing a summerset before it made its final plunge."

And there revealed on the plank was the culprit of the affair, a large projecting nail, which had been snagged in the shroud. "This, I say, is the only time I have ever witnessed anything like levity or irregularity during the burial ceremony at sea," Coulter added hastily, the sensitivities of his audience in mind, but there is an inescapable impression that the recollection gave him a reminiscent grin.

7

Battling Scurvy

We have now 37 whaleships in port and outside,
and others arriving daily. . . . Quite a number have lost spars and sails,
but the saddest scene of all is the number of seamen we see
carried through the streets to the hospital painfully afflicted
with the scurvy. Oahu diet and balmy breezes will soon renovate their
diseased frames. . . . Two men have died since getting into port.

Polynesian *of Honolulu,*
November 20, 1847

$\mathcal{A}$FTER LEAVING EDGARTOWN IN NOVEMBER 1837, THE *AURORA* sailed in company with another Nantucket whaler, the *Phoenix* (possibly because Captain John Hussey's relative, Isaac B. Hussey, was in command of her), to the Cape Verde Islands, where the *Aurora* took on fresh provisions before sailing south and tackling the tough westward route round Cape Horn to the Pacific coasts of South America. Finally, in April 1838, they dropped anchor in Paita, Peru, where the men were given liberty—days off—to go on shore. It was the first of many similar visits.

"The small pox is prevailing in Paita to an alarming extent," wrote Dr. King in May 1839; "at least it would be so thought in the U. States; but here they seem to give themselves very little trouble about it." More than two hundred deaths had been reported in the last month, a large number "for so small a place," and definitely a cause for worry. As it happened, though, King's only patient was a man with a cough, whom he treated with antimonial wine and tincture of opium in water and honey. However, as the months and then years of voyage took their toll, an ever-increasing line of patients arrived at his door—so many, in fact, that he began to make note of them in his journal, keeping up an almost continuous record for the three months from August 17 to November 22, 1840 (see Appendix B). Obviously, the men were growing less fit.

Because of a fight or an accident, a man named Gow sustained a wound ("vulnus") on his thigh that refused to heal, developing into an abscess which required daily treatment for a month. Wearing rough, dirty clothing and working aloft in wet, salt conditions led to boils ("eruptio") and ulcers ("ulcus"), another indication that the men had lost their natural resistance. Because of the coarse diet, there were many episodes of "foul stomach" and gastrodynia, countered with magnesium sulfate and ipecac.

There were three cases of testitis—inflammation of the testicles—which seems a high number, considering that it represents 10 percent of the crew over a sampling of just three months. This could be the result of a slip while straddling a spar, a common accident on a pitching ship, but in at least one case it was perhaps a side effect of gonorrhea. A water-based poultice ("cataplasm") was the usual treatment, with an opium pill if the pain remained severe. Cases in general of venereal disease became more numerous, being treated with piperine, Dover's powder, Epsom salts, and a mysterious patent mixture, "Mistura Adamsi."

Other shipboard slips—or fights—resulted in bruises ("contusio"), which were treated with simple fomentations of vinegar, ("lotio acetic")—probably lifted from general stores. And then there was the skipper's headache. Captain Hussey suffered badly from pains in his head ("cephalalgia") and also from insomnia ("vigilance"). Dr. King seemed to be somewhat at a loss to know what to do about this; his remedies ranged from Epsom salts, mercury pills, opium pills, and cupping to making up hot punch, presumably by commandeering the ingredients from the pantry. However, considering the circumstances, the state of the crew was a credit to the young Nantucketer's medical skill. In the whole of the three-month medical record he had only one case of dysentery, which he successfully treated with opium, arrowroot, blistering, Dover's powder, and calomel. And he did not lose a single patient—something that not many South Seas surgeons could say.

Captain John Hussey Jr. must have felt quite pleased with his surgeon, even if Dr. King did fail to cure his severe headaches and insomnia. However, a major benefit to the overall health of the crew of the *Aurora* was that the ship dropped anchor so often. Ironically, while calling at ports like Paita involved drunkenness, diarrhea, and the pox, along with wounds sustained during fights and accidents that were all too likely to have been "fixed" by an incompetent port physician, *not* dropping anchor risked the scourge associated with long voyages: that insidious destroyer of health, spirits, and eventually life itself—sea scurvy.

Scurvy is not unknown on land, particularly in the early spring after a long, hard winter, due to a simple deficiency of vitamin C (ascorbic acid). At sea this deficiency was complicated by deficiencies in thiamin, niacin, and riboflavin as well. Old seafarers, despite a lack of knowledge of this scientific complexity, understood the hard fact that men sickened and suffered and died when they had been away from land for a certain length of time. During Drake's circumnavigation of the Atlantic in 1585, he lost a quarter of his 2,300 men through scurvy. In 1657 a Manila galleon, *San José*, was found drifting off Acapulco, a ghost ship manned by dead men, all victims of this horrible affliction; and on Anson's voyage of 1741, only 626 of the original roster of 961 survived. Richard Hawkins, the Elizabethan sea rover, very aptly called this dreadful curse of long voyages "the plague of the sea, and the spoil of mariners."

Few realized how quickly the disease could develop. The *Tuscan*, with Dr. Frederick Debell Bennett on board, set out from Honolulu on May 22, 1835, on the way to the Sea of Japan whaling ground, and as early as July 7 Dr. Bennett began to express concern about the health of the crew. "Chronic or mild diseases became acute or aggravated," he reminisced later; "inflammatory sores were quick in forming and slow to heal; and glandular affections were numerous. But the most general and salutory complaint was a profuse eruption on the skin of minute vesicles, attended with intense tingling or itching upon exposing the person to cold." He attributed all of this to leaving the tropics and entering a cooler latitude, and certainly did not entertain the notion that the men might be suffering from the first stages of scurvy. How could it be so when they had left Oahu just forty-six days previously? It was far too early.

If that was his logic, he was wrong. The first symptoms of increasing weakness, tiredness, and depression could appear as soon as six weeks after the ship's stocks of fresh fruit and vegetables had run out. Small purple spots erupted on the legs and arms and then ran together until the limb was swollen and black, all this accompanied by severe pains in the joints of the knees, ankles, and toes, particularly at night. Because vitamin C is necessary for the body to produce collagen, which glues scar tissue together, wounds that had been healed for years opened up, and fractured bones that had knitted broke apart. The stomach and breath became foul, and gums became so soft and spongy that the teeth dropped out. Blood trickled from the eye sockets and nostrils, and vomit was bloody, too. Given lemon juice to drink or fresh fruit and vegetables to eat, the recovery was miraculous. Without it, death was inevitable, as bleeding inside the skull compressed the brain and crushed it down into the spinal canal.

That scurvy was something to do with shipboard diet had been recognized for hundreds of years. Back in the thirteenth century, Gilbertus Acquila suggested that it could be blamed on faulty feeding, and as early as 1593 Sir Richard Hawkins noted that the remedy "most fruitfull for this sicknesse, is sower oranges and lemmons." In 1601, on an epoch-making voyage to the East Indies, Captain James Lancaster's *Red Dragon* was supplied with "certaine bottles of the juice of limons, which he gave to each one as long as it would last, three spoonfuls every morning." The three other ships of his little fleet, which did not carry the juice, were so devastated by scurvy by the time of arrival that their crews had to be assisted by Lancaster's men, who were in very much better shape.

John Woodall thought the prevention and treatment of "this lamentable disease" so crucial that he included a treatise, "Of the Scurvy called in Latine Scorbutum" in *The Surgions Mate*. "The use of the juice of Lemons is a precious medicine and wel tried, being sound & good," he wrote; "let it have the chiefe place for it will deserve it." He recommended that two or three spoonfuls be taken each morning, perhaps mixed with a little aqua vitae, which should have saved the lives of countless sailors, along with cheering their spirits. Unfortunately, Woodall thought the beneficial element was the acidity, and recommended useless prophylactics like "good oyle of Vitrioll" as well. This misunderstanding had far-reaching effects: Dr. John King asserted that salts of lemon (number 13 in his list) "is good in scurvy when fresh fruit and vegetables can not be

Captain James Cook.

When Lieutenant James Cook was given the command of the *Endeavour* at the relatively young age of forty, he was known as a quietly competent seaman and a gifted navigator. All his commanding officers had spoken well of him. That first exploratory voyage made him famous, for it was then that, as well as charting much of the Pacific, including New Zealand, he established his reputation for good housekeeping, ransacking landfalls for antiscorbutics, releasing animals into the wild in the hope that they would multiply into a food source for mariners, and establishing gardens in eccentric places. On his return to England in 1771 Cook was promoted to the rank of commander and sailed again in charge of the *Resolution*, accompanied by the *Adventure*. His third voyage began in July 1776, and in the course of this he discovered and charted the "Sandwich Islands" (later named "Hawaiian Islands"), the place where he met his death, during a skirmish with natives.

obtained." Salts of lemon is citric acid, which has none of the antiscorbutic qualities of ascorbic acid, the ingredient present in the raw fruit or its juice, so in the fight against the disease, King's concoction was nothing more than a pleasant drink. However, many of his brethren made the same assumption.

Crank theories concerning the disease abounded. As late as 1845 the shipping paper in New Bedford, after noting that the ship *Hydaspe* had limped into port under the control of just the captain, mate, and one man—all the rest of the crew being dead or dying of scurvy—supplied a "cure of scurvy." Whale flesh, it seems, was the answer. If a scurvy seaman should wrap a piece of whale meat about his affected limbs, then a swift cure was guaranteed. Such hokum persisted despite the fact that as far back as 1753 a naval surgeon, Dr. James Lind, had published the results of a famous experiment that had proved once and for all that the remedy for scurvy was citrus fruit. In May 1747, while serving as the surgeon of the *Salisbury*, a fourth-rate (fifty-gun) man-of-war, Lind selected twelve men with scurvy for special treatment. All twelve were given sweetened water-gruel for breakfast, mutton soup or "duff" (a flour-and-water pudding) for dinner, and barley, rice, or sago with currants and raisins for supper. Additionally, two were given a quart of cider to drink, while two others had elixir of vitriol. Two more drank vinegar, and two were given seawater, while another two were dosed with an elixir of garlic, mustard seed, horseradish, balsam of Peru, and myrrh. The last couple were given oranges and lemons, and these were the men who were up and about and nursing the others six days later. It is considered by some to be the first clinical trial in history.

The man most famous for his obsession with scurvy-free crews is Captain James Cook, the commander of possibly the most important discovery voyage to the Pacific, in the *Endeavour* from 1768 to 1771. Quite apart from navigating his way through uncharted waters in the greatest sea on earth, he dedicated an enormous amount of thought and energy to what his "people" ate. Not only did he stock his stores with sauerkraut, portable broth, and citrus juice, but he was a forager on an epic scale. Everywhere the *Endeavour* dropped anchor, he sent a boat on shore to collect local flora, and then he experimented with the harvest. Thus one of his instructions to his colleague, Furneaux, on a later expedition, ran: "you are hereby required and directed, whenever vegitables are to be got, to cause a sufficient quantity to be boil'd with the usual allowance of wheat or oatmeal." He also set great store by a beer made from the bark and tips of sprucelike trees "by boiling them three or four hours, or until the bark will strip with ease from the branches, then take the leaves or branches out," he instructed. This liquor was to be mixed with "the proper quantity of melasses and

Inspissated Juice" along with the right amount of yeast, and "in a few days the Beer will be fit to drink."

His men detested it all, starting with the sauerkraut. Cook countered this particular problem by craftily decreeing that sauerkraut should be reserved for the cabin table alone. "The Sour Krout the Men at first would not eate untill I put in practice a Method I never once knew to fail with seamen," he wrote:

> and this was to have some of it dress'd every Day for the Cabbin Table, and permitted all the Officers without exception to make use of it and left it to the option of the Men either to take as much as they pleased or none at all; but this practice was not continued above a week before I found it necessary to put every one on board to an Allowance, for such are the Tempers and disposissions of Seamen in general that whatever you give them out of the Common way, altho it be ever so much for their good yet it will not go down with them and you will hear nothing but murmurings gainest the man that first invented it; but the Moment they see their Superiors set a Value upon it, it becomes the finest stuff in the World and the inventer a damn'd honest fellow.

By such devious ploys he manipulated his men into cramming down their assorted throats a strange miscellany of manuka leaves, kumara roots, "sellery" (*Apium australe*), and "scurvy grass" (actually a kind of cress), with the result that he was able to report, on reaching Batavia (modern Jakarta), that "I have not lost one man by sickness the whole voyage." Alas, he spoke too soon, for the same agues, fevers, and dysentery that finished off so many sailors on South Seamen in the Timor Straits carried off thirty-four of his crew.

The crews of South Seamen were particularly vulnerable to scurvy, for they cruised such long distances in search of their prey. Dr. John Wilson calculated that on his voyage on the *Gipsy*—a matter of "3 years, 4 months, 24 days"—they sailed on passage "courses *306°* of Latitude or *18,360* miles, and *229°* of Longitude or *13,740* miles, in the whole *32,100* miles!" Then he amended the figure, already impressive enough, saying that "it may be doubled, at

H.M. Endeavour.

ARTIST, RON DRUETT

At two o'clock in the afternoon of August 26, 1768, the 369-ton cat-built *Endeavour* sailed from her anchorage in Plymouth Harbour. She was carrying 94 persons, provisions and stores for eighteen months, a goat, and two greyhounds, and was bound on the first of James Cook's three historic expeditions to the Pacific. Two years, nine months, and fourteen days after departure, she anchored in the Downs again. Sold out of the navy in 1775, *Endeavour* returned to her old trade as a collier (coal freighter), finally running ashore and breaking up in Narragansett Bay.

the least, to allow for the space run over during the cruizing, as we were constantly on the move, going to and fro, and from one place to another" in the hunt for whales.

Because of this, while dropping anchor in exotic ports involved drunkenness and disease, these sojourns were vital for the health of the crew. "Light winds and fine; we are all anxious for port," wrote Dr. John Wilson in October 1841, toward the end of a season's whaling in the Sea of Japan; "all are fagg'd and wearied, with incipient tokens of scurvy, pains and weariness of the limbs &c." Whales were abundant, however, and Captain Gibson insisted on lingering, so that Wilson recorded a sad scene while trying out, of "poor scorbutic wretches [who] move about languidly, though willingly: many covered with papulae, or boils: some with oedematous legs, or indolent unhealable Sores, or each or all. It is now time we were

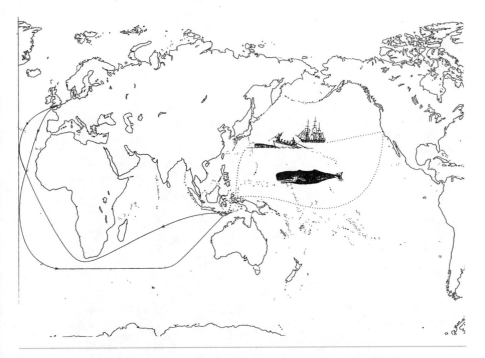

Route sailed by the *Kingsdown*, 1829–1832, a typical London South Seaman voyage.

in Port," he emphatically concluded. There the *Gipsy*'s men might indulge in "frolic and boisterous mirth," but they would also eat the fruit that would save their lives.

It was best of all for the general health of the crew (not to mention the skipper's peace of mind) if the landfall was uninhabited, or virtually so. One such place was "Elphinstone's Bay" in the Island of Celebes, where the captains liked to take on firewood, coconuts, and fresh water, simply because it was impossible for the crews to get drunk, there being no grogshops. In March 1839, the *Warrens* dropped anchor in Elphinstone's Bay in company with the *Kent*, so that Dr. Robert Smith Owen had the unusual privilege of going on shore in good company—the surgeon of the other ship. Taking a boat, they went about fifteen miles up a stream and fell "in with a canoe with several natives in, who on catching sight of us run the canoe ashore & took to the woods as fast as their legs would let them." Further along, the surgeons came across a small village surrounded by land that had been recently burned off. Beyond that, the jungle was "so thick that if you get in but a little way you are obliged to crawl on all fours to make your way, at the same time standing a chance of meeting some unpleasant sort of companion who would like as not leave with your flesh & bones." However, it was a pleasant adventure and a very good chance for observing local fauna and flora while the seamen reprovisioned the ship in a state of laudable sobriety.

In the eastern Pacific Ocean, the Galápagos Islands had this same rare virtue of being free of grogshops, and giant tortoises could be collected there as well. Once on board, the great reptiles roamed the decks for weeks without needing care—or even producing ship-soiling dung—until the time came when fresh meat was needed, a walking larder, as it were. The week or so on shore while the men were hunting the tortoises (called "terrapin" by the whalemen), meant that they, like their counterparts in Elphinstone Bay, were eating local herbs and fruit.

Dr. William Dalton, who sailed from England on the *Phoenix* in January 1823, recorded: "July 2^d we anchored off Hoods Island [Española] in 13 fathom of water." The island was "about 15 miles long and six broad," and consisted of "craggy rocks and large loose stones as if cleft asunder by the violence of an earthquake: when you step on them they make a sonorous noise as if they contained some metallic substance." There were plenty of small bushes, but the "prickly pair tree is the only tree growing on this island; there is no weed, or fresh water here. This Island is inhabited by Terrapin, Guaners [iguanas], Lizards, Centipedes, and small serpents; also Doves, Pelicans, and a variety of sea fowl; there are also a few Seals."

It was all very interesting and educational. Dr. Dalton had ample opportunity to roam about and observe, while the men collected "200 Terrapin." However, matters did not go as well as anticipated. "The writer of this unfortunately lost himself on Hoods Island," Dalton confessed:

and suffered for want of food but more particularly for water; the intense heat of the weather and the difficulty of travelling having created great fatigue: I slept in a prickly pair tree to avoid the reptiles infesting this Island. On my return I learned three of our crew had also lost themselves but had fortunately returned in safety.

Dr. John Coulter—who held the strange theory that salt provisions *caused* scurvy, which could be cured simply by strolling about on land—was another to visit these unusual islands. In 1833, when "a feeling of debility" started "creeping through the crew," the *Stratford* dropped anchor in the Galápagos, and a large tent was set up on shore for the men to enjoy three weeks of walking about to shake off the scurvy—an even easier matter than Coulter envisaged, for "the only thing required to be brought from the ship was biscuit, as everything else was in abundance on shore." Green turtle could be caught with ease, along with wildfowl; there were fish in the rocks and "herbs in great variety," such as a very palatable mint. Obviously, in a place like this, nothing was going to happen to prove Coulter's theories wrong.

However, shaking off the scurvy, while a sure thing, was going to take a couple of weeks, so Coulter took it into his head that he would like to walk round the island in the meantime. "As we were to lay here some time now, and nothing for me to do professionally, either on board or on shore," he obtained the captain's permission, shouldered his gun, and set off on "an exploring excursion." The men delivered three cheers as he went, but none of them volunteered to keep him company, probably because they were well aware that they could not keep up with his pace. "They said it was all a humbug to be tramping about on an uninhabited island from morning to night," Coulter grunted, and set out to prove them wrong.

In true frontier style he crawled through tangled bush and hacked down trees to make overnight huts. Every dawn, "without being annoyed by exorbitant hotel charges," he again commenced his march. Not for him the scientific observation or detailed wildlife notes; instead he used his gun, shooting game for his supper and then battling with buzzards for the result. The big birds "seemed to think that I actually came there to butcher for them, for they would light on the ground and hop around me, sometimes would even jump on the carcass, have the impudence to look me straight in the face, and grapple the meat in their claws." Finally, he compromised by killing something for them first and then, "when the chief body of them were engaged, I would start off and transact business for myself."

And so he trekked on in Indiana Jones fashion, pausing to shoot a seal and make moccasins from its rubbery hide when his boots fell apart; swimming across inlets, despite the abundance of sharks; exploring a ghostly encampment that was inhabited only by the skeleton of its previous owner, which fell apart at his touch. This last proved to be a dire omen, for when Coulter arrived back at the beach where he had left the men, it was to find both sea and strand deserted—"picture my feelings when there was neither man, or boy, or ship, to receive me—all gone; the tent was still standing. What can this all mean?"

A note in a bottle explained it all. "DEAR DOCTOR," it read:

> There has been a flaw in the chain cable—it has parted; the ship's adrift, leaving her anchor and some of the chain behind; there is not wind, the current strong and setting her off to the N.W. At the back of the tent, under some brushwood, you'll find something I brought on shore for you. As soon as we get a breeze again, I will beat up for you and the anchor, &c.; stay where you are until we come up. All hands on board have been well since you left. The current has got a fast hold of the ship, and we have now to pull five or six miles after her. In haste.
>
> Your friend,
>
> A. LOCK

Captain Abijah Lock was a friend indeed. The "something" brought on shore for Dr. Coulter was a cache containing frying pan, gunpowder, duck shot, biscuit, and a change of apparel. And he was as good as his word as well, for two weeks later the ship hove into sight. However, as we shall see, this was by no means the last of Coulter's strange reunions with Captain Lock and his crew.

Other surgeons who enjoyed stalking the countryside with a gun were John Wilson and Robert Smith Owen. As soon as the *Warrens* raised Timor in September 1837, Owen took a boat on shore for coconuts to give to those "affected by the Scurvy," and at the same time hunted goats—"somewhat ludicrous" looking animals, for they were "of a sooty carrotty color & beards nearly to the ground." How palatable their meat was is doubtful in the extreme, but in the meantime the coconuts would have done the good work. Dr. John Wilson was a firm believer in "cocoa-nuts and taro, most excellent *preventatives of Scurvy*," and all the ships collected the former, for fodder for shipboard animals as well as for the men. The problem, as John Coulter once mused, was that coconuts were not easy to harvest.

When the *Stratford* arrived at an uninhabited island in the South Pacific, Dr. Coulter was sent on shore with a boat and boat's crew to procure a supply of coconuts, which meant that he became intimately acquainted with this problem. Finding a grove of the palms was easy enough. Coulter could see lots of nuts, too—sixty feet up in the air. So he asked a Tahitian seaman to climb what he considered the most promising tree, though that fellow protested that those nuts were "Ita miti," no good, being too old and hard even for hogs. Coulter refused to listen, so up went the Tahitian, "steadily, but gracefully," perched in the top—and heaved a hail of coconuts at the surgeon and his shipmates. As he had promised, they were all very hard. John Coulter retaliated by telling two men to fetch their axes. It proved a tough job, the trunk being so fibrous, and the result was disappointing in the extreme, for there were only five usable nuts in the heap that eventually arrived on the ground. "This is wig-making with a vengeance!" one of the men joked. "We'll fill the ship in no time. Two men, two axes gapped, half an hour's work, and five nuts!" Luckily, the Tahitian had finished enjoying his own jest and decided to cooperate, with the result that "he saved us from being well laughed at on our arriving alongside the ship with a cargo of five nuts, and spoiling two axes in getting them!"

Dr. William Dalton, on the other hand, was such a great advocate of the antiscorbutic qualities of the potato that he wrote a treatise that was published in 1843 by that influential medical journal, *The Lancet*:

> On our arrival at Valdivia, on the coast of Chili, one of our men was observed by a female to take a potato from a heap, and very unceremoniously and eagerly eat it. She called his attention to a quantity of apples, and tendered some to him; but although he accepted the apples, he assured her that he had not make a mistake. We remained at sea, on various cruises, during periods of from six to nine months each. On one occasion we were exposed to all the consequences arising from damp and moisture for six months, having been cruising near the equator in the wet season, and I believe that during that period we never passed a day without rain; at the same time, we were living on salt provisions, with a very scanty allowance of "scurvy-grass." We returned to England after an absence of two years and ten months, never having had scurvy among the ship's company, and had the satisfaction of seeing every individual that embarked with us return to his native land.

In 1824, when Dalton was at the Bay of Islands, New Zealand, the *Francis* of London came in flying the flag of distress. "The whole of her crew, excepting the captain, first, second, and third mates, surgeon, and the man employed to wait upon them, were confined to their beds with scurvy," he recounted. The men, helpless to save themselves, had to be hoisted onto deck with pulleys to be conveyed to a camp hospital set up on shore. There, they were fed with a "liberal supply" of potatoes and "all happily recovered." That the after gang of the ship had escaped the ravages of the awful disease was directly attributable to the superior food set on the cabin table: they had potatoes, while the common crew did not. As Dalton went on to declare, it was most eloquent evidence that scurvy could be avoided by the simple precaution of supplying the ship with "a bountiful supply of that inestimable prophylactic, the potato."

To get a good supply of articles such as the potato, however, the whaling skippers were forced to trade with the natives of the islands they touched. Thus throughout the Pacific and Indian Oceans, providing the South Seamen with fruit, meat, and vegetables became an industry, and a major source of rum, tobacco, gunpowder, and muskets. On Saturday May 9, 1835, Dr. James Brown was sent from the *Japan* with a party of three boats to find what he could on a Timorese shore. "We Purchased 52 sheep," he recorded. The sheep being alive, ferrying all this mutton to the ship was no easy matter. The "best scene," however, happened back on board—"viz., that of butchering, every mess being allowed to kill what number of sheep they considered would satisfy them for that night, eating or rather devouring, this being the first fresh meat" they had enjoyed in quite a while. "The Galley fire and armourer's Forge, was set underway for cooking, and in less than 3 Hours after the Sheep were eating on the Island our Crew were *eating* them for supper."

Captain Hill being a fellow who believed in keeping his surgeon busy, Dr. Brown was sent on many a similar mission. He hunted for seals, and fished for cod, and dealt with local rajahs. In the East Indies transactions with local rulers were usually managed by an agent, or "compradore," a fellow who was likely to have an interesting history, more often than not being a British seaman who had left his ship to marry a local woman and make a fortune out of the visiting ships. It was not the idyllic existence it might seem. Dr. John Wilson remarked in tones of pity that he had met a Englishman living under these circumstances at Roti, on the southern coast of Timor. This fellow, who had been a boatsteerer on the *Eleanor*, was "married to a daughter of the Rajah or King: he looked ghastly—fever & ague had nearly worn him out." The work, too, involved long hours, for the agent had to dance attendance on the captain and his wife (if there). Meetings with local dignitaries had to be organized, mail fetched and delivered, and diplomatic little gifts of local delicacies presented. In return the compradore took a percentage of the trade goods he obtained—for most masters of South Seamen made money on the side by bartering manufactured items such as scissors and clocks for commodities such as brocades, precious stones, and intricate gold- and silver-work that could be sold at a profit, once home. For the captains, paying the commission was well worth the outlay. As Eliza Underwood of the *Kingsdown* once remarked, it would have been almost impossible for her husband to do any business at all without the compradore's knowledge of the country, the language, and local customs.

When Dr. Frederick Bennett dickered with the Rajah of Sûtarano, Timor, for supplies, his compradore was a man named Brown, who was half-Dutch, half-Malay. The rajah's palace was "a large wooden edifice, erected close to the beach, enclosed by lofty palisades" with an anteroom below, where the surgeon and the agent waited to be summoned. Eventually they were invited to ascend a ladder to the reception room, where they "found the rajah seated on a mat, surrounded by pillows and cushions." Chairs, however, were provided for Europeans, and the business went forward smoothly. "Purchased a number of Pigs, Fowls, Cocoa Nuts, Indian Corn," wrote Dr. James Brown, after dealing with the same local king. His business had gone quite well too, for the rajah had graciously invited him to a banquet—"but only water to drink." If Dr. Brown had known that Dr. Bennett had been regaled with "arak [native liquor] and coconut milk" in the same circumstances earlier, he might have felt a little piqued. However, it made a pleasant change from life on board.

When the *Tuscan* weighed the anchor after a spell in the Society Islands, Dr. Frederick Bennett likened the ship to Noah's Ark:

> Pigs and poultry were crowded into every spot capable of supporting animal existence; cocoa nuts, feis [small native bananas], and bananas hung in rich festoons from the stern and rigging; oranges, sweet potatoes, and pumpkins occupied nets stretched across the quarterdeck; and in addition to the more perishable

prophylactics against scorbutic troubles, a large supply of lime-juice had not been omitted by our provident Commander.

Ironically (and frustratingly for that "provident Commander"), within days the crew petitioned for a return to salt meat, having quickly got tired of fresh messes. Oddly, Dr. Bennett approved, saying "seamen can maintain their health and strength, and live more contentedly upon [salt provisions], than upon any two kinds of fresh meat." Obviously, Dr. John Coulter would have debated this vigorously, but whatever the theory about the cause of scurvy, in the end it made no difference, for in due time the fresh provisions ran out. After that, months of salt provisions loomed ahead, for the ships were steering to the whaling grounds, where they cruised slowly back and forth, and life was regulated by the migratory patterns of the prey.

This was the stage of the voyage where the prospect of the dread scourge really raised its ugly head. Knowing how to prevent and cure the disease was no guarantee of a scurvy-free ship, for no matter how wise and knowledgeable the surgeon, there was nothing he could do once the citrus juice had gone and the potatoes, taro, or coconuts had all run out. As the famous experimenter James Lind once remarked, this was the part of the voyage when the "ignorant sailor and the learned physician will equally long, with the most craving anxiety, for green vegetables and the fresh fruits of the earth." The "learned physician" of a South Seaman on a whaling ground was particularly prone to this "craving anxiety," for how long a whaler lingered there depended entirely on the whales. If they were plentiful, then the ship stayed to take as many as possible, and if there were no whales to be raised, the vessel set sail for a more promising place, which could be thousands of miles away.

The *Kingsdown* was one of these, for in October 1829, after whaling unsuccessfully in the Timor Straits, she steered a course for San Francisco on the far side of the Pacific, arriving there in April 1830. At the time, this landfall was nothing much more than a spectacular but largely deserted bay, known to the whalemen as "Yerba Buena" ("good grass"), for here they could replenish stocks of firewood and fresh water, and buy much needed fresh beef and live bullocks, from rancheros in the hinterland. Dr. John Coulter went on shore here at one point in the voyage of the *Stratford*, being very ill with some kind of rheumatism that was probably exacerbated by the early symptoms of scurvy, for he was unusually depressed. While Captain Abijah Lock took the ship off on a cruise—declaring that he could do without a doctor for a while, as he "prided himself on his surgical and medical skill, in dressing wounds, setting fractured limbs, reducing dislocations, or administering medicine"—Dr. Coulter restored his health with steam baths, good food, and fresh air, with the result that he was soon up and about and as lively as ever, stalking the wild animals of the land with his gun.

So we can assume that with plenty of strolling about at Yerba Buena, the crew of the *Kingsdown* regained their health at the same time that the ship refreshed her provisions. Captain Underwood steered west to spend a season whaling in the so-called "Sea of Japan," which was in fact a vast stretch of sea extending from about 160° East to 156° West in about 28° to 34° latitude North. As Dr. John Wilson wrote, it included "the greater part of the Eastern Ocean, all that great Sea which washes Niphon or Japan, and its numerous Isles." The cruise generally started in April and ended in October when the typhoon season began.

This area had a very bad reputation for scurvy, for the Sea of Japan was a poor place to reprovision, there being so few friendly landfalls. Yet many vessels congregated there, including at least eighteen from London alone in that season of 1830. As well as the *Kingsdown*, there was the *Wildman*, with Andrew Skelton (brother of the owner of the *Kingsdown*) in command, along with the *Venelia*, commanded by Captain Minor (the same ship and captain that so nearly ran into the *Japan* while gamming, five years after this date), the *Sarah*, with Captain William Edmund Hill in charge (in his pre-*Japan* days), and the *Ranger*, commanded by Captain Garbutt, whose surgeon was a young Scot by the name of John Lyell.

Twenty-two-year-old Lyell had gained his license from the

Royal College of Surgeons of Edinburgh in 1829, just before joining the ship in London. They sailed on October 29, heading for the
Pacific via the Cape of Good Hope, the Indian Ocean, and the
Timor Straits, where the ship was reprovisioned. A course was then
steered for the Sea of Japan, where Captain Garbutt chose to linger,
despite Lyell's growing alarm. The crew developed symptoms of
scurvy in August, but the whales were plentiful, and so it was not
until September 18 that Captain Garbutt consented to leave the
ground and head for the Marianas.

Their progress was slow, baffled by calms and unsteady
breezes, "at which we were much distressed on account of our
crew," Lyell wrote in his characteristically highly colored style;
"which was so crippled by scurvy, that not only had we ceased to
look for whales, but feared the loss of some of them ere the products of the land rescued them from its putrid jaws." At long last,
on September 23, Saipan hove into sight. Hauling up close to the
northwest coast of the island, Garbutt instructed his surgeon to
take two boats on shore, "for the purpose of ascertaining whether
we might obtain any pigs and fruit for the relief of our distress
from scurvy."

After traversing the lagoon, Lyell and his men hauled their craft
up onto a sandy beach at a place "where a few dogs indicated the
exist'nce of inhabitants," and indeed, they were almost immediately "greeted by a few uncouth beings, nearly in a state of nudity."
These shabby folk were not locals. Instead, as they apologetically
explained, they had been sent from Guam to hunt wild pigs, and
had express orders not to deal with any ships, "under pain of
imprisonment & the lash." In response to the surgeon's eloquence
they relented and loaded up the boats with fruit and hogs, consenting to take payment for the pigs but donating the harvest of the
wonderfully abundant wild bush:

> The beach on which we landed was cro'ded with cocoanut trees
> loaded and dropping with fruit, behind which the lemon bushes
> were weighed to the earth with their acid loads. Abundance of

John Lyell.

John Lyell was born in Newburgh, Fife, Scotland, on August 14, 1807, the son of David Lyell and his wife Betsy. Though he hailed from a predominantly rural community, John opted for the sea, signing up as the surgeon of the South Seaman *Ranger* very soon after gaining his surgeon's license from the Royal College of Surgeons of Edinburgh, and leaving England in October 1829 at the start of a voyage that was to last almost exactly three years. Not only did his adventure overlap the voyage of the *Kingsdown*, but he sailed in the same seas as well. However, the two ships never spoke. After return, Lyell set up in practice in his hometown, at the same time furthering his studies, and completed a degree in medicine in 1850. In April 1879 he died, leaving both his practice and his lifelong interest in natural history to a son, another John.

papaw trees erected their naked stems, studded round at the top with green and yellow apples, and various species of capsicums exhibited their splitting scarlet pods. With these products of the soil, which were a ready & certain cure for scurvy we soon filled the boats, and had we been inclined, might in a little while have filled the ship also, so plentifully did they exist.

Coincidentally, this was the same island group where Lord Anson had been saved from the grisly prospect of his entire crew expiring from scurvy in August 1742. "As soon as we had loaded our boats with pigs, coconuts, limes, lemons, papaw apples, bread-fruit, chilis &c., we left the shore and made the best of our way towards the ship," Lyell recorded, "which we gained an hour after sunset, and spread a salubrious feast for our scorbutic crew, which would soon renovate their exhausted strength." And so it proved. On September 29, the *Ranger* reached Guam, where "three of the seamen that were most affected by scurvy were sent on shore to recruit their health and strength," though two of them, who had been so close to death that they could "scarcely stir themselves" six days earlier, "were now so much recovered by the fruit and fresh provision we had received on board from Saipan, that they were able to waddle about the deck without assistance: so powerful are limes & young coconuts in dispelling this putrid malady!"

John Lyell had two reasons to feel highly gratified. Not only did he have the satisfaction of seeing men who were under his care return to health, but he was not forced to ask Captain Garbutt to leave the sick men on shore under the care of a port physician while the ship continued on her cruise. All too often, this shore doctor would be a man whose professional standards were dubious, for the surgeons who set up their shingle in some far-flung spot were much more likely to be there by accident than by intention. They had been fired after a quarrel with the skipper, or had been bullied into handing in their notice, or had simply deserted the ship. John Wilson had direct experience of one such case, for on April 16, 1840, while on the coast of Timor, he was sent for by Captain Blyth of the bark *Rover*, who "was in a dilemma about the medicine chest." Blyth's surgeon had deserted the ship in Kupang, and so Blyth "begged I would examine it & ascertain what were missing, & to furnish the doses & uses of what remained, that he might pre-scribe himself, & benefit the sick, in the absence of any Surgeon. I did so: There was no calomel, no blue-pill, no Quinine, no cin-chona bark, no adhesive plaster! I was informed," Wilson added with an almost audible sniff, "the young man used to get drunk, & conduct himself in an unworthy manner."

For a man like the surgeon of the *Rover*, leaving the ship

might have seemed a much better option than going on with the voyage. The prospect of settling in the tropics might have seemed adventurous—glamorous, even. Like the seamen who left their ships to become compradores in the East Indies, any one of these beachcomber doctors might have started out with high hopes. A significant number succumbed to hopelessness, however, quickly corrupted with tropical fevers and the local rotgut liquor—a real concern for any captain who was forced to leave his seamen in the questionable care of any one of these fellows.

This danger was particularly evident in Guam. In April 1841 the *Gipsy* was lying in the anchorage when Dr. John Wilson was roused from sleep "by the Surgeons of the 'Vigilant' & 'Indian', they having received an express signed by their respective Captains, to make all speed up to Town, bringing with us Amputating Instruments, &c." A man had fallen out of a coconut tree and was seriously hurt; "on examination we found a compound fracture of the lower third of the Ulna, with a dislocation of the os Magnum: besides a severe bodily concussion." The port doctor was an Englishman by the name of Cass, "who has resided on the Island a great many years, married a native woman & has a family: he left a Whaler at this Port: He is a drunken, worthless character: with every opportunity to amass money & secure to himself reputation & respectability, he has become the boon companion of sailors & an outcast from all good society." What Dr. Wilson saw that midnight did nothing to improve this harsh judgment. The surgeons found the patient's arm bound up "so tightly, as to impede the circulation and endanger the limb; the fractured end of the bone sticking out, & no attempt having been made at reduction: splints of bamboo were also used! The limb was tumefied & painful: the patient was sensible."

Mercifully, Wilson spared the readers of his journal the "sensible" patient's screams as the surgeons jointly "replaced the ends of the broken bones in apposition, & reduced the Dislocation." Perhaps the poor man was grateful that they decided, after some discussion, not to amputate—"yet it might have been better," Wil-

Dr. Charles Frederick Winslow.

As Dr. John Wilson aptly observed, if a shore physician had the sense to remain sober and shrewd, he had every opportunity to make a tidy fortune.

Dr. Winslow (1811–1877), a native of Nantucket, was a prime example of this. In 1844 the Seamen's Hospital in Lahaina, Maui, Hawaiian Islands, was leased and operated by the U.S. State Department, and Winslow was given the position of physician in charge. An enterprising and energetic man with nerves of steel, he administered to a growing list of patients, as attested by the huge bills he was sending along to Washington—such a swelling list, in fact, that rumors sprang up that he was collecting fees for men who had departed or were dead.

In 1846 Winslow abruptly left Lahaina in the midst of a flurry of gossip, carrying along a windfall that was reliably estimated at twenty thousand dollars. Despite these dire suspicions (and the uneasiness expressed by Mr. Pleasanton, the State Department auditor), it took fourteen years for the government to do something about it. Meantime, Winslow was enjoying a colorful career, speculating in gold-rich California, writing books, and setting up another Seamen's Hospital in Paita, Peru, where he had scooped the job of U.S. Consul as well. In 1860, it looked as if his luck had run out, for Captain Hunt of the U.S. Sloop of War *Levant* was assigned the responsibility of collecting up Hawaiian medical records. Hunt did this, and the documents were loaded aboard. The ship departed from Hilo in September—and was never heard of again. The *Levant* had gone down with all hands, and by an incredible stroke of luck Winslow and his ill-gotten fortune were safe.

son continued: "as we subsequently learned the man had died; if I mistake not, from Locked-Jaw." And why had the poor man not had better treatment? Because "Mr. Cass, the Medical-resident, is nearly blind, & so enervated from excessive drinking, that the natives dare not to trust him."

Arriving in Lahaina, Maui, in November 1838, Dr. Eldred Fysh recorded with palpable distaste that when "King Kamehameha the 3rd and his officers came on board twice and got most infernally drunk," the island monarch's "doctor in chief, an American [sic], was the greatest brute of the lot." In Honolulu, in October 1841, Dr. John Wilson had more to say. The name of the "brute" was Ford. He was a fellow "now advanced in years," who had been the first surgeon to settle on Oahu. A very sad case, Ford was now "a drunken dissolute man without, almost, the necessaries of life, he wanders about begging grog from every one: In him is exemplified the uselessness of splendid talents without Moral conduct, for had he been steady, he would by this time have been one of the richest on the Island: as it is, he is the poorest, and all through drunkenness." His dissolute ways must have prematurely aged him, too—Dr. Richard Ford (who was not, in fact, American, having hailed originally from Shrewsbury, England) was forty-six years old, just fifteen years Wilson's senior!

8

Encounters
with Native Peoples

Ships engaged in the sperm whale fishery are out
seldom less than three years, some of them four,
according to their success, and other adventures.
They are all well armed and have plenty of all sorts of
ammunition, as they have often to defend themselves
from the hostilities of natives.

Dr. John Coulter

$\mathcal{B}$ECAUSE OVERSEEING THE SHIP'S PROVISIONS WAS SUCH AN important part of the sea surgeon's job, the doctor came in frequent contact with native rulers and colonial officials and traders. He was usually the skipper's right-hand man when formal visits had to be made or received, perhaps because he was more cultivated than the other men on the ship or perhaps because the first and second mates were too busy. After the *Japan* dropped anchor in the Timorese port of Sûtarano on May 12, 1835, Dr. James Brown "prepared to go on shore along with the Captn." for an audience with "His Majesty," the rajah of the port. They got tired of waiting, however, so "shoved off and went on board a prow that was lying at anchor, had some aniseed, returned to the ship." This prau was a floating grogshop—a profitable institution and an enduring one, too, for up until quite recent times big outrigger *perahu* sailed out from the island of Paloe and stood off the coasts of Timor as mobile bars, selling *"moki"* to boats' crews and villagers.

Just a few years before Dr. Brown's time, Dr. Thomas Beale took a lively interest in the manufacture of this *moki*, describing a "toddy-cutter" climbing a coconut palm to cut off "the end of the fructifying bud that projects from the head of the tree"—a destructive process, because this was the bud that would have produced the flowers and nuts. A bamboo container was set beneath the wound, and by dawn, when the cutter returned, it was full. "It is then sold to any one who chooses to purchase; and it is much used by the inhabitants themselves, who obtain from it the ardent spirit, called by them aquadente, which they procure by distillation, after the juice has been fermented." This *aguardiente* or *moki* was the same "aniseed" that Dr. James Brown tippled on board the Timorese prau, for—like the *pastis* of France, the *raki* of the Middle East, and the *ouzo* of Greece—it was flavored with anise.

Timorese Village.

FROM *LIFE ON THE OCEAN*,
CHARLES NORDHOFF (CINCINNATI, 1874)

Despite the lack of an audience, the party from the *Japan* was not forgotten by the rajah they had come to see. "Don Pedro, son of the King, came on board in the afternoon in a very rude made canoe," Dr. Brown noted. This village prince had "no more dress than the other natives," but at least they were able to conduct business— which would inevitably have included arrangements for selling *moki* to the crew of the *Japan*. In April 1840, Captain Gibson and Dr. John Wilson of the *Gipsy* negotiated with this same fellow, "the Rajah's son, Don Pedro, who had been sent by his father, & was accompanied by some of his females." As well as doing trade with the master of the *Gipsy*, Don Pedro made money by turning his dwelling place into a grogshop and supplying the men "with Aniseed, an ardent spirit of a fiery taste and potency."

This spirit was so very ardent that Dr. Wilson theorized it could well have been adulterated with a dangerous narcotic, "nux vomica," the seed of an Asian plant, *Strychnos nux-vomica*. Usually prescribed in very small doses for fevers, dysentery, and the bites of sea snakes, one of the constituents of nux vomica is strychnine. Wilson may have had it wrong; it was customary for a particular species of dried fish to be served with *moki*, a combination that was notorious for causing extreme intoxication. Whatever the cause, the *Gipsy* men became crazily pugnacious. Wilson, who was strolling the beach with his fowling piece, "stepped in" to help the second mate subdue them: "we managed at last to load the boat, & a pretty load we had; squabbling, quarrelling, & blows exchanged & attempts to stand up all very unpleasant at the best but particularly so, now, when a very little, would capsize the boat, laden almost to the gunnel."

The surgeon "prepared for a swim," but somehow they got to the ship in safety, "for a wonder." Some of the men had to be hoisted up the side of the *Gipsy*, but they all made it to the deck in one piece. No sooner were they all aboard, however, than they were "at it" again, "fighting like incarnate devils," said Dr. Wilson:

> such a noise & ferment—it was terrible: then, there came the cry, they had got hatchets & sung out murder; the Mates immediately ran forward & plunged amongst the men & contrived to disarm them. . . . I verily believe, had the Mates not interfered when they did, some one or more would have been killed.

"The men appeared more than drunk," he added, their condition a frightening "compound of frenzy & inebriety." Next day they were "suffering so severely from yesterday's debauch" that they nearly let the ship run ashore. However, just as wrecking seemed inevitable, a light breeze sprang up, wafting them free. "The anchor was with much difficulty 'hove up' by the motley crew—motley's the wear, black eyes, faces cut, scratched, bruized, swollen & bloody, looking miserably ludicrous: hands shattered & battered & the entire body stiff & sore."

Bearing such scenes in mind, it may seem surprising that more men did not adopt the East Indies alternative to liquor, the custom of chewing betel nut (*sirih*) with areca leaf (*pinang*) and lime paste (*chinam*). The resulting appearance may have inhibited them from adopting the habit, for it "makes them look as if they always had a mouthful of blood," Dr. Fysh commented. John Wilson tried out a chew for himself, finding that it produced "exaltation of the spirits, & an agreeable flow of ideas," at first, but that this agreeable effect was soon succeeded by "feelings of lowness & discomfort." The Malays, he said, "imagine it braces the stomach & gives them an appetite & digestion: the juice that exudes from its mastication is of a blood-red colour, & stains everything it comes in contact with"—including the chewer's teeth, which turned black.

In nearby Sumba, James Brown observed the same habit, "which makes their lips and spittle red." The Malay men he saw there were rather inadequately clad as well, he thought, having "no clothing farther than a piece of cloth wrap'd round the loins." The women appeared to be wearing rather more than their menfolk, but the doctor did not have a good chance to make sure, because the instant the captain's boat touched the beach, every female vanished as if by magic. Captain William Edmund Hill's reputation had preceded him, it seems, for he "is a dear boy for a girl—to use a sailor's phrase," wrote his surgeon dryly. John Wilson had a better chance to study them, possibly because Captain Gibson did not have the same notoriety as a girl-chaser. "The women weave [wind] a broad shawl, or dungaree fixed around the waist," he wrote, "the breasts & arms being quite bare, excepting among the better class who wear a jacket"—thus completing a picture of the traditional attire, the *sarong kebaya*.

When in port, it was common for sea surgeons to be called on to help with medical problems on land. Back in December 1832, John Coulter had been made most welcome by the Portuguese governor of Brava in the Cape Verde Islands because the unfortunate old fellow had toothache. And three years after that he assisted the people of Tacames—a watering place in the Gulf of Guayaquil—during an epidemic of dysentery. In October 1841, Dr. John Wilson was called on shore at Honolulu to vaccinate the small children of a wealthy merchant, Mr. Skinner, against smallpox, making himself so popular that he was welcome all over town, inoculating citizens

A Victorian View of
Timorese Natives.

FROM *LIFE ON THE OCEAN*,
CHARLES NORDHOFF
(CINCINNATI, 1874)

here, there, and everywhere. Smallpox had been introduced to
Tahiti by the merchant vessel *Don Quixote* earlier that year, resulting in a terrible epidemic, and so the inhabitants of Honolulu were
naturally very nervous.

At Batu Gadeh in Timor, Dr. Robert Smith Owen was called on
shore to see "2 or 3 invalids which I did & prescribed for them.
They die here for actual Medical Assistance," he commented. One
was a prominent Chinese merchant, who was in a shocking state
with a diseased liver and advanced edema of the legs, and Owen
was not at all surprised to hear next morning that the patient had
expired. His conscience was clear, for he had done all he could, and
he had no hesitation in attending the obsequies, even though there
was a servant with a gun stationed at the door. Similarly, in Guam,
Wilson was called out to see a man who had been taken ill while
deer hunting. While he "took a few ounces of blood from him," it
was an equally futile gesture, for the patient was moribund already,
dying a few hours later. Just as with Owen, it never occurred to
Wilson to refuse to help out in his professional capacity, even when
the case was hopeless.

Coulter, by contrast, found it a good idea to exercise discretion
on occasion, bearing in mind the well-known instance of a surgeon
who treated a Maori patient while his ship was in New Zealand.

Despite that doctor's best attention, the patient expired, upon which the physician was promptly "and without appeal, sacrificed" by the relatives of the deceased, to provide the main course in the funeral feast. "In fact, amongst such a people," Coulter continued, "though they may be warmly attached to him, a strange man is very critically situated, and cannot be too careful."

John Coulter was by no means the first to cogitate along these lines. In July 1786, when trader Captain James Strange was getting set to weigh the anchor after bartering for furs at Nootka Sound, on the Northwest Coast of North America, the Indians asked him to leave a hostage as surety against his return. Captain Strange cooperatively volunteered his surgeon, an unfortunate fellow by the name of Mackay. And then, he blithely sailed away, leaving Mackay with two instructions—to learn the lingo so he could make himself useful as a translator next season, and to avoid doctoring if humanly possible. For, as Strange phrased it, "if unfortunately an accident had happened to any of his patients, in consequence of his failing in the means for their recovery, there is no doubt but that his life would pay the forfeit. I therefore most earnestly recommended to him, on no account whatsoever, to administer to those whose Complaints were of an alarming nature."

Dr. John Coulter's time for caution came in the South Pacific, when he was on shore in the Marquesas Islands as the reluctant guest of a warring chieftain. There, "the only instance in which I practised my profession among them was the cutting out of two bullets which were immediately under the skin." He carefully avoided any more ambitious surgery, for the same reasons that Captain Strange described.

Again, he was in a fix that was the fault of his daredevil nature. Despite the generally held opinion that the Marquesas Islands were very risky territory—it being considered wise practice for ship captains to "to take the precaution of first having one or two of the head chiefs on board before the boats go in to trade, to keep them as hostages for the boat's security"—Coulter had gone on shore to meet the locals and explore the scenery.

When Dr. William Dalton first arrived at the largest island of the Marquesas group, Nukuhiva, in December 1823, he recounted that: "A canoe came from the shore and paddled repeatedly round the ship having a native standing up and making a hideous noise and several antics." This apparition was a shaman, decorated with feathers, and with "several human sculls and bones suspended to different parts of his body, making a most frightful appearance." This was gruesomely in accordance with what Dalton already knew—that the Marquesans were "complete heathens and desperate cannibals." The native girls were a lot more friendly, taking off their clothes and swimming to the ship in hordes, but it would seem understandable if Captain John Palmer of the *Phoenix* had ordered the anchor to be weighed the minute his stocks of fresh water and firewood had been replenished, and quit the island group.

Instead, Palmer steered for another Marquesan island, Hivaoa. Here, he traded for "a large supply of Hogs, Cocoa-nuts, breadfruit, bananas, plantains, pumpkins, papaw-apples &c. &c.," paying one musket for each dozen hogs and flint and cartridges for the vegetables and fruit. This was general practice, despite the inherent risk. Dr. Dalton noted that formerly the natives had been armed with "only clubs and spears, now they have muskets, which they procure from English shipping in exchange for refreshments, Sandal-wood and Cocoa-nut Oil"—a situation that the captains must have recognized as dangerous. During this visit, in fact, "the natives made an attempt to take our boats, but luckily did not succeed," for the *Phoenix*'s men fired upon them. Less than thirty months before, ten crewmen of the ship *Coquette* had been massacred here.

But then again, if Palmer wanted to buy provisions, he had little choice about what to barter, for the warlike Marquesans were so hungry for European arms that they would resort to capture and killing to get them if peaceful trade did not avail, being so obsessed with intertribal feuds that diplomacy and caution did not have a chance. In January 1824, Dalton noted that the Marquesans were

South Seas Natives.   FROM *MISSIONARY WORLD*

Dr. William Dalton's first visit to a "savage" island was made remarkable by a
ceremonial visit from a shaman, who stood up in a canoe bedecked with skulls,
"making a hideous noise and several antics." This kind of stirring description was
readily adopted by editors of missionary periodicals, eager to point out to the lay
reader the dangers faced in the foreign field.

"continually at war one tribe against another tho' living only a mile
or two apart"—and this was still the case three years later, when he
returned as surgeon of the *Harriet* of London, commanded by
Captain Edward Reed. He found that the "natives of this Island are
as wild and savage as ever," and a year after that: "They continue to
feed on their enemies as usual."

"This is a dangerous island," John Coulter admitted when the
Stratford dropped anchor at Hivaoa. However, having gained the
sponsorship of one of the chieftains, "Toomova," by the simple
expedient of rubbing noses, he shouldered his gun and a bag of
ammunition, stepped into a canoe, and landed on shore. For four
days, all went swimmingly. The scenery proved as delightful as the
hospitality. Then, however, he discovered something that gave him
pause—"an extensive defence, or breast-work, recently repaired,

with a warrior lurking here and there behind it." Could his hosts be at war with another tribe?

Coulter cautiously looked around, and saw Toomova watching him with a very broad grin. "Very good man you," said he, "pointing significantly" at Coulter's double-barreled gun. The surgeon promptly informed him that he had nothing to do with any local conflict, but then was silly enough to rise to the challenge when asked to show off his marksmanship. No matter how many pearl shells they put up as targets, John Coulter unerringly blew them to pieces. Accordingly, he should not have felt at all surprised when two days later the chieftain who had been left as hostage on the *Stratford* walked into the hut with a guileless smile, and the news that the ship had sailed off and left him.

Naturally, Coulter's hosts "were quite pleased at the idea that I might be with them always," and promptly invited him to a council of war. It was a group that:

> Presented a strangely wild and romantic appearance. . . . The fine athletic forms, the rich head-dresses, the entire body being tatooed over; no covering but the "mara," or rool of native cloth about the loins; the guns, spears, or clubs of each chief lying either beside or before him; the great body of warriors hovering at a distance around, the fluttering of the feathers in the head-dress, the waving of the leafy veil overhead, all gave an impressive effect to the scene.

Coulter was given a headdress of his own as evidence of his new high status and invited to give an opinion. After due thought he suggested that there should be a military parade and inspection of arms so that he could assess their resources. This was considered an excellent notion—with the proviso that he would take on the dress of a chief. The doctor did not want to do this at all, but they took his clothes away, and so he had no choice but to array himself in an assortment of bark-cloth wraps and human hair adornments. This metamorphosis was hailed with great delight, expressed in yells, drumming, and a war dance. So far, so good. The problem was that the omens proclaimed that he should be tattooed all over as well.

Understandably, Dr. Coulter felt very strong reservations indeed—but, as with the clothes, he had no choice: "therefore I made up my mind to accede to the wishes of the chiefs and people with as good a grace as possible, and to bear any pain inflicted by the operation as manfully as I could." His only proviso was that his face should remain unmarked—a very wise move. Dr. Frederick Bennett described the "harlequin-like appearance" of Marquesan men, three broad bands of black being tattooed across the forehead, eyes, and mouth. A circle of untouched skin was left around each eye, lending a "peculiarly glaring and almost terrific effect" to the visage.

At the news that Coulter had agreed to be decorated in their traditional fashion, the tribe became more excited than ever; guns were fired in the air and "conchs sounded in all directions." And, forthwith, the "operation" started. There were two "tatoo-men" with two assistants who bore the instruments, which were pieces of flat bone in all different sizes, each with a cane handle and serrated at one edge for incising the skin and inserting the pigment. After stabbing patterns into the skin with these comblike tools, wads of fine bark cloth were used to wipe off the blood, "in order to see if the impression is perfect," and then the dye was beaten in with the rapid hitting of a stick on the slanted handle of the tattooing tool. The process was just as uncomfortable as it sounds. "The constant hammering at the skin, or into it, with considerable violence, irritates the whole frame, and the constant wiping off the blood with the tappa [bark cloth] is worse. However, as the work proceeds, the flesh swells up, which gradually benumbs the part."

Harrowingly, Dr. Coulter was very conscious of possible complications, everything he had ever learned about tumors, abscesses, ulcers, and erysipelas progressing through his mind. Nonetheless, he took it like a soldier for four hours the first day and three hours the second. Then he was rubbed all over with coconut oil and, after another ceremonial round of musket firing and conch-blowing, he was propped up in the cool shade of a tree to recover. Unsurprisingly, he felt "a little faintish," but managed to be polite to the stream of people who came along with congratulatory presents. A few days later, "the swelling all went down, the outer skin peeled off," and he was as good as new, if somewhat unrecognizable.

Inevitably, however, there came the day when the "war-conchs" blew, and he had to gird himself for battle. It was a brutal affair, much of it hand to hand, finally resolved by tricking the enemy into a redoubt that was then set on fire, "the whole scene a downright picture of hell." However, Coulter's side had won and he had acquitted himself well, and so he had every right to join in the carnival feast that followed. He did watch some of the preparations—the butchering of the enemy slain and the digging of the earth ovens—but did not stay long. Instead, he "left the arena sick to loathing" to sit in his house, close his ears to the ghastly sounds outside, and put his mind to the problem of getting back to his ship.

This was no small dilemma, for Toomova was positive that the whole tribe wanted him to stay for keeps. Diplomatically, Dr. Coulter "turned the conversation," but spent as much time as he could with the fishermen of the tribe, so that he was on the spot when the loud boom of a ship's gun echoed from the fog-bound lagoon. And lo, when the mist cleared away, there lay the *Stratford*, to the surgeon's delight. Being John Coulter, however, he could not resist a joke. Tattooed and near-naked as he was, he commandeered a canoe and paddled across, and to his glee they kept on firing a gun for their doctor.

He was finally recognized by his distinctive guffaw, at which the crew delivered three hearty cheers. "Amidst the most tremendous and unrestrained laughter I ever heard, I got over the side and on deck once more." Captain Abijah Lock strode up and shook Coulter's hand, but also shook his head. "Come off to the ship naked and tatooed as a Marquesan?" he demanded. "Well, if this is not the fag-end of a cruise among savages, I don't know what it is."

THE SOUTH SEAMEN WERE ALL AWARE OF THE RISKS OF OFFENDING warlike people by unintentionally straying into sacred space or otherwise breaking taboos. Some of the blunders were resolved with laughter, others with bloodshed. One can readily imagine the terror of the moment when it was uncertain which way the encounter would go. At the island of New Ireland, Dr. Wilson recorded wryly, "I chanced to take my hat off." Sighting his bald head, the natives "set up a bellowing." One, who was standing in the main chains and leaning over the rail where Wilson stood, "took me by the hand & gave vent to his wonderment, admiration, or whatever might be the emotion, in an extempore song, & dance: such a song & such a dance!"

Dr. Wilson surely must have had the unsettling thought that the dance might be a war dance, and must have blessed his luck that they were not at Ceram, where the head-hunting natives could well have considered a bald head a capital prize. There, as Dr. James Brown observed, "A man does not obtain a wife until he has brought the heads of some of his enemies as a present to his intended. One head would entitle him to a wife, but the more he can produce the more he is esteemed."

"I certainly had a very narrow escape here," wrote Dr. Eldred Fysh in February 1838, after going ashore for fresh stock at Gardiner's Island in the Bismarck Archipelago. One of the boat's crew had lighted his pipe and begun smoking as he leaned on his oar. "No sooner did the natives see this man than those who were unarmed made off and those who had spears leveled them at us." The smoker threw his pipe overboard, "which pleased the poor fellows very much. I have no doubt if they know anything about 'Old Harry' [the devil] they took the smoker for one of his brothers." It was not the only time Eldred Fysh noted that the savages were just as frightened of the visitors as the Europeans were of them, if not more so. A year later, at Ocean Island, Captain William Aldiss Bond fired a musket in the air when the ship was plagued with thievish natives, and "one poor devil was so alarmed that as he jumped into the water he made a long yellow ray which hung behind him like the tail of a comet."

According to Dr. Wilson, the natives of the islands of Ombai, Pantar, and Lomblen were especially notorious—"in disposition, as far as is known, they are bloodthirsty & cruel; they speak a language

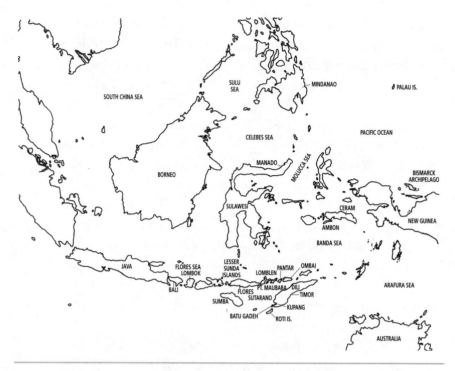

Moluccan Ground and Timor Straits.

peculiar to themselves; & they go destitute of clothing: I believe they have not even canoes. Ships dare not venture to trade with them," he declared. Though the islands were beautiful from a distance, "sprinkled with clusters of luxuriant shrubs, & lofty trees and are very pleasant to the view," their charm vanished "at the thought that human beings little better than the brute & of a nature more relentless & savage, are the possessors. I may mention before quitting *Timor*," Wilson added, "that upon the little shrub covered rock called Pulo-Batto or Batto rock, a merchant-captain lies buried who was slain in defending his vessel against an attack made by a set of Malay Pirates."

Piracy was (and is) endemic to the East Indies and the South China Sea, it being traditional to supplement the family income with a little looting. Indeed, in times of strife and privation it was often the only means of economic survival. In a huge sea dotted with remote islands, it was so easy to get away with it, too, for once the seized vessel was set adrift or sunk, the pirates were indistinguishable from innocent fishermen. Thus any little fishing prau was an object of nervous suspicion, for the captains of South Seamen were acutely aware that knives, pointed bamboo stakes, and the local curved sword, or *kris*, were standard equipment on such craft.

In August 1831, Eliza Underwood was regaled with a sensational account by Mr. Burns, a compradore on the island of Celebes (modern Sulawesi), of a close scrape on his way home from Ambon after conducting some very satisfactory trade in muskets. Because the business had proved so profitable, he was carrying an unusual amount of cash—three thousand rupees (about £300, or $1500)—and a large amount of gold as well. Naturally, then, his heart plunged into his boots when he spied "seven Maggandanna prows" steering straight for his leaky old prau.

These Maggandanna pirates, who hailed from Illana Bay in Mindanao, had a particularly savage reputation, for "their custom is when they take prisoners to braise their knees and elbows every day by hard blows so as to keep them too stiff to make their escape till they can dispose of them." Mr. Burns took the best evasive action he could think of, steering close to the nearest beach in the hope that the large pirate vessels with their deeper draft would not be able to follow. However, the instant his prau made shallow water, his entire crew jumped overboard. As they dashed to the shore and vanished into the jungle, he sat aghast, "looking on them in utter despair."

In true pirate fashion, the Maggandannans hove to within gunshot and called out to him to surrender and deliver. Instead Mr. Burns gathered his wits, a cutlass, and "a great parcel" of rupees, and jumped overboard himself. He made it to shore only a few yards ahead of the pirates, and promptly demonstrated the stuff of which resourceful traders are made. Dumping the coins from his bag at the edge of the trees, he sprinted off into the jungle in the wake of his crew—and "as he had hoped, they staid scrambling for the money," allowing him to escape. It was a desperate (and expensive) ploy, but it worked. Mr. Burns had lost his money, his muskets, and his prau, but at least—like John Coulter—he came out of it with his hide intact. We can imagine Eliza Underwood clasping her hands to her breast in mingled sympathy and congratulation. Just three weeks later, however, the story came back to her vividly with all its ghastly connotations.

Matters could scarcely have been worse. Captain Underwood was bedridden with another attack of gout and in such agony that Eliza was forced to allow the surgeon to give him an opiate. Being in need of fresh fruit and vegetables, the ship had ventured too close to the Lesser Sunda Islands—the same ones that were inhabited by the "inhuman savages" Dr. John Wilson described nine years later—"a very savage tribe," as Eliza testified, "said to be cannables." Instead of getting to a place where a boat could be sent on shore to fetch the corn and coconuts they hoped for, the ship had become becalmed in "a bay or bite as the sailors call it. . . . To my great dismay," she wrote:

> I perceived we were even in a worse situation than last night, the breeze only just enabling us to stem the current . . . and the ship going about, thus giving me reason to fear that we shall yet be some days confined here, during which time I shall continue in dread of the ship drifting on shore here among these savages— wild wretches who spare not even those of their own colour, but sacrifice life in mere wantonness or to furnish their horrible meal; no wonder that a timid woman should dread falling into their hands.

This, the entry for Saturday, September 24, 1831, is the last in this journal, the only book that survives. Eliza ends: "I hope I shall close my next book with a more pleasing reflection, surely I shall for the next will close in London, but yet I have much to dread." Did she start another book? It is impossible to tell.

The *Kingsdown* was reported back in London in April 1832, with 2,300 barrels of oil—72,450 gallons, or 287.5 tuns—worth close to £20,000, or $100,000. It was a highly gratifying return to the owners, particularly considering the value of such a sum at the time. The captain's share would have amounted to £1,000, while the surgeon's share would have been a little less than £170—not much for three years' work and certainly not enough to set up in private practice. We do not know what he did with the little cache, nor what became of the *Kingsdown*'s surgeon afterward.

Exactly three months later, the *Kingsdown* set out for the South Seas again: on July 10, 1832, the Lloyds List reported that "*Kingsdown*, Sim[m]ons," was dropping down the Thames. Captain William Simmons was very young—at only twenty-four—but had already demonstrated that he was a talented South Seaman. He had taken out his first command, the leaky old *Essex*, in December 1829, and had brought her back with a full cargo of oil within three years. The 1832 *Kingsdown* voyage was to prove equally successful. Simmons was reported at Kupang in August 1833, and in May 1835 he was in the English Channel bearing up for Gravesend with a full cargo, having been out just thirty-four months. Philip Skelton and the other owners—his brother Andrew, Limehouse shipbuilders Curling & Young, John Boulcott & Son of 80, Wapping Wall— must have felt pleased with their choice of master. On August 25, 1835, Simmons took the *Kingsdown* out again, but this time he was to meet his nemesis—Captain William Edmund Hill of the *Japan*.

9

"Motley, Reckless & Profligate":
Troubles with Captains and Crews

Ship Sharon of Fairhaven put into
Sydney N.S.W. Dec. 22nd for fresh hands,
the crew having mutinied and killed the captain.

New Bedford Whalemen's Shipping List,
June 6, 1843

On sunday june 21, 1835, dr. james brown went to captain Hill with the bad news "that I did not expect Cooper's mate to survive above 3 Hours at the farthest." The poor fellow, an Irishman by the name of David Sweeney, did not last even that long, for he "died in the Course of Two Hours and in the afternoon was buried ashore on the Timor Coast." Then, the instant he was back on board, Dr. Brown scrambled up the foremast to do extra lookout duty, for the very good reason that he wanted to avoid the skipper's attention. Otherwise Captain Hill was all too likely to order him to learn how to set up barrels so he could take over the job of the man he had failed to cure.

Earlier that month, Dr. James Brown had wryly noted that he had "turned out this morning as I've done these several days to wash decks in consequence of Jacobs [one of the apprentices] being laid up with the Fever." This was no small burden, for washing the decks began at eight bells, four in the morning, and was not very dignified for a surgeon, either, for it involved getting down on all fours and scrubbing the dirty planks with a block of sandstone. It would not be unnatural if Dr. Brown resented this. No doubt, like Dr. John Wilson, he thought that doing common seamen's work was "far beneath the dignity of the office" of ship's surgeon. However, he had little choice, for this was Captain Hill's eccentric way of making sure that his doctor did the best job possible of medicating the men. If a hand was off duty, someone else had to do that man's work, and it was only logical that the surgeon should do it, for he was the one to blame. If the doctor wanted to avoid such labor, then all that was necessary was for him to make sure that none of the crew got sick. It was infuriating, but Hill refused to even discuss it.

James Brown was by no means the only doctor to have trouble

with the boss. Dr. Thomas Beale, who sailed from London in October 1830 as the surgeon of the *Kent*, quickly became disillusioned with Captain Laughton, who proved to be such "a mean and contemptible tyrant" that Beale was delighted to exchange situations with the surgeon of the *Sarah & Elizabeth* when the two ships gammed in June 1832. Considering that Laughton had "estranged from him every soul in the ship, by his cruel and tyrannical conduct," it seems rather odd that Dr. Hildyard, surgeon of the *Sarah & Elizabeth*, should have offered to trade jobs. However, Captain Laughton expired just a few months later and was dropped unmourned into the sea, so Hildyard did not suffer too long from his incautious generosity.

"The Chief Mate conducted himself very unbecoming towards the Captain," wrote Robert Smith Owen on the *Warrens* in November 1837, "and declared himself off duty, and requested in my hearing when in his berth to be put ashore in the morning." This foreboded a crisis for the surgeon—not because Mr. Mortimer, the chief mate, had fallen out with the skipper, but because the doctor was the only other man on board who was keeping a log. Captain George Gray already had Dr. Owen mounting the mast and keeping lookout—so did this mean that he was fated to be rerated as one of the ship's officers? It looked ominously likely.

Next day Dr. Owen recorded that "The Captain wish'd me to go to Masthead," all the crew being busy. No sooner was he up there, though, than Captain Gray called him down again because he wanted to discuss the problem "respecting the Mate's Conduct of last night." The surgeon did not particularly want to hear the grubby details, but nonetheless was forced to stand and listen. "It appears that Mr. Mortimer when reproved by the Captn. for not paying attention to the helm, that he damn'd him & the Ship." When Captain Gray threatened to "push him off before the mast" (disrate him to the rank of common seaman), Mortimer retorted, "Let me get my shoes on & I'll soon settle you."

"The Captn. is determin'd that he shall not come again into the Cabin at his Table," Owen continued. And so the row dragged on

for a couple of days. Captain George Gray ranted and the first officer sulked; there were threats to put the offender on shore and to
stop the monthly allowance to his wife back home. Finally, Dr.
Owen took matters into his own hands; first he had a private word
with Mr. Mortimer, advising him "to apologize to the Capt. which
he did," and then he approached Captain Gray and talked him into
letting "his better feelings sway him," with the result that "tonight
all was forgiven—and he [Mr. Mortimer] resumes his duties."
Before long, however, Dr. Robert Smith Owen got involved in a
row of his own. It was dramatic stuff that in an earlier age would
have led to a duel.

"Last night, because the Captn. could not have his way in play-
ing at Cards, which I objected to as unfair play," he wrote, "he said
I cheated." Owen was already depressed and irritable. "I threw up
my cards, and left the Table."

Mr. Mortimer, perhaps hiding a grin in his whiskers, followed
him, with the sage advice to pay no mind to this little eccentricity on
the part of the captain, his practical counsel being that "it was better
to let him win." Just like the earlier row, the unpleasantness sim-
mered on. A couple of days later, Dr. Owen grudgingly consented to
share a glass of grog with the captain, and Captain Gray agreed to
spare him the games of cards in the future. However, this was not the
last of the ructions between the surgeon and the skipper.

To be fair to the masters of South Seamen, they were operating
under a lot of pressure. Not only had the owners trusted them with
a piece of valuable property that was being deliberately risked in
hazardous waters, but their own incomes depended on the luck of
the voyage. Additionally, the men they commanded were some of
the roughest plowing the seven seas. "The men who constitute the
bulk of South Seamen are of the very lowest dregs of society, the
refuse of Ratcliffe Highway & New Gravel Lane," wrote Dr. John
Wilson. This meant a constant challenge for the master, who "has
one of the most arduous tasks to perform, that of keeping his motley, reckless, & profligate crew in due order & subordination."

Fights and rows were common, often the direct result of drink.

"There is a singular fact to be noticed with regard to those who are long at sea, namely the strange propensity to excessive drinking!" Dr. John Wilson exclaimed. "Men who are as sober as Anchorites when located on shore, have a strange & apparently quite overpowering tendency to intoxicating drink, and will commit almost any folly to obtain the stimulus!"

"Being Christmas Day, there was no work done," wrote Dr. Eldred Fysh on the *Coronet* in 1837, just seven months after leaving London. Captain William Aldiss Bond had given permission for a good dinner and a ration of grog, but "there are some sailors not fit to be call'd men on any ship, for they are more like brutes. Well," he went on:

> we have 2 or 3 of this sort—who not contented with drinking their own Grog, but must steal the boys', & buy the other men's if they would sell it. In this way they got just so, as to fill them up with Dutch courage—I speak of 3 men, Mitchell, Neale, & Brown—who after getting their pluck up came aft & kicked up a row, Mitchell began it, the others assisted, Mitchell struck Mr. Kenney & beat him about the head & face till I jumped forward & defended him, the Capt. came down from aloft & Neale squared off at him—but did not strike. Brown did nothing but use abusive language & urge the others on. Mitchell vow'd he'd murder me, if he could get hold of me in the Forecastle, but as I told him, it would take a man to do that.

"And that was how our first Christmas day pass'd, in Rows, Blasphemy & Intoxication," Dr. Fysh concluded. Captain Bond had been remarkably lenient in allowing a treat to the men, for two months previously one of these miscreants, Neale, had boldly declared to the quarterdeck as a whole "that he would sooner swing at the Yardarm of a Man of War than obey the officers of the *Coronet*." Little wonder James Brown noted that the master of the *Eleanor* took the precaution of locking up the grog and carrying the key in his pocket whenever he left the ship.

While the crews of South Seamen were particularly notorious, American skippers were certainly not immune from trouble. When the *Coronet* spoke the *Jefferson* of Nantucket in October 1838, the American captain came on board, but Dr. Fysh recorded that he stayed only a very short time, "as he swore he could take no comfort [i.e., relax] out of his ship." Dr. Tom Noddy recorded a major ruckus on the *Java* of New Bedford, in January 1855. When the second mate "told a man named Domingo Pues to get a broom and sweep off decks," the fellow flatly refused to do it. Captain John Lawrence was fetched to mediate, but Pues, who was Chilean, would only answer in Spanish—infuriatingly, for everyone on board knew that he could speak very good English. Falling out of patience, the captain "struck him in the face two blows, neither of which was sufficient to knock him down."

Domingo ran forward to the forecastle, "followed by the officers and nearly all hands." Captain Lawrence called him back, but instead a "scuffle ensued between the officers and some of the crew on the forecastle and Domingo drew a large knife and made a thrust at Mr. Smith." The mate dodged aside, and "the Captain sang out to the Steward for his pistols which were loaded and brought to him." Leveling these, he grimly watched from the quarterdeck as the Chilean was overpowered and brought aft—followed, however, by most of the crew, who declared they wanted "to see fair play."

Lawrence, however, was made of tougher stuff than Pues had reckoned (and had his two savage Russian hounds to back him up), and so the Chilean was speedily tied up in the rigging. When his shipmates promptly threatened mutiny, "saying they would do no more work on board the ship," they were seized up one by one too, until "there was 12 or 14 of them lashed up," and left there for the night. Dr. Noddy, "having no watch on deck"—this being one of the few advantages of being the ship's surgeon—"went below and turned in and was soon in as sound a slumber as though no more than usual had happened."

Next morning, Captain Lawrence inspected the men who were still tied up in the rigging, and then announced to Domingo, "I am going to flog you for drawing a knife." And, forthwith, he carried out the punishment personally, with a doubled "piece of seizing

A flogging.   ETCHING BY J. HALPIN, 1846

stuff." Within a dozen strokes, Pues was completely subdued and
was released after promising "to behave himself in future, and
never draw another knife." Then a second man, "John Spaniard,
[who] seemed to be a ringleader throughout the whole fracas," was
stripped and flogged likewise. "After making the man promise that
he would be a good man as long as he went to sea," John Spaniard
was released too, and so John Lawrence worked through the ranks
of troublemakers, and the mutiny was successfully put down.

As voyages dragged on, insurrection became the particular
nightmare of every skipper. Loyalty to the ship, captain, and officers was considered so crucial that the earliest signs of rebellion
were immediately countered with boots, fists, and the lash. In January 1841, a man on the *Gipsy* by the name of Collins refused to
obey an order. When Captain Gibson strode up to take charge, "he
struck the skipper a blow on the left eye, wounding him in two
places." Blood flowed freely, and "Collins was immediately seized
by the Mates, tied up to the main rigging, & received a dozen blows

from a stout rope's end, upon the bare back." After that, he was put in handcuffs and leg irons, and chained up in the steerage to be fed on bread and water until the first opportunity to put him ashore. Dr. John Wilson, an attentive observer of all this, did not disapprove at all, despite the fact that Collins was "married & has a family in England." Furthermore, the man had been tipsy. However, "Such things cannot be allowed on Board a ship."

As Wilson pointed out another time, because the crews were only "with difficulty kept in subordination," the caliber of the officers was crucial: "unless the Mates & boatsteerers are competent men, there is sure to arise great dissatisfaction, the economy of the ship deranged, and all hands grumbling, discontented, & unhappy." Naturally, then, a shipmaster was likely to become tense and illhumored if he ever harbored the notion that his officers were unreliable. The particular *bête noir* on the *Gipsy* was William Gill, the second mate. Back in October 1839, when John Wilson first made Gill's acquaintance, he noted that he had "the look of a creole, thick bushy black whiskers, an impudent look & a swaggering reckless manner—by no means prepossessing." The surgeon found no reason to alter this first impression. Eight months later, they discovered that Gill was a murderer—for so he openly boasted. Worse still, he was a "Jonah," or so the first mate averred: "There is a witch in the ship, & while he remains there will be no whales got, & that happens to be the right honorable William Gill." The chief officer had learned about these satanic leanings from no one else but Gill himself: "such was the confession, & he coupled it with language the most foul & disgusting." Captain Gibson determined to put him ashore at the first opportunity, a decision that Wilson heartily endorsed:

> this Wm. Gill is a great scoundrel & contemptible blackguard, always quarrelling & swaggering & conducting himself as disagreeably as possible. He is an old inveterate beachcomber, & in my opinion is making himself as disagreeable as possible that he may have permission to leave the ship, as in that case he will be allowed to take his things with him.

Three weeks later, Gill was put on shore at the Bonin Islands. "It is not the first time he has been turned out of a ship," noted Dr. Wilson darkly. As it happens, William Gill did rather well for himself. When the *Gipsy* returned to the islands a year afterward, it was to find that Gill had established himself with a native "helpmeet" and the position of *"Pilot* of the *Port!"* Captain Gibson, on the other hand, seemed doomed to be unlucky with his officers. To fill out his roster after Gill had departed, he promoted his third officer to the second mate's position and shipped a man named John White as third mate. This was quite a step down the ladder for that fellow, for he had been chief officer of the *Alert*—which probably accounts for the lack of surprise in Wilson's entry when he noted six months later, in Tinian, Rota, that White had got so drunk when sent on shore with a message that his boat returned without him. Staggering on board in the dead of night, he was promptly disrated and sent to the forecastle, and was discharged from the ship four days later.

On the *Japan,* trouble had started early in the voyage. They were only six weeks out of London when Dr. James Brown recorded that the blacksmith, or "Armourer," had been "found out in having stolen knives, handkerchiefs &c &c." Justice was swift and surprisingly democratic, though definitely supervised by Captain William Edmund Hill. "Was what the Sailors call *Split* to the Windlass & sentenced to receive *two whacks—blows—bastadoe*—or whatever term may be given it, from each of the men with the Carpenter's hand saw, over the breach, which was speedily performed, commenced with the Carpenter, and ending with the boy Bill." In May 1835, at Kupang, one of the men was seized for inciting insurrection. Dr. Brown noted that Captain Hill "found it necessary to put Thomas Ball in Irons, he was taken from the ship in charge of a Serjeant from the Fort and lodged there, being a mutinous and dissatisfied man."

In his own opinion, Captain Hill was having a lot of trouble with his stiff-necked Scot of a surgeon, too. In January 1836, when he was on board the *Eclipse* gamming with Captain Allen, he summoned Dr. James Brown to give an opinion on a seaman's double rupture, as a favor to the other master. Hernia was a common complication of seafaring, usually the result of hauling heavy tubs of saltwater up over the bows for washing the decks. James confirmed that the man was indeed ruptured "on both sides—these I found properly secured by trusses." He also "found that he had been labouring under inflammation of some of the viscera and I found the abdomen still very tense, but did not take any particular notice as Mr. Hill, Surgeon [no relation of Captain Hill of the *Japan*], was well aware of this disease and had bled him for it—my opinion being only requested [to say] if he was fit for duty."

The reason for this was that the crew of the *Eclipse* was mutinous. The ruptured seaman had declined to do any work on the grounds of his physical condition, so Captain Allen had given him a "rope's ending" (flogging) for refusing duty—and this despite the fact that "the boys had threatened to not to do any work if he (the Captn.) ever thrashed him." Having absorbed this information, Dr. Brown gave the problem his due consideration, and then (very bravely) gave his professional opinion that the man "was not fit for work, in consequence of the state of his bowels—but fit as far as Hernia was concerned." For obvious reasons, Captain Allen of the *Eclipse* was not at all pleased to hear this bit of news, and neither was Captain Hill. The silence in the boat on the way back to the *Japan* must have been deafening. When James Brown arrived on board, he was busy in the forecastle for a while, for two of the hands were sick with dysentery, but then Captain Hill summoned him into the cabin.

Ostensibly, the invitation was for a glass of grog, but no sooner had the doctor got his glass in his hand than his skipper "commenced about the sick as if I could help them from getting bad." Captain Hill—like Captain Allen—reckoned he had shipped a doctor to keep the men fit for work, not for putting them off duty so they could loaf about the decks. What the devil use was a surgeon if he could not keep them hale and healthy?

"I told him I could not prevent a man being taken bad," Dr.

Brown returned—which was nothing less than the truth. "My duty was to attend them when sick—which I had always had." It was no easy task, either, but it would have been of no use whatsoever to point that out to a master like William Edmund Hill. And so it was not a happy ship that sailed in company with the *Kingsdown* the following month, February 1836.

They were cruising off the northern coast of Timor. When day dawned on Saturday, February 27, both South Seamen were lying close to "Point Mobar" (Point Maubara). It was a good opportunity to refresh provisions, so Captain Hill sent Dr. James Brown on shore in the third mate's boat. Then Hill had his own boat lowered, pulled up alongside the *Kingsdown*, and invited Captain Simmons to keep him company.

When the two captains arrived on the beach, the rajah was waiting to welcome them in a most jovial manner. The bargaining for "3 Buffalo, 10 Sheep, 18 goats, 1 pig, and 3 dozen fowls" had gone well, and he was happy with the price, which was a certain amount of gunpowder. Business was over and it was time to have some fun. While the livestock was loaded into boats and ferried to the ships under the supervision of the two third mates, the rajah personally escorted the two captains to his palace, which was about fifty yards above the high-water mark. The two surgeons, James Brown of the *Japan* and Mr. John Marshall of the *Kingsdown*, were invited along too. And there the king regaled them with a banquet.

By the time Dr. Brown got up to measure out the agreed amount of gunpowder due to the rajah, the atmosphere was merry. The local king had amply demonstrated that he was delighted with his visitors by making Captain Hill a present of some coffee and giving Captain Simmons "a young dog of the greyhound kind." There was a slight hitch when a message came back that two of the goats had not been delivered, and a bit of an argument occurred because Dr. Brown had neglected to write down the terms of the original agreement, much to his skipper's irritation. However, eventually the captains consented to accept a couple of sheep in the place of the missing goats. The rajah pointed out a flock that was grazing nearby, and told them to take two of those. A hilarious scene ensued, with eight sailors running at the madly scattering sheep, throwing themselves full length as they tried to tackle the jumpy animals to the ground, at which the rajah laughed as heartily as the captains and the surgeons.

No sooner was this merriment over and the sheep safely in the boat, however, than the rajah abruptly changed his mind. As Dr. Brown went on to relate, the king did not want to lose his sheep after all (possibly because they had proved so entertainingly agile), and so he wanted them back. Instead, he would find them a couple of goats, "as originally agreed upon:

> By this time I had got into the Japan's boat, when Capt[n]. Simmons asked me to go off with his Surgeon and he would come along with Capt[n]. Hill—having received a goat and given up the sheep which was in the Kingsdown's boat Dr. Marshall and I shoved off—when we were about 50 yards from the beach I observed the natives make a rush up to their huts. . . . Capt[n]. H. entered his boat, the crew shoved off, Capt[n]. Simmons was steering her; they had not pulled 30 years from the beach when natives came running down armed with muskets, and fired at both boats.

The boat with the two surgeons would have been out of range if they had not paused to see why the captains were detained. As it was, with balls splashing all about the boat and whistling past their ears, they got out of there "as fast as the flurried state of the crews would permit." Then, belatedly, Dr. Brown heard Captain Hill hollering for him to come back—"that he wanted assistance, Capt[n]. Simmons and our carpenter being shot."

There was no way the two surgeons wanted to be within range of that hail of musket balls again. What would be the point? The doctors could hardly give assistance if they were being shot themselves. So it was with great reluctance that "we pulled alongside our boat and I and a sailor jumped into her—but it was of no use, both men were quite dead." Forthwith, they hastily pulled for the *Kingsdown*.

It was after sunset before they arrived. The bodies were hoisted on board, and Dr. Brown "examined them along with Mr. John Marshall, and found that a ball had entered Captn. Will Simmons' right arm about 6 inches below the shoulder; passing through the fleshy part of the arm it entered the chest betwixt the 3rd and 4th ribs." The carpenter, Samuel Edward Aldwell, had been shot in the back. The ball had penetrated "about 2 inches from the spine, betwixt the 7th & 8th ribs of the right side." In both cases, death had been instantaneous.

"I have no idea of what might have been the cause of the Rajah thus firing on us," Brown added in his usual circumspect fashion. "Until I left the beach everything appeared as friendly as ever I had seen with any other Rajah on the coast." Dr. John Wilson, that assiduous recorder of South Seaman gossip, had different ideas. In April 1840 the *Gipsy* was cruising off Point Maubara, just where the *Kingsdown* and the *Japan* had been standing on and off while the captains and surgeons feasted on shore, reminding Wilson of the "bloody tragedy [that] occurred there, some 4 years ago."

According to the tale as he had heard it, the party "had partook rather freely of liquor, and were somewhat inebriated." Not only that, but "some insult or other, had likewise been offered to some of his women: the chief became greatly excited & seeing that a rumpus was likely to ensue;—the *carpenter* snatches up *Capt. Hill* & put him in the boat & he & *Capt. Simmons*, together, push off from the beach, when several shots were fired at them by the natives."

Dr. John Wilson's details of the fatal wounds match Dr. Brown's account closely. Wilson, however, added the extra comment that the shots "were intended for *Capt. Hill* & his *carpenter*—they had no intention to hurt *Capt. Simmons*." James Brown could very well have found this understandable—in the case of the girl-chasing William Edmund Hill, at any rate. However, he did not mention it, probably because it was impossible to prove such a statement. "Simmons was but 28 years old, & was greatly lamented," Wilson went on. "He was buried at *Atipoopa*, a little higher up than *Maubara*."

"At daylight calm," wrote Dr. Brown on Monday February 29, 1836. "Captn. Hill went on shore at Atapoopa [Atapupu] and obtained leave from the Commandant to bring the bodies on shore for interment, at 3 o'Clock they were put into one boat and towed by another three on shore—the burial service of the church of England was read over them and a salute of 12 good Muskets fired also 9 Minute guns—Flag half-up—then 7 Minute guns—Flag up—a few minutes before six we left the beach and returned to the Kingsdown, at 8 I returned on board the Japan."

The offending rajah had fled to the hills. The Dutch governor posted a reward for his capture, and he was handed in and summarily hanged at Kupang.

THE MURDER OF THE CAPTAIN OF THE *KINGSDOWN* LEFT CAPTAIN Hill in charge of both ships, partly because there was a lot of illness among both crews and partly because the *Kingsdown*'s first mate, Mr. Edwards, was rather inexperienced. Altogether, William Hill had a peck of trouble, which was abruptly worsened the day after he got both ships to Kupang. A vicious storm blew up, and when a boat from the *Japan* was sent on shore, it was dashed on the rocks with the loss of a boatsteerer and three men. To lose so many at once was a calamity, considering that the ships were shorthanded already. Naturally, Captain Hill's temper was shorter than ever, and he proceeded to take it out on his surgeon.

"The Captn. being dressed for going on shore," Dr. Brown assumed that he should get ready to keep him company, as he had done so many times before. Instead, however, Captain Hill called him to the cabin, "and said that he would ask me to go along with him but that he was ashamed of me, and unless I was to work &c. &c. &c. I should no longer be in the ship—and that he would take the keys of the medicine chest." Astonished, James Brown started to point out that he had in fact done rather a lot of work, but Hill shouted him down, claiming "that I had never had done anything for him but a little writing and he was sorry he had ever asked me to write a line."

And off the skipper stomped, but that was not the end of the matter. Next day, Captain Hill called his surgeon into the cabin again, where he brusquely informed him that "unless I wrought hard and lent assistance at all times, I should be sent on shore." There Brown would be allowed a rupee a day to keep him going until he got a job or a berth on another ship—a particularly nasty jibe, one rupee being the going price for a bottle of aniseed in Kupang. Sailing without a surgeon might be breaking regulations, but that did not matter to Captain William Edmund Hill, who had managed very well without a doctor in the past—"he had formerly been Surgeon and could be so again."

The old salt had really got into his stride now, and the wincing surgeon was forced to stand and listen as his sins were listed and elaborated upon: "that I went on shore the night we arrived here, and got beastly drunk, thus I was obliged to keep my bed all next day &c." It was on the *Favorite* that Dr. Brown had learned his "bad practices," or so he was informed, for it was on that ship he had learned how to get "beastly drunk"—that humiliating term again, and with the first and fourth mates witness to the tirade, too. And with that, Dr. Brown was dismissed, for Captain Hill reckoned he had said it all.

For the whole of the next week, it seemed as if that would be the end of the unpleasant affair, and that the doctor had avoided the fate of Hill's past surgeons. James Brown went on shore a few times, either with the first mate, Mr. Martinson, or in the company of the surgeon of the *Kingsdown*. On board, he supervised the division of fresh meat between the two ships, and on shore he played a few games of billiards at the place of a local merchant, Mr. Tillman. Otherwise, he carried out medical duties—"Several of our crew very bad with the dysentery—also some of the *Kingsdown* men." As for Captain Hill, "with regard to me, no word."

The idea of leaving the ship and escaping all this aggravation would have been most tempting, but Dr. Brown was experienced enough to know that this was exactly what the old salt wanted. If he left the ship of his own free will, he would forfeit his lay—his share of the profits of the voyage. It was quite common, in fact, for some skippers toward the end of a cruise to harass their men, to drive them into deserting the ship and abandoning their share of the money. Once the whaling was finished, it was easy enough to recruit ordinary seamen who would be paid just a wage for the homeward voyage—or might even be pleased to work their passage home for no money at all. Dr. Brown's problem, however, was solved in an unexpected manner. One afternoon when he was on board the *Kingsdown*, "to see the sick, had not been there half an hour when I was sent for to our Captn.—he having been taken bad while at dinner." No sooner was Captain Hill up and about than another crisis developed, again taking the skipper's mind off his surgeon's sins. He was called on board the *Kingsdown* because the men had mutinied.

Usually, as we have seen, this was the kind of situation that was put down with swift and drastic action. On the *Kingsdown* in March 1836, however, this mutiny was different, being a strangely dignified affair. The crew had made a formal declaration "that they would not proceed on the voyage under the command of [first mate] Edwards—but that they would proceed with the ship to Sydney or any other British port for the purpose of getting another Commander." Their reason, they said, was that they had seen Mr. Edwards "two or three times tipsy or intoxicated." In their estimation, too, "M^r. E. was not capable of navigating a ship or of taking proper care of her upon whaling ground." The humiliated officer "offered to throw all the grog overboard, provided that would satisfy them," but they remained adamant. What could one do to counter such a tidy revolution? Captain Hill compromised by getting Dr. Brown to write out a long deposition detailing the situation. He signed it, the surgeon witnessed it, and Hill returned to his ship.

The *Kingsdown* men were as good as their word. In December, the ship was reported in Sydney, where a replacement master by the name of Lazenby was found. However, the crew knew they had muscles now, and were willing to flex them. The ship was reported at Vavou in October 1837 with only 600 barrels of oil, so they directed the *Kingsdown* to New Zealand, where yet another master was found, this one named Jenkins. Captain Jenkins brought the ship home, but not until May 1839, so that the total length of the voyage was nearly four years, a loss and a distinct disappointment to the owners.

BACK ON THE *JAPAN*, DR. JAMES BROWN'S PROBLEMS WERE CONTIN-uing. "At suppertime" one evening in October 1836, Captain Hill abruptly attacked him again:

> saying, it was a bloody good thing that the ship was nearly full as there was now some prospect of getting soon home, other-wise he would be obliged to make alterations in this Cabin—as for you D^r., you never put your hand to work to do either one thing or other, and I am determined you shall no longer mess at this table. I told him that I had always done what I came here to do—after a deal of abusive language I was ordered to prepare to move my things to the Forecastle, saying "you can go and mess with 'Jack' I dare say he loves you better than I do—I give you till tomorrow morning—and if you don't go I shall have to use force—that's all—and bring the Keys of the Medicine Chest to me here" (striking the table with the handle of his Knife).

"After retiring from supper, I did not enter the Cabin again this night," Dr. Brown merely wrote, but as he sat in his little stateroom he must have been acutely aware of the mess cabin just the other side of his louvered door. Being fired from one's job is bad enough at any time, but in the middle of the ocean it takes on the nature of a crisis. In Kupang he had been saved by the skipper's timely ill-ness, but he certainly could not rely on that happening again. Brown decided to call Captain Hill's bluff. Accordingly, he spent the next morning packing his clothes into his chests, "and at dinner time went in to the Cabin, and delivered him some numbers of the 'Lancet,' Bateman's on diseases of the Skin Synopsis &c." Doubt-less hoping to make a point, he also returned the quadrant, "which I have had the use of for some time," Captain Hill having put him to navigational duties since early in the voyage. Then "I put the Keys of the Medicine chest on the table—He immediately got up in a passion—not to come and disturb him at dinner, after working all day—I was ordered out preemptory and the keys hove away."

And Dr. Brown returned to his stateroom. Presumably, the pangs of hunger were really gnawing by this time. However, worse was to come. "At a little after 4 P.M. all hands were called aft," and the grievance was aired before the whole of the crew in such dramatic style that it reads like a play:

> *Captn. H.*—Now, this is a disagreement between me and my Surgeon—he says he doesn't have to do anything but carry out the antics of a Surgeon, and refuses to do anything else— Now I am determined he shall not any more mess at my table—this is what I have called you aft to tell you—do you all hear it?
>
> *Crew (shuffling about and glancing at each other)*—Yes.
>
> *Captn. H.*—Now, if any of you have any complaint against him, speak out."
>
> *Silence.*
>
> *Captn. H. (promptingly)*—I have often heard that the Dr. was negligent and inattentive, and refused medicines when asked for them.
>
> *All silent.*
>
> *Captn. H.*—I appeal to my officers.
>
> *Officers*—Yes, we have often heard the people complain of him.
>
> *Captn. H.*—Well then, point them out.
>
> *Silence.*
>
> *Thomas Ross*—The Dr. once refused me "sweet oil" when I asked for it.
>
> *Dr. Brown (no longer able to keep still)*—But why was it refused?
>
> *Captn. H.*—Be quiet.
>
> *More silence.*
>
> *Joe Howes (after clearing his throat)*—During the time I was unwell I believe the best was done for me.

Captn. H.—That'll do.

Robert Jarman—I never asked for any medicine but what it was
always given.

Captn. H.—Is there anyone else has anything to say?

All silent.

Robert Jarman was exhibiting a spirit of justice and fair play, for
during the previous voyage of the *Japan* (1831–1834) his best friend
had died in agony some time after breaking both legs in a whaling
accident, for the inexperienced surgeon (unnamed) had botched the
necessary amputations. This is described in an account he wrote of
this earlier voyage, titled *Journal of a Voyage to the South Seas, in the
"Japan"* . . . and published in 1838 by Jarman himself, who became a
journeyman printer in the town of Beccles, Surrey, after leaving the
sea. Unfortunately, at no time did he mention the second voyage, or
describe Captain Hill, Dr. Brown, or this dramatic little scene.

At this stage, it having become so apparent that the men felt
sorry for the surgeon, Hill began to bluster. Well, he said, as of
tomorrow the surgeon would be in a place by himself, and if he
wanted to put himself off duty, then he was welcome to do it. At
this, Dr. Brown (very much aware that his share of the profits of
the voyage was in danger) protested he had never suggested such a
thing. "But you gave me the keys," the captain argued. "Yes," Dr.
Brown pointed out, "but it was by your own orders."

"You delivered books and quadrant—but not the carpenter's
property," the old salt snapped. The carpenter was the man who
had been shot at Maubara, and evidently his tools had been
entrusted to the surgeon. Brown, aghast at this virtual accusation of
theft of a dead man's belongings, exclaimed that he had put them on
board the *Pacific* to be taken back to London. But how could he
prove it?

"Man the mastheads," the captain ordered, his point made, and
stumped away.

"Thursday 27th," wrote James Brown next day:

Fine weather—I visited the sick as usual and kept myself in my

birth until about 2 P.M.—when the Captn. called me and said now
there is a birth for you in the half deck—take your own things
and your medicine chest and do with it *as you have done before.* I
will never ask another dose from you—I'll sooner die—you can
buy what you want I shall give you only what Mr. Bennett [the
owner] allows—and I shall never ask you to do a "hand's turn" as
long as you are in the Ship even if she were sinking—you have
now I consider £140 worth of property in [the] ship & I consider
you never have done a hand's turn to get it.

So now it was in the open. Captain Hill begrudged the doctor
his lay—the £140 that was Dr. Brown's share of the money from
the whales that had been taken thus far in the voyage. At least he
was not going to lose that, but if any more whales were raised during the rest of the voyage, he would not have any part of the profits
from those. And as far as rations were concerned, he would be
given the basic seaman's allowance to eat, but he would have to buy
any extras for himself.

As time would tell, ten more months of voyage stretched ahead,
but there was nothing Dr. Brown could do about it. The steward
and one of the apprentices, William Jacobs (the same man who had
been laid up with fever when the surgeon took his place washing
decks), helped him shift his chests into the room in the "half
deck"—which was, in fact, a small storeroom that had been cleared
out, its contents to be stored in the stateroom that the doctor had
vacated—and there he took up residence.

From then on life must have been remarkably lonely. On Christmas Eve and Christmas Day the men were "dancing and singing
until midnight," but Dr. Brown had nothing to celebrate. If Captain Hill went on shore, he seized the opportunity to visit another
South Seaman, if there was one nearby, and socialize with the surgeon. Otherwise, he went to a beach to have a solitary bathe. If Mr.
Martinson, the first mate, was going on shore, Brown might keep
him company, for he knew that the ship would not sail without the
chief officer. Otherwise, he did not dare leave the *Japan.*

"Just Landed."   FROM *NIMROD OF THE SEA*, WILLIAM DAVIS
(NEW YORK, 1874)

He medicated sick men if they specifically asked for him, but others, presumably, were treated by the captain. On April 20, 1837, a seaman by the name of David Michie died of anasarca (a form of dropsy), but he did not seem to be one of Brown's patients. They arrived at St. Helena in July that same year. Dr. Brown did not go on shore. On the thirteenth, they hove the anchor, leaving "one of our men, Thomas Jones" on shore:

> he being unable to proceed with us, not having sufficiently recovered of the Scurvy. He was the only one that was under my care and it was by my advice that he remained on shore—the others after being a few days on shore, either put themselves under the care of a D^r. Reed, or D^r. Reed got orders to attend them, which I cannot say—but I know that he has sent two men on board who are quite incapable of doing their duty—nor will they most likely be able to do anything during our passage to England, viz.: Peter Green a Swede (Scurvy) and Richard Wheeler, diseased liver, and chronic diarrhoea—received from the Captn the Medicines I ordered at St. Helena, and had to give him a receipt for them.

Finally, on Saturday, August 5, 1837, the *Japan* arrived at the mouth of the Thames River, and Dr. James Brown wrote, "the *Tam O'Shanter*, Tug Steam Boat made fast to us, and towed us to the London Docks." At 3.15 P.M., the ship was secured, and at long last he was able to walk away with his draft for £140 firmly in his hand. It was pretty poor pay for thirty-three months of aggravation and hell, but at least Dr. Brown was on his way home.

Epilogue
The Fates of Our Surgeons

On the morning of the 27th of November, 1836,
we arrived at Gravesend, and were truly thankful
to an Almighty Providence,
which had permitted us thus happily
to complete a voyage of three years and twenty-four days,
without the loss of one of our crew
either by disease or accident.

Dr. Frederick Debell Bennett

"THE A/C [ACCOUNTS] I SHALL BE ABLE TO GIVE YOU," WROTE DR.
Robert Smith Owen to his brother, "will be quite interesting, *scorn-
ing* as I do embellishing them anything of the marvellous." Perhaps
a little flexibility would have served him better, for his path seemed
so dogged by ill luck. In September 1838, after seventeen months of
voyage and constant dreaming of marital bliss, he received a letter
that his brother had penned exactly a year before, which utterly
dashed his hopes.

"You state that Emma is to be *married & that shortly*," he
exclaimed. He refused to believe it: "it would be too unkind & too
unfeeling to say that in so short a space of time she could be wanton." The "space of time" and wanton cruelty were even worse
than Robert imagined. Another letter, dated April 3, 1838, casually
informed him that Emma had been a married woman for ages, having wed his rival *within* six months of the departure of the *Warrens*.
"Surely my Destiny cannot be so wayward that evil luck ever
attends on my planet," Robert mourned. Exactly a year previously,
he had heard in Kupang that a ship's doctor had cut his throat and
had been buried the next day, "no friends to follow his remains to
the grave, neither any coroner's inquest held." The cause, it seemed,
was a love affair, and when he read his brother's news, Robert
Smith Owen must have known just how that surgeon felt.

Nothing about this adventure seemed to be going well. It was in
December 1838, three months after receiving the dread news of
Emma's marriage, that Captain Gray accused him of cheating at
cards. George Gray was tense and irritable himself, for other ships
were doing so much better than the *Warrens*. In Elphinstone's Bay
in March 1839 they were in company with the *Kent*, which had
taken 1,200 barrels, one thousand of them in a three-month period
of hectic whaling off the stormy western coast of New Holland,

while the *Warrens*, which had been out three months longer than the *Kent*, had just 600 barrels to report.

Dr. Owen, like the mate, Mr. Mortimer, knew exactly whom to blame for the poor performance of the *Warrens*—the captain himself. As Mr. Mortimer remarked, they always seemed to be in port or making passages instead of whaling. George Gray was altogether too fond of grog and socializing—singing, "smoaking," and drinking were the order of the day, and "Looking after oil is out of the Question!!!!"

Leaving the ship was a distinct temptation. Robert Smith Owen had found that he loved the tropics, often noting in his journal that he was, "Sweating profusely & in excellent Health, thank God— never was better." He liked the Malay people, recording in Sûtarano that his manner "so delighted them that they would not let 'Mr. Doctor' go." When in port, he was "inundated with invitations" from the foreign residents. In July 1839, for instance, ten months after learning about Emma's infidelity, he spent a couple of weeks on shore at Manado, in the northern part of the Celebes, as the guest of the resident surgeon.

Owen was extremely impressed with the port, for the people were so civilized. Their daily routine suited him to perfection: "rise at 5 in the morning, & take a Cup of Tea, strong, sometimes with bread or a small biscuit—then to the bath—dress for the morning walk or amusement till 11 a.m.—at 12, lunch or Dinner—bath— then sleep till ½ of 2—then bathe again, then Tea or Coffee—4 or 5, gentle exercise, & about 6 pay a visit to the Billiard room which is the general rendezvous of an Evening for Gentlemen." Cards, cigars, wine, and soda water were all available, and a slate was kept so that the bill could be paid at leisure. The women were beautiful, if one overlooked "the Dutch characteristic of thick ancles & heels," and their children were "without doubt the finest I have seen." The houses were clean, spacious, and elegantly furnished. There was good money to be made here, too, for though his host was retained by the Dutch Commandant at 250 rupees (£23) a month, he was allowed to keep a private practice as well. In a year's time, as Owen learned from this medical friend, retirement on a pension of 100 rupees a month beckoned. This shore surgeon was going to change his course and go into the gold-trading business, so the position of medical attendant would be open if Dr. Owen wanted it.

It was a remarkably tempting proposition. In the event, however, Robert Owen returned on board the *Warrens*, although how long he remained on the ship is uncertain. The *Warrens* arrived home in May 1840, but there is some doubt that the surgeon was still on board. The last entry in Owen's journal is dated February 12, 1840, on the verge of going on shore at St. Helena. He was very concerned about the state of the crew, fearing that three of them would die. The first signs of scurvy had appeared as far back as December, when some of the men had started complaining of "sponginess of the gums." When he had reported this to the captain, George Gray had flown into a rage, declaring that "they should have nothing from him" as it was their own fault—"they would bring it on themselves" by mere laziness—and it was the surgeon's job to make sure it did not happen. This was impossible, for the medical chest was "impoverish'd," but when Dr. Owen informed Gray that he could do nothing for the men without fresh food and medicine, it only led to a row.

The poor state of the crew's health was bad enough, but the situation was made still worse by the fact that the ship had taken no more oil. Her report was still 600 barrels, so that Owen's lay was worth the miserable sum of £20—less than one month's stipend in Manado. Shifting to another berth could have appeared a good alternative, and indeed, Owen had already received an offer from the captain of the trader *Mandane* of Sunderland. At the time he had turned down the proposition, but at this date he could well have had second thoughts. In England he would be an object of pity, a penniless and jilted man, while returning to the Celebes Sea held out the promise of an adventurous, glamorous future.

Because of the prevailing winds, most of the homeward bound South Seamen called at St. Helena to make report and take on a few fresh provisions for the final leg of the voyage. Naturally, then, it was an excellent place to learn news of the fleet. Owen undoubtedly would have heard of the *Rochester*, which had arrived from South Seas four months previously with a most gratifying report of two thousand barrels. Now, she was going out again under the same master, Captain Kenney, who had taken his departure from Deal, Kent, on January 7. Thus the *Warrens* and the *Rochester* were in close proximity, one heading south, and the other north—and it seems very likely that they spoke. If they did gam, Kenney could well have offered Owen the surgeon's berth, perhaps because the man he had shipped was unsatisfactory, had regretted his bargain, or was sick.

It may seem a long shot. However, evidence indicating that the *Warrens* did gam with the outgoing *Rochester*, and that Kenney did make the offer—and that Robert Smith Owen accepted it—can be found in Dr. John Wilson's journal. The *Gipsy* arrived at the island of Rota in the Marianas on March 29, 1841, almost exactly one year later, and there Wilson recorded that the *Rochester*, *Indian*, and *Vigilant* were at anchor in Port Apra. After going on board the *Vigilant* to play chess with the surgeon, Mr. Morris, he noted, further, that they were "joined by M^r. *Hawkes, Surgeon* of the '*Indian*,' & by M^r. *Owen,* Surgeon, of the '*Rochester*.' The day was passed with mutual satisfaction & pleasure," he went on.

Then, four days later, Wilson remarked that he had joined a lively party staged by Captain Kenney at the house of a local compradore, Don José. There, "M^r. *Owen,* & a large company of *ladies*—the elite of the place, nearly all of them young," were enjoying themselves. Music was provided by a fiddle and a guitar, one young lady sang an English song, and the fandango was danced. Dr. Wilson declined to hop with the locals, but not so Dr. Owen, who was having a first-rate time.

Was this the same young man who had been treated so shabbily by Dear Emma? Owen, after all, is a common name. However, Dr. Robert Smith Owen was not in England, for he appears in none of the surgeons' lists. Neither does his name feature in the registers of

Cirencester, his hometown, or in any subsequent census. And so, the likelihood persists, and the reader hopes that that is what truly happened.

> No one but those who have been long at sea can conceive the delight that all on board experience on first making the English coast.
>
> *Dr. John Wilson, on arrival at the Nore, March 1843*

The *Gipsy* entered the London Docks on March 20, 1843, when Wilson went ashore with a draft for his share of the voyage in his pocket. It would not have been much, perhaps even less than the £140 that Captain Hill had so begrudged Dr. James Brown, for the value of oil had declined since. However, it was a great deal more than Robert Smith Owen had earned, and in other respects Wilson seems to have done quite well for himself. He graduated M.R.C.S. in 1844, and as he already had his L.S.A., he was able to describe himself as a general practitioner. He set up in practice in Golden Square—a Bohemian area at the time, beloved of novelists, artists, and opera singers, but nonetheless very convenient, being in the heart of Westminster, London.

Five years later, he was affluent enough to move to 66 Albany Street, Regent's Park, part of the gorgeous Nash-designed redevelopment that had been completed in 1828. Bustling markets were just a street away and the Zoological Garden was within walking distance, while Wilson would have been able to watch barges gliding up from the Limehouse on the Regent's Canal. Here, he set up in practice as a surgeon-accoucheur ("man-midwife"). In June 1846 he married Eliza Riviere, the daughter of a well-to-do and artistic Huguenot family of jewelers, artists, and bookbinders. A son, John Henry Parker Wilson (who later became a surgeon himself), was born nine months later. Over the next thirty years the family moved from one house to another as the Wilson fortunes improved. Midway through his career John Wilson gained the coveted rank of physician, having been elected a Licentiate of the Royal College of Physicians of Edinburgh in 1860. About 1876 he retired, moving to fashionable Brixton, where he died in 1879 at the age of sixty-eight.

While unpublished during their lifetimes, the journals of Dr. John Wilson and Dr. William Dalton are now in print because of the dedication of two noted scholars, Honore Forster and Niel Gunson. Very different in style, they are valuable for different reasons. John Wilson was very much the social commentator, not just noting events and impressions in detail and illustrating them with gentle watercolors, but adding memoranda later as whaling news of interest hit the papers, thus creating a remarkably complete record of the British enterprise in the southern fishery in the middle of the nineteenth century.

William Dalton, on the other hand, kept a concise, objective, and businesslike journal, and was very much the scientist. He became the most distinguished of the group professionally, contributing several articles to medical journals, as well as letters that were published in *The Lancet*. Like John Wilson, he eventually attained the high status of a physician, becoming a Fellow of the Royal College of Surgeons in 1854, and being elected to the Royal College of Physicians of London in 1869. When he died, in 1873, he merited an obituary in the *British Medical Journal* that conveys a tantalizing glimpse of William Dalton the man:

> After obtaining his qualifications, he served for several years as a surgeon to a whaling ship in the South Pacific. He used to be very fond of narrating his stirring adventures and experiences whilst in this capacity; and, indeed, he became so thorough a sailor, that he was offered command of a ship.

One who actually walked the quarterdeck—as second mate—was Eldred Fysh. It was very fortunate that he became such a thorough officer under Captain Bond's tutelage, for in December 1839 the *Coronet* arrived in Mauritius and apparently never left. The ship was still in that port in February 1840, and after that no more was heard of her. The conclusion is that she was condemned, leaving the crew to make the best of their own way home. Eldred

Fysh shipped out as the second mate of the passenger ship *Eliza-beth*, keeping a journal on board that ends off Beachy Head, East Sussex, on November 2, 1840.

According to this, he was happy enough, but nevertheless he did not pursue a life at sea. Instead, he returned home to Newmarket, Norfolk, where he set up in practice as a surgeon, living with his widowed mother and spinster sisters until March 27, 1845, when he married a schoolmistress, Elizabeth Peek, and moved to the town of "Magdalen Bridge, nr. Lynn." How well he did there is debatable, for in 1847, the same year his second daughter was born, he advertised in the *London & Provincial Medical Directory* as a "Surgeon & Chemist." Somewhat mysteriously, he claimed to have been a military surgeon in the past, so perhaps he had eked out his income with a retainer from the army. Then, just two years later, he found a last resting place in Watlington churchyard, where the inscription on his stone reads, "Eldred Edmund Fysh who died 11 January 1849. *Iacet in pace.*" Dr. Fysh was just thirty-seven years old. The cause of his death is unknown.

THE *SARAH & ELIZABETH*, WITH THOMAS BEALE ON BOARD, WAS reported at Deal in Kent on February 4, 1833. In 1835 he put the journal he kept on voyage to good use, publishing a sixty-page pamphlet called *A Few Observations on the Natural History of the Sperm Whale, with an Account of the Rise and Progress of the Fishery*. This aroused such interest that in 1839 it led to a book, *The Natural History of the Sperm Whale: Its Anatomy and Physiology— Food—Spermaceti—Ambergris—Rise and Progress of the Fishery—Chase and Capture—"Cutting in" and "Trying Out"— Description of the Ships, Boats, Men and Instruments Used in the Attack; with an Account of Its Favourite Places of Resort. To which is added, a Sketch of a South-Sea Whaling Voyage; Embracing a Description of the Extent, as well as the Adventures and Accidents that Occurred during the Voyage in which the Author was Personally Engaged.*

Thomas Beale's *Natural History of the Sperm Whale* was in fact a travelogue rather than a book of natural history, but it was extremely well received, a prominent admirer being the artist Joseph Mallord William Turner, who produced a number of powerful paintings on the strength of it. The honor of receiving a medal for a paper on *Physeter macrocephalus* (the scientific name for the sperm whale) meant still more prestige, but Beale, a deeply religious and philanthropic man who joined the Paris-based *Institut d'Afrique*, an organization devoted to the welfare of African slaves, spent the rest of his life as a poorly paid medical officer attached to the Stepney Poor House of the City of London Union. On August 21, 1849, at the age of forty-two, he contracted Asiatic cholera, and twenty-seven hours later he was dead.

"There are only two books in being which at all pretend to put the living Sperm Whale before you, and at the same time, in the remotest degree succeed in the attempt," wrote Herman Melville. "Those books are Beale's and Bennett's; both in their times surgeons to English South-Sea whale-ships, and both exact and reliable men." Dr. Frederick Bennett's ship, the leaky old *Tuscan*, arrived home at the end of 1836. His book appeared a year after Beale's—at the same time, coincidentally, when the *Tuscan* was condemned at the Bay of Islands, New Zealand. It had an equally comprehensive title—*Narrative of a Whaling Voyage Round the Globe, from the Year 1833 to 1836. Comprising Sketches of Polynesia, California, the Indian Archipelago, etc. With an Account of Southern Whales, the Sperm Whale Fishery, and the Natural History of the Climates Visited*—and attracted considerable public attention, too. Evidently a man of means, Bennett pursued a number of scientific hobbies as well as attending to his medical practice in Southwark. He had been a member of the Royal Geographical Society since 1831 and had an active interest in the Zoological Society of London and the Devon and Cornwall Natural History Society. He was another to die young, passing away in 1859 at the age of fifty-three.

Another surgeon to publish his experiences was Dr. John Coulter, the flamboyant Irishman who in 1845 published *Adventures in*

The Whale Ship.

JOSEPH MALLORD WILLIAM TURNER, CA. 1845
COURTESY METROPOLITAN MUSEUM OF ART, NEW YORK

Exhibited at the Royal Academy in 1845, this painting was named "Vide Beale's Voyage p. 175," having been inspired by Dr. Thomas Beale's stirring description of a battle with a very large whale.

The bull sperm pictured was an unusual specimen, in that he repeatedly "peaked his flukes" as if to sound, but breached in different directions instead. After many attempts Captain Swain managed to pitch a lance into him. At once he sounded, but only briefly, for then he "rose to the surface with great velocity," catching the boat and throwing it high into the air, "fracturing it to atoms and scattering its crew widely about."

While the men floundered desperately out of the way, the bull whale swam in tight circles, crashing the water with his flukes. Then, to make the situation even more precarious, several large sharks arrived, "attracted by the blood that flowed from the whale." It took a full three-quarters of an hour for another boat to arrive to the rescue, but no sooner had the men been hauled into the bottom (meaning that the whaleboat was now grossly the Pacific; With Observations of the Natural Productions, Manners and Customs of the Natives of the Various Islands; Together with Remarks on Missionaries, British and Other Residents, etc. etc. Despite the rather forbidding title, Coulter did not seek to educate, but rather to entertain, and in this he certainly succeeded. By coincidence, *Adventures in the Pacific* came out at about the same time as Herman Melville's *Narrative of a Four Months' Residence Among the Natives . . . of the Marquesan Islands* or *Typee*, and so, inevitably, the two books were compared. The critic in the *Dublin University Magazine* lauded Coulter for his maturity and pithy prose, while Melville was dismissed as that "nondescript young American."

Adventures in the Pacific is an incomplete account, coming to an abrupt halt two chapters after the lively descriptions of his tattooing and the gory war between the cannibals—deliberately so, for Coulter was no sluggard in business. The last paragraph promised

overloaded with a crew of twelve instead of the usual six), than the attack on the "immense creature" recommenced.

"We, who were on board the ship and had observed from a great distance, by means of the telescope, the whole of the occurrence, were employed in beating the ship towards them," Beale recounted, "but they were to windward, and the wind being rather light, we had even our royal sails set." Meantime, a third boat arrived to join the fray. Repeatedly lanced, the whale at long last went into his flurry—and sank when he died, never to be seen again.

Turner painted this scene for Elhanan Bicknell, an oil merchant who made his fortune from woolen mills and whaling ship shares, but the work was returned after some disagreement, possibly because of its inaccuracy. The whale is anatomically incorrect; the whaleboats have too much beam for their draft; there are three when the account lists only two intact boats; and the ship has not set any of her royals (small square sails at the summit of each mast). Nevertheless, the scene is unmistakably dramatic, in the true tradition of the master.

that with encouragement he might, "at a future time, bring the reader across the meridian 180° into east longitude, and tell him of the adventures and occurrences at islands, and other places, where a civilized trader seldom, and a missionary never landed"—evidence of John Coulter's sure assessment of his audience. As expected, his readers could not get enough of such bloodcurdling stuff, and in 1847 a second book was published. Again, in the style of the time, the title told the prospective purchaser exactly what he would find between the covers—a stirring account of *Adventures on the Western Coast of South America and the Interior of California: including a Narrative of Incidents at the Kingsmill Islands, New Ireland, New Britain, New Guinea, and Other Islands in the Pacific Ocean; with an Account of the Natural Productions, and the Manners and Customs, in Peace and War, of the Various Savage Tribes Visited.* The public had made it obvious that they wanted lots more sensational accounts of savage encounters, and that is exactly what Coulter delivered.

The promised additional encounters with untamed tribes were made possible when an acquaintance, Captain Trainer, arrived on the Californian coast in his smart new Baltimore-built brigantine *Hound.* Coulter had just recovered from the rheumatism that had compelled him to leave the *Stratford* for a while, and had a few weeks' grace before he was scheduled to meet his ship in Tahiti. Coulter shipped on the *Hound* and forthwith steered for the western Pacific and the islands listed in the title.

The natives of "the Kingsmill Islands" (in modern Kiribati) had a reputation for treachery that surpassed even the Marquesans, but nonetheless Coulter ventured on shore for a lengthy expedition— and this despite his observation that his hosts wore long necklaces made up of the finger and toe bones of the ingredients of past meals. It is odd how much his experiences there mirror his adventures in the Marquesas, though this time when he was stripped to the hide the warriors backed off smartly, no doubt understandably impressed. Coulter even played the same joke on the crew when he returned to the brig. Altogether, it is very likely that Coulter succumbed to the temptation of embroidering his yarn to include lots more of what his audience had relished earlier. At that time it was respectable publishing practice to leaven fact with fiction. He may even have been telling the unvarnished truth, for there are many strange tales told of the beachcombers of the Pacific, and the voyage of the *Stratford* is easily authenticated. However, it is probably safe to say that *Adventures in the Pacific* is a lot more reliable than the sequel.

With his sharpshooting and his tattoos, John Coulter could have successfully joined the circus after leaving the sea, and he would not have been the first seafarer to do that, either. Instead, however, he settled in Dublin, where he became a surgeon-accoucheur attached to the General Lying-In Hospital, an institution usually known as "The Rotunda" that was famous for its work in obstetrics. It may seem a strange avocation for an adventurous ex-whaling surgeon who was very much a man's man, but, as we have seen, he was not the only one of our sea surgeons to enter the field of obstetrics. One cannot help but wonder, though, what Coulter's patients thought when he rolled up his sleeves for a delivery. The date of his death is unknown, but may have been in the early 1860s, for in 1862 his name disappeared from the membership list of the Royal College of Surgeons. There is also the chance that he merely retired, for he was about the age of sixty, having been born at the start of the century.

Oddly enough, a somewhat more flamboyant fate was in store for John B. King of Nantucket, the man who had shipped as a sailor on the old *Aurora* but was elevated to the much more boring status of surgeon. On December 2, 1840, the *Aurora* reached home, and Dr. King, three years older and infinitely wiser than the day he had left, resumed practice in his old hometown of Nantucket. Eight years later, the whole eastern seaboard of the United States was electrified by the news that gold in legendary quantities was lying about for the digging in California, and thousands of men packed up and set off on long arduous journeys to get a share of the bonanza. "There's lots of lawyers in these diggings," remarked Dr. Tyrwhitt-Brooks (a man who had jumped ship in San Francisco and headed off to the mother lode)—and there were plenty of fellow surgeons, too. John King decided to join the horde, which is not surprising when his earlier attempt to join the common crew of a whaler is considered. However, his participation had a lot more to do with making money out of the forty-niners than with digging. He bought a half-share in the old *Aurora* and sailed her around Cape Horn with a company of gold-seekers on board. Though Captain Seth Swain had been hired to take command of the ship and the crew, the responsibility of the passengers was all Dr. King's, for he was traveling as the managing owner.

And at last he was experiencing adventure, for an exciting trip he had of it, according to the journal kept by one of the prospective miners, "James M. Bunker 2d." The passengers washed for themselves, bought their own provisions in port, and fought with each other and the cook. "Dr. King offered a resolution that the passengers abstain from spitting on the floor when spittoons were provided," Bunker recorded after one of the many meetings. Some said they would comply only if the captain and officers refrained from spitting too, but this amendment was lost. Every man on board was armed to the teeth, and marksmanship was practiced on deck, enlivened by the occasional duel. "A sea voyage is very tedious," Bunker meditated, despite all this excitement, "especially if you are in a hurry."

After arriving in San Francisco, Dr. King put the ship into the Oregon lumber trade, apparently with some success, but he made no attempt to settle on the West Coast, instead returning home eleven months later to resume his solid medical practice and play an important part in Nantucket affairs. He became Medical Examiner for the island when that office was created, and also one of the Board of Trustees of the Nantucket Institution for Savings, and was a founding member of the Agricultural Society. When he passed away in 1872, his obituary lauded him as a "sturdy, sterling, and honored" citizen.

Meanwhile he had outlived the era of the south seas whaling surgeon, simply because of the enterprise of his fellow citizens. The British—who, unlike the Americans, had made it a legal requirement that a doctor should be on board their ships—had relinquished the southern fishery in the face of strenuous American competition. In 1829, when the *Kingsdown* sailed from London, 151 American vessels were cruising the Pacific. By 1843, when John Wilson disembarked from the *Gipsy*, there were more than 700, leading to the popular claim that the energetic Yankees were whitening the great sea with their sails. According to a contemporary estimate, the fleet was catching more whales in one day than the British South Seamen had caught over the last ten years.

There was a brief, ill-fated effort to revive the business in 1849, when the Southern Whale Fishery Company, founded by the Enderby family of whaling merchants and backed by oil merchants such as Elhanan Bicknell, sent out its first ship. Within just a handful of years, however, the capital ran out, the company was wound up, and with that, the South Seas fishery was abandoned by the British. The requirement to ship a surgeon for South Seas went with them, and so, except for eccentric episodes like the shipping of Tom Noddy on the *Java*, the medical care of any whaling crew was left to an American captain, his medical chest, and some guide that would have been a direct descendant of Woodall's *The Surgions Mate*.

APPENDIX A
MEDICAL CHEST COMPARISON

ITEM	WOODALL'S CHEST—1617	DR. KING'S CHEST—1837
Emplastra [Plasters]	Stipticum Paracelsi (stimulating) Diachilon Magnum cum gummis (for abscesses) Diachilon simplex (litharge, oil, lard) Diacelsitheos (diachylon with palm oil) Oxicroceum (saffron, burgundy pitch, wax) Melilot & splene ("dissolveth windinesse") Meliotum simplex (melilot, resin, wax, oil) De Lapide Calaminari De Minio (red lead oxide, cinnabar) Callidum or strengthening plaster	Strengthening plaster Adhesive plaster "Rob & Ass"—diachylon with asafetida and frankincense
Unguentum [Ointments]	Basillicon (oils, resin, and lard) Apostolorum (litharge, turpentine, myrrh, wax) Aureum (gold) Ægyptiacum (copper acetate and honey) Album Camphoratum (white wax, camphor) Diapompholigos (belladonna, litharge, red lead) Pectorale (chest liniment)	Basilicon Ointment ("Ung. Res." "cerat res.")

ITEM	WOODALL'S CHEST—1617	DR. KING'S CHEST—1837
Unguentum **[Ointments]** *continued*	Rosarum (with oil of roses) Nutritum (with lead acetate) Populeon (with herbs including poplar buds) De Melle & Sapo (honey and soap) Contra Ignem (Dorstenia wood) Contra Scorbatum (antiscorbutic) Dialthea composita (hollyhock) Dialthea simplex Potabile ("drinkable ointment")	
	Mercury	Mercurial ointment
	Linamentum arcei (retaining, bracing liniment)	
	Aragon (stimulating)	Liquid Opodeldoc (soft soap, essential oils)
	Martiatum ("soldiers' ointment"—ferric chloride) Axungia porcine (pork lard) Axungia Cerui (lard, lead acetate) Mel simplex (honey)	
		Simple ointment Turner's cerate
Aqua	Calestis (lime water) Dr. Stevens' patent cordial Rosa solis (rosewater) Cinamon (cinnamon water)	
	Limoniorum (lemon cordial)	salts of lemon
	Rosemary Sassafras (from sassafras root) Anniseed	
	Absinthe (wormwood water)	absinthe
	Mellissa (water of lemon balm) Angelica	
	Minthe (mint water)	Essence of peppermint
	Cardui sancti (blessed thistle) Theriacalis (opium water) Rosa Damascki (Damascene roses) Rosa Rub (red roses) Odiferæ (sweet water) Plantaginis (plantain) Falopy (mercury) Viridis (verdigris water) Aqua fortis (nitric acid) Verjuice (crab apple juice) Lotion (alum with herbs or mercury) Lixinium forte (sodium hydroxide)	

Aqua *continued*	Lixinium commune (lye)	
		Tincture of rhubarb
	Acetum rosarum (rose vinegar)	
	Acetum vini (wine vinegar)	vinegar (acetic lotion)
	Spiritus vini (brandy)	hot punch
	Spiritus vitriol (oil of vitriol)	Elixir vitriol (sulf'acid, alcohol, ginger, cinnamon)
	Spiritus Terebinthine (turpentine)	
	Causticke liquid	
Sal [Salts]	Absinthe	
	Gemmæ (rock salt)	
	Nitræ (saltpeter)	nitre
Oleum **[Oils]**	Rosarum	
	Anethinum (oil of dill)	
	Chamomeli (chamomile)	
	Lumbricorum (earthworms)	
	Liliorum (lilies)	
	Hipericonis simplex (St. John's wort)	
	Hipericonis cum gummis	
	Balmi artificialis (probably citronella)	
	Sambucorum (elder flowers)	
	Lini (flaxseed)	
	Ovorum (eggs)	
	Laurini (bay)	
	Absinthe	absinthe
	Papaveris (poppy)	opium pills
	Petroleum ("oil of Peter"—parsley)	
	Scorpionis (probably broom tips)	
	Amgidalarum dulcis (sweet almonds)	
	Amigdalarum amararum (bitter almonds)	
	Balsami naturalis (costmary)	
		Castor oil (ol. ricini)
		Olive oil
Chymical **Oyles**	Vitrioli	Blue vitriol
	Sulphuris per campanum (brimstone)	flowers of sulphur
	Gariophilorum (oil of cloves)	
	Macis (mace)	
	Philosophorum (tilestones and bricks)	British oil
	Annisæ (anise)	
	Terebinthinæ (turpentine)	
	Juniperri	

ITEM	WOODALL'S CHEST—1617	DR. KING'S CHEST—1837
Chymical Oyles *continued*	Antimonii (antimony) Succini (amber) Absinthii Origani (oregano)	Antimonial wine absinthe

Syrups	absinthii
	Limoniorum (syrup of lemons)
	Papaveris (poppy)
	Cinamomi (cinnamon)
	Rosarum simplex
	  (syrup of rose petals)
	Solutium (rosarum solutium,
	  solution of roses)
	Violarum (syrup of violets)
	Oxymell simplex (clarified honey)
	Mel rosarum (rose honey)
	Diamorum (mulberry syrup)
	Raphanæ sylvestri (horseradish)
	Prunellorum (sloes)
		salts of lemon
		
		Syrup of Squills

Conserves	Rosarum Anthos (rosemary conserve) Berberorum (barberry) Citoniorum (quince pulp) Luiule (fennel fruit) Prunellorum (conserve of sloes)	

Electuaries [Elixirs]	Diacatholicon (purging elixir)
	Diaphenicon
	  (purge made of dates)
	Diaprunum
	  (purge based on prunes)
	Conf. Hameck (witchhazel)
	Desucco Rosarum
	  (rose-juice cathartic)
	Diatrionpiperion
	  (black pepper elixir)
	
	Theriace Londini
	  ("London treacle")
	Conf. Alkermes (egg whites)
	de Ovo (eggs)
	Mithridatum Damocrites
	Theriac Andromace
	  ("Venice treacle")
	Theriac Diatesseron
	  ("Greek treacle")
		
		calomel and jalap
		
		piperion
		Mistura Adamsi:
		  "Adams's mixture"
		
		Elixir ad longam vitum
		  (tincture of aloes
		  composita)

Opiates	Laudanum paracelsi (opium, henbane, coral, hartshorn, bezoar, spices)	Laudanum (opium, saffron spices, wine)
		Ether (ethyl oxide)
		Spirits of nitre
	Diascordium (opium with garlic germander)	Opium pills
	Diacodium (meconion, poppy juice)	
	Philomum romanum (spiced opium)	paregoric
	Persicum (peppered opium)	
	Tarsensi (Turkish opiate)	
	Auria Alexandrine (opium and gold)	
		Dover's Powder
Succus [Juices]	Absinthe	absinthe
	Acatie (acacia)	Gum Arabic
	Licorice ("succus glycyrrhizzae")	
	Limoni (lemon)	salts of lemon
	Pulpa Tamarindarum (tamarind pulp)	
Pils [Pills]	Agaricum ("Pilulae Aggregatinae," with mushroom agaric)	
	Aurea (called "golden" because of the saffron)	
	Cochia (aloes, scammony, absinthe, alhandal)	
	De Euphorbia (for scurvy)	
	De Cambogia (gutta gambier, a purge)	
	Russy (myrrh, saffron, aloes)	
		Blue pill; mercury pill
		Calomel pill
Puluis Laxatus	Benedict Laxatine ("Blessed laxative," purge)	
	Arthreticus (purging powder)	Epsom salts— "Sulph. Magnes."
		Cream of Tartar
		Emetic tartar
		castor oil
Trochiseus [Pastiles]	Absinthia	absinthe
	Alhandall (pulp of *Citrullus colocynthus*, a purge)	
	De Spodio (ivory; powdered calcium carbonate)	
	De Minio (red lead)	

ITEM	WOODALL'S CHEST—1617	DR. KING'S CHEST—1837
Simples	Foliorum sena (senna leaves)	
	Rhabarbaræ	rhubarb
		Ipecac
	Agaricum (mushroom agaric)	
	Scamoniæ (scammony)	
	Hermodactils (witch aloes hazel)	
	Polipodium (Peter Podgam fern)	
	Dent Elephantis (elephant's ear plant)	
	Cornu serui (hartshorn, carbonated ammonia)	Spts. (spirits) Hartshorn
	Euphorbii	
	Turbith (a compound of sulfur and mercury)	
	Cambogia (Camboge, Garcinia gum, a purge)	
	Cassia fistula (Cassia pulp, laxative)	
	Mirabulanorum (Glauber's salt)	Glauber's salt
Certaine Other Simples	Crocus (saffron)	
	Opium	
	Chinæ (root of Smilax china)	
	Sarsaparillæ	
	Sassafras	
	Guiacum (resin of *Guaiacum officinale*)	tincture of guaiac
	Cortex guaiaca	
	Cortex granatorum (pomegranate rind)	
	Licorice	
	Hordia commune (common barley)	
	Hordia gallica (French barley)	
	Semen anisæ (anise seeds)	
	Feniculi (seeds of fennel)	
	Carraway	
	Cumini (cumin seeds)	
	Petrocelini (parsley)	
	Lini (flaxseed)	flaxseed
	Fenigrece (fenugreek)	
	Anethæ (seeds of dill)	
	Papaveris (poppy)	
	Plantaginis (plantain seed)	
	Semina quatuor frigide Majoris (four major cold seeds: cucubita, cucumber, citrullus, melon)	
	Sem: quatuor frigide minoris (four minor cold seeds: lettuce, portulaca, chicory, endive)	
	Saccacum (sugar)	

Certaine Other Simples *continued*	Amigdalarum (almonds) Una passa (currants) Amillum (starch)	
Spices	Sinamone (cinnamon) Macis (mace) Piper (pepper) Nuces Muscats (nutmegs)	piperine Cloves
Gummes	Guiace Opopanax (root of *Opopanax* sp.) Bdelium (gum from Balsamodendron sp.)	
		Balsam Copaiba

	Amoniacum (resin of Dorena
	  ammoniacum)
		linimentum ammoniatum
		  forte

	Sagapenum (resin of sagapen,
	  Ferula sp.)
	Galbanum (another Ferula—
	  asafetida—product)
	Myrrha (resin of
	  Balsamodendron myrrha)
	Masticke
	Laudanum
	Storax calamintha
	  (liquidambar resin)
	Liquida (see above)
	Benjamen (belzoin)
	Tragacanthum (Astrolagus
	  gummifer gum)
	Pix navalis (navy pitch)
	Resina (pine resin)
	Succinum (amber)
		Emplast. Roborans
		
		Myrrh
		
		Laudanum
		
		Burgundy pitch
		
		Quinine

Other Needfull Simples of Divers Kindes	Cera citrina (yellow beeswax)
	Mummia (Egyptian mummy,
	  powdered)
	Sparmaceti (spermaceti oil)
	Sanguis Draconis
	  (dragon's blood resin)
	
	Lupines (hops)
	Cantharides (Spanish fly)
	
	Camphora
	Spodium (burned ivory)
	Sumach
		Cerat. simplex
		
		kino
		
		Blister plaster (emplast
		  vesicet.)
		Camphor gum

ITEM	WOODALL'S CHEST—1617	DR. KING'S CHEST—1837
Other *continued*	Galls (oak tree galls) Bolus veræ (kaolin) Bolus comunis (clay)	
Mineralls	Antimonium or Stibium (antimony)	Antimonial wine
	Sulphur	Flowers of sulphur
	Alumen rochæ	Alum
	Vitriolum commune (copper sulfate; copperas)	Blue vitriol; copper sulfate
	Vitriolum album (zinc sulfate)	White vitriol
	Cerusa venetia (lead carbonate)	
	Plumbum Album (white lead carbonate)	
	Plumbum minium (red lead oxide)	
	Lithargum aureum (lead monoxide, white lead)	
		Sugar of lead (lead acetate; acet. plumb.)
	Viride aes (verdigris)	
	Tutia (zinc oxide)	
	Arsenicum (arsenic)	
	Argentum vivum (quicksilver)	
	Mercurius sublimatus (mercurous chloride)	calomel
	Mercurius Precipitatus (red mercuric nitrate)	
	Cinabrium (mercurous sulfide)	
	Flores Anthos (rosemary flowers)	
	Flores Balaustiarum (pomegranate flowers)	
	Rose rubea (red rose petals)	
	Flores Chamomille (chamomile flowers)	chamomile flowers
	Flores meliloti (melilot clover blossom)	
	Flores centaurus (centaury flowers)	
	Flores Hyperici (St. John's wort flowers)	
	Flores Sambuci (elder flowers)	
Baccae **[Berries]**	Juniperi Lauri (bay)	
Ferni **[Flour]**	Tritici (wheat flour) Fabarum (bean meal) Hordei (barley meal) Fursuris (wheat bran) Volatalis (mill dust)	
		maranta—arrowroot

Herbes	Rosmarinus	
Most Fit	Mentha	
to Be	Melilotum	
Carried	Salvia	
	Thimum (thyme)	
	Absinthium	absinthe
	Carduus benedictus (blessed thistle)	
	Mellissa (lemon balm)	
	Sabina (juniper)	
Radices [Roots]	Althea (hollyhock)	
	Raphana silvestris (horseradish)	
	Peritrum (pyrethrum, Spanish pellitory)	
	Angelica	
	Consolida (comfrey)	
Misc.	Calx viva (quicklime)	Chloride of lime
	Album grecum (stercus canis: dog feces)	

APPENDIX B
DR. KING'S PATIENT LIST, *AURORA*, 1840

Note: the ship was at sea throughout this accounting.
Explanatory notes are in italics; missing letters are in square brackets.

DATE	PATIENT	CONDITION	TREATMENT
Aug. 17	Gow	wound on thigh	poultice
	Wm. Folger	discharge from the ear	Tinct[ura] opi[um] & Bal[sam] (*laudanum*)
	Easton	Contraction of Spermatic cord	Lini[mentum] ammon[iatum] F[or]te (*Compound liniment of camphor with alcohol and lavender oil*)
	Henry Hinckley	Foul stomach	Sulph[as] Magnesia (Epsom salts)
	Martin	Gonorrhoea	Mist[ura] Adamsi (Adams's mixture)
Aug. 18	Jean Coroff	Testitis (*inflammation of the testicles*)	Poultice
	Gow	Vulnus (*wound*)	Turner's cerate (*calamine ointment*)
	F. G. Coffin	Gastrodynia (*gastric pain*)	Tinct. Aloes C[omposita] ("*Elixir ad Longam Vitam*") et T[inctura] Lav[andulæ Composita]

DATE	PATIENT	CONDITION	TREATMENT
Aug. 19	Gow	Vulnus	Poultice
	Wm. Thompson	Constipat[ion]	Sulph. Mag.
Aug. 20	Gow	Vulnus	Ung[uentum] Res[inæ] (*Basilicon ointment*)
	Easton	Cephalalgia (*headache*)	Sulph. Magnes.
	F. G. Coffin	Foul Stomach	Pulv. Ipecac
Aug. 21	Gow	Vulnus	Ung. Res.
	Dunham	Constipat.	Sulph. Mag.
	B. Morton	Cephalalgia	Pulv. Ipecac
Aug. 22	Gow	Vulnus	Res[inæ] Cerat[um] (*Basilicon ointment*)
	Simpson	Gastrodynia	Pulv. Ipecac
	J. Reed	do.	Vinum Antimo. (*antimonial wine*)
Aug. 25	[Capt.] J.H.H.	Gastrodynia	Cal[omel] et Jal[ap]
	J. Reed	do.	Diet
	J. Boho	ulcus (*ulcer*)	ung[uentum] Hyd[rargyri] (*mercury ointment*)
	Maitings	Gonorr.	Mist. Adam.
Aug. 26	Gow	Vulnus	Ung. Res.
	Martin	Gonorrhea	Mis. Ad.
	Steward	Gastrodynia	diet
Aug. 27	E. G. Coffin	Contusio (*bruising*)	Fomento vinegar (*bathe in warm vinegar*)
	Martin	Gonorrhea	Piperine to Mis. A. (*black pepper oil in Adams's mixture*)
	Gow	Odontalgia (*toothache*)	Gum opii
Aug. 28	Gow	Vulnus	Cerat. Simp[lex] (*simple cerate— benzoated lard with yellow wax*)
	E. G. Coffin	Contusio	Lotio Acetic (*vinegar*)

Date	Patient	Condition	Treatment
Aug. 29	Kimball	Haemorrhoids	Opii et Plumb[i] Ac[etas] (*lead acetate*)
	Gow	Vulnus	Cerat. Res.
	E. G. Coffin	Contusio	Acetic lotion
	Ben	Eruptio (boils)	Sulph. Sublim[atum]. (*flowers of sulfur*)
Aug. 30	Gow	Vulnus	Cerat. Res.
	Jean Roy	Diarrhoea	Opii
	E. G. Coffin	Contusio	Acetic lotion
Aug. 31	Gow	Vulnus	Cerat. Res.
	Jean Roy	Diarrhea	Opii
	Jean Canoff*	ulcus	Cerat. Res.
	Jean Bohe	Testitis	Cataplasm (*poultice*)
	Sylvia	Palpitatio (*palpitations*)	Empl[astrum] Rob[orans] (*compound plaster with frankincense*) & Asef[etida]
	E. G. Coffin	Contusio	Acetic lotion
Sept. 1	Jean Canoff	Testitis	S. Mag. & Cataplasm
	Jean Bohe	Ulcus	Ung. Res.
Sept. 2	Jean Bohe	Ulcus	Sulph. Mag. & Ung. Hydr.
Sept. 3	Gow	Vulnus	Cerat. Resino
	Bohe	Ulcus	Cerat. Simplex & do. at night
	Alex	[blank]	Emplast. Rob
Sept. 4	Bohe	ulcus	Simpl. Cer.
	Gow	vulnus	Sulph. Cupri (*copper sulfate*)
Sept. 5	Alex	Dysentaria	Pill Opii
	J. Canoff	Testitis	Cataplasm
	F. Sylvia	Palpitatio	Tinct. Lav. C. et opii
Sept. 6	Alex	Dysentaria	Dovers powd. & Cal.
	Bohe	Testitis	Pill opii & Catapl.
	Martin	Stricture	Pill opii

*Evidently there is a confusion between Jean Bohe and Jean Canoff in this day's entry.

DATE	PATIENT	CONDITION	TREATMENT
Sept. 7	Alex	Dysentaria	Opii & Maranta (*arrowroot*), Emplast. Vesicet. (*blistering plaster*), Pill opii
	Gow	Ven. Ulcer (venereal ulcer)	Acet. plumb
Sept. 8	Sylvia	Ischioria (*sciatica*)	Ol. Rici[ni] (*castor oil*) Tinct. Al[oes] & Cal et Jal.
	Alex	Dysenteria	Pill opii & diet
Sept. 9	Alex	Dysenteria	Pill opii
	Capt. J.H.H.	Cephalalgia &c &c &c	Hot punch
Sept. 10	Ben	Vulnus capitis (*head wound*)	Tinct. Antim. Absin[the]
Sept. 11	Ben	Vulnus capitis	Tinct. Antim. Absin.
Sept. 12	Capt. J.H.H.	Cephalalgia &c	Sulph. Mag.
Sept. 14	Capt. J.H.H.	Cephalalgia &c &c	Pill. Hyd. (*mercury*) & Sul. Mag.
Sept. 15	Capt. J.H.H.	Cephalalgia &c	Cupped him
Sept. 16	Gow	Diarrhoea	Pill Opii
Sept. 17	Martin	Testitis	Cataplasm
	Capt. J.H.H.	Cephalalgia & vigilance	Pill Opii
Sept. 18	Ben	Gastrodynia	Pill Opii
	Martin	Testitis	Cataplasm
	Sylvia	Palpitatio	Pill Opii &c
	Capt. J.H.H.	Vigilantia (*insomnia*)	Pill Opii
Sept. 19	Martin	Gonn. & testitis & stricture	Cataplasm & Mist. Adam. &c
	H. Hinckley	Bubonocea (*hernia*)	Foment. &c
	Capt. J.H.H.	Cephalalgia &c	Diet
Sept. 20	Martin	Testitis &c	Cataplasm
Sept. 22	Kimball	Haemorrhoids	Opii & Plumb.
	Folger	Gastrodynia	Tinct. Absinthe
	Martin	Testitis	Cataplasm
	Jno. Cariou	Paronychia (*abscessed fingernail*)	Cataplasm

	Capt. J.H.H.	Cephalalgia &c	Pill Hydr.
Sept. 23	Capt. J.H.H.	Cephalalgia	Mist. [?]
Sept. 24	J.H. Gardner	Vomiting &c	Pill opii
	Martin	Testitis &c.	Foment. Acetic
	Gow	Chancre & diarrhea	Sulph. Cupri

Though the diary is still kept daily, with brief notations of wind and weather, the next six entries have no medical content.

Oct. 1	F. Coffin	Odontalgia	Ext[racted tooth]
	Bill Thompson	do. yesterday	do.
	H. Hinckley	Gastrodynia	Emet[ic] Ipecac
Oct. 2	Kimball	Haemorrhoids	Fumigation
Oct. 3	Gow	Diarrhea	Pill Opii
	H. Hinckley	Gastrodynia	Pulv. Ipecac
Oct. 4	Bill Thompson	Anem [Anemia?]	Sulph. Mag.
Oct. 6	Martin	Gonorrhoea	Mist. Adams, Piperine and dose Coch[ia] Mag. (*coccia major, a cathartic*) bis dies (*twice daily*)
Oct. 9	Folger & Jack	Running from ears	British Oil (*mineral oil*)

No medical material in the next eleven entries.

Oct. 22	J. Reed	Gastrodynia	Pill opii, flour gruel, ginger tea
Oct. 25	Martin	Gonorrhoea	Piperine aqua
Oct. 30	H. Hinckley	Vulnus	Emp. Ad[hesive] et Simplex Cer.
	Cook	Ophthalmia	Acet. Plumb.

Another long gap without medical notations, though Dr. King does mention that the provisions have been reduced to salt meat and flour.

Nov. 21	Jos. H. Gardner	Bubonocele &c	Sulph. Mag.
	Charly	Secondary Venereal	do.
	Cook	ulcus maris ("*sea sores*")	cerat. Simplex
Nov. 22	Charly	Venereal Rheumato.	Pulv. Dover

Diary finishes December 1; ship arrives home December 2.

APPENDIX C
GLOSSARY

Aback To haul aback is to adjust a sail so that it sends the ship sternward. To lie aback is to adjust the sails so they are pulling against each other and the ship lies relatively still.

Abroad Spread, usually as in "all canvas abroad."

Absinthe Wormwood, *Artemisia absinthium*. A cerebral stimulant, poisonous in excess.

Acetic Lotion Vinegar.

Aft Toward the stern of the ship.

After Cabin Also known as the transom cabin; a narrow cabin set across the stern. The captain's private sitting room, furnished with a large settee, a chart table, and lockers.

After Gang Also known as the after guard. The people who live in the after quarters of the ship.

Agaric *Agaricus albus*, a species of fungus found growing on larches. Cathartic.

Aguardiente Rough liquor distilled from wine (in Spain, Portugal, and South America) or from arak (in the East Indies, where it is also known as moki). Literally "burning water," from the Spanish *agua ardiente*.

Album Graecum Dog feces, also known as Stercus Caninum. According to Woodall, grated dog feces were useful for dysentery and hemorrhoids when boiled in salad oil. The calcium content was probably the effective element. (The feces were white because the dog had been eating bones.)

Alhandall See citrullus.

Aloes Juice of *Aloe Barbadensis* or *Aloe Socotrina*, a bitter tonic and slow-acting but efficient purge. Anthelmintic when used as an enema.

Alterative Medicine that gradually changes and corrects a morbid condition.

Althea "*Radix althea* Hollihocke roots are hot and drie to the first degree," wrote Woodall. This is *Althea rosea* (used to reduce inflammation), a direct relative of the marshmallow, *Althea officinalis*—which Woodall called "dialthea." Both are members of the very useful mallow family (okra, balsa, kapok, durian, cola, and cocoa plants all belong to this order). The roots of *A. officinalis* can be boiled to make a marshmallow confection (the modern version has none of the herb). Both are emollient.

Alumen   Alum, salt of either potash (aluminium and potassium sulfate) or ammonia (ammonium and aluminium sulfate). Astringent, used as a gargle.

Amber   Oleum succini is oil of amber, the fossil exudation of various pines. Mixed with camphor and spirit of hartshorn as a liniment for whooping cough. The tincture was given in water for headaches.

Amidships   In the waist or middle part of a ship.

Ammoniacum   Gum of *Dorema ammoniacum*, a stimulant and expectorant.

Amygdala   Bitter almond (Amygdala amara) or sweet almond (Amygdala dulcis). Both fruits of different varieties of *Prunus amygdalus*. Demulcent and nutrient. The oil is used as a carrier for other medicines. Bitter almond oil ("English oil") is laxative.

Analgesic   Medicine that alleviates the sensation of pain by lessening the sensitivity of the nerves and brain. Also called an anodyne.

Anesthetic   Painkiller. A local anesthetic numbs sensation in the patch of tissue where it is applied, while a general anesthetic induces complete unconsciousness during surgery.

Angelica   *Angelica officinalis*. A decorative garden plant. Carminative, tonic, antibiotic; fish wrapped in angelica leaves keeps longer. Flavoring agent in Chartreuse liqueur.

Anise   Dried ripe fruit of *Pimpinella anisum*, aromatic and carminative; used to relieve flatulence and to diminish the griping of a purgative medicine.

Anthelmintic   Medicine that destroys intestinal worms (vermicide) or expels them from the gut (vermifuge).

Antimony   A metallic element also known as stibium or kermes, mostly used in medicine in the form of tartarated antimony, which is also known as tartar emetic. Diaphoretic, expectorant, alterative, emetic, a circulatory and nervous depressant. Useful in treating delirium tremens. Can be used in blister plasters as an alternative to cantharides.

Antipyretic   Medicine that controls and reduces temperature in fevers.

Antiscorbutic   Medicine that prevents or treats scurvy.

Antiseptic   Agent that prevents decomposition by inhibiting the growth of microorganisms.

Aperient   Laxative.

Aqua   Watery infusion of herbs, simple solution of inorganic compounds, or water-based cordial.

Aqua Fortis   Nitric acid, literally "strong water."

Aqua Vitæ   Brandy or whiskey, literally "water of life."

Arak   Native liquor fermented from coconut palm juice.

Armourer   English name for a shipboard blacksmith.

Articles   Ships' papers, signed by all hands when shipping.

Asafetida   *Ferula assafoetida*, Soothing, expectorant, diuretic, diaphoretic. Useful as an enema in cases of extreme flatulence.

Astringent   Medicine that contracts tissues, including blood vessels, checking bleeding and mucous discharge and cleansing ulcers.

Atropine   Obtained from the leaves and roots of belladonna. As an ointment, used to relieve muscular spasm and neuralgia. Atropine sulfate is used to dilate the pupil of the eye.

Balsam Copaiba   *Copaifera* species. A South American native unknown in Europe until the seventeenth century. Cathartic, diuretic, antivenereal.

Bark (naut.)   Three-masted vessel with square sails on the fore and main masts, but with fore-and-aft rigging (triangular sails) on the mizzen mast.

Barrel   A unit of measurement for oil, 31½ gallons.

Bdellium   Gum of *Balsamodendron* (see myrrh), used for plasters.

Beakhead   A small open platform forward of the forecastle, where the sailors eased their bowels while perched over holes that had been cut for this purpose. These "seats of ease" were found only on large ships.

Belladonna   Deadly nightshade. The leaves contain atropine and hyoscyamine. A poison used as a narcotic, diuretic, and diaphoretic.

Benzoin   Resin obtained from *Styrax benzoin*, the Benjamin tree. Expectorant, styptic, antiseptic, useful for severe bronchitis. The compound tincture is Friar's Balsam.

Betel   Leaves of *Piper betle*, chewed in conjunction with lime and the nut of *Areca catechu*.

Black Skin   Outer slimy coat of a whale's skin.

Blanket Piece   A long strip of blubber hoisted up from the whale.

Blessed Thistle   *Cnicus benedictus*, formerly known as *Carduus benedictus*. A thorny plant related to all the other thistles, but with large heads of yellow flowers. Used from antiquity for plague treatments and as a stimulant of the liver and of mother's milk. Tonic and diaphoretic. When steamed, the leaves can be eaten (with care).

Bloodletting   Bleeding as part of medical treatment, also known as venesection or phlebotomy. The vein is lanced, usually in the bend of the elbow, and an amount of blood released. It could also be carried out by applying bloodsucking leeches to the skin, often in the inside of the nostrils. Once considered a means of reducing the activity of the body, it is now out of fashion, save for the use of leeches in plastic surgery.

Bloody Flux   Dysentery.

Blubber Room   Space between decks above the main hold reserved for temporary storage of horse pieces during cutting in. Some cutting work goes on in here as well.

Blubber   Thick oily coat of fat on the whale, which insulates it from the cold of the depths of the sea.

Boat's Crew   Six men who crew a whaleboat, headed by an officer or a boat-header.

Boatheader   Man in charge of a whaleboat, usually one of the officers.

Boatsteerer   American name for a harpooner.

Boom   Spar to which the lower edge of a fore-and-aft sail is attached.

Bougie   A long slender instrument made of metal or whalebone, used for dilating orifices such as the urethra or rectum, or a slender stick of medicine embedded in lard or some other hard fat, which is inserted up the urethra.

Bow Boat   Boat that hangs from the forward davits on the larboard (port) side of the ship.

Brail   A small rope fastened to the lower edge of a square sail or the after edge of a fore-and-aft sail. To brail up is to clinch the sails ready for furling.

Breach   A whale's leap out of the water.

Brick-Bat   A fragment of brick, usually employed as a missile.

Bubonocele   Hernia.

Burgundy Pitch   Technically, resin from the trunk of spruces, but more often a substitute made from pine resin, turpentine, and palm oil. Used in stimulating plasters and ointments.

Burthen   Ship's carrying capacity; tonnage.

Caboose   English name for a galley, pronounced "camboose" on whalers.

Calamine   Native zinc carbonate. Mildly astringent, used in lotions, dusting powders, ointments, and plasters.

Calomel   Mercurous chloride.

Calx   Lime, calcium oxide, used as a disinfectant. Calx viva is quicklime, which is unslaked, or dry, lime.

Camphor   Resin of *Cinnamomum camphora*. Carminative, expectorant, diaphoretic, still used for the relief of hay fever and the common cold. An important ingredient in paregoric.

Cantharides   *Lytta vesicatoria* or *Cantharis vesicatoria*, a dried and crushed beetle generally known as "Spanish fly." A blistering agent. When mixed with benzoated lard, it formed an ointment which was used to keep a blister seeping.

Carminative   Medicine that disperses ("discusseth") wind and relieves colic. Also known as an aromatic.

Cassia Fistula   Pulp from the fruits of *Cassia fistula*. Laxative. Often given in combination with figs, prunes, and tamarinds as confection of senna.

Castor Oil   Oil of *Ricinus communis*. A mild, safe, and speedy cathartic.

Cataplasm   A watery (not oily) poultice.

Cat-built   A ship built with a very broad beam for its draft.

Cathartic   A purging medicine, a laxative, also known as an aperient.

Caustic   Substance that burns off skin tissue such as chancres. Also known as escharotic.

Cauterize   Seal off a wound (usually an amputation) with a red-hot iron or boiling oil or hot pitch. Can also be done chemically, e.g., with silver nitrate.

Cephalalgia   Headache.

Cera   Beeswax. Cera flava was yellow beeswax; cera alba, white beeswax, which was beeswax that had been bleached by exposure to the air. Used as a base in ointments and plasters.

Cerate   A mix of oil and wax used as a base for externally applied drugs.

Camomile   Dried flower heads of *Anthemis nobilis*, the common chamomile. Tonic and carminative, treasured from antiquity as a tea. Often added to aperient medicines as a softener or to opiates as a dilutant.

Chancre   Venereal ulcer.

Chandler   A dealer in maritime goods and provisions.

Cinnamon   Dried inner bark of *Cinnamomum zeylanicum*. A carminative, astringent stimulant, also used to flavor food.

Citrullus   Pulp of the fruit *Citrullus colocynthis*, otherwise known as colocynthis or alhandall. A powerful cathartic. Was usually prescribed in conjunction with henbane, which prevented excessive griping. Not to be given when the intestines were inflamed.

Clew   A clew or clue is a lower corner of a sail to which ropes called tacks and sheets are attached for manipulating the setting and tension of the sails. To clew up is to draw the bottom of the sail up to the yard or mast, and to clew down is to release (unfurl) a sail. Clew-garnets are used to clew up the lower square sails.

Cloves   Dried flower buds of *Eugenia caryophyllata*, Aromatic, carminative. The oil is a mild counterirritant.

Clyster   An enema, also known as a glyster.

Comfrey   *Symphytum officinale*. Woodall called the root "consolida." Emollient, used for wounds, ulcers, abscesses, both internally and externally.

Conserve   Fruits or flowers pounded up with sugar.

Convolvulus   A family of strongly twining and climbing plants commonly known as bindweeds.

Costiveness   Habitual sluggishness of the bowels.

Counterirritant   Substance that stimulates, inflames, and irritates the place where it is applied. Rubefacients cause redness and heat, while vesicants or epispastics raise blisters.

Course   The largest and lowest square sail on a mast. That on the foremast is the fore course, that on the main, the main course.

Creole   A native of Spanish America or the West Indies who is of European or mixed parentage.

Cruise   In whaling parlance, a deliberate search back and forth across the whaling ground.

Cutting Spade   Long-handled shovel with a sharp cutting edge for cutting blubber.

Cystitis   Inflammation of the bladder.

Demulcent   A substance that soothes mucous membranes, such as in the mouth and intestines.

Dessicant   A drying agent, used on seeping ulcers and wounds.

Diachylon   Basic plaster composed of lard, oil, and litharge (lead monoxide), invented by the ancients to hold medicines against the skin and prevent them from rubbing off or evaporating.

Dialthea   *Althea officinalis*. Marshmallow. See althea.

Diaphoretic   Medicine that promotes sweating.

Diet   A dietary regime, usually based on cereals and broth, with little or no meat.

Dill   The dried ripe fruit of *Anethum graveolens*. Carminative, a gentle remedy for flatulency, often prescribed with sodium bicarbonate (baking soda).

Disinfectant   Substance that destroys microorganisms.

Diuretic   Medicine that promotes the production of urine.

Dock (verb)   To crop short, e.g., a lamb's tail. Also to moor a ship in an artificial enclosure known as a dock.

Downhaul   Rope attached to an upper corner of a sail that pulls it down when shortening sail.

Dragon's Blood   A garnet-colored resin obtained from a number of plants, including the agave and the rattan palm, ground up into a powder. "Sanguis Draconis is colde and drie in the first degree, it is of an astringent quality, [and] it closeth up wounds," wrote Woodall. It was also used to make varnish for fine violins.

Dropsy   A morbid collection of fluid in the body cavities.

Dysentery   Painful inflammation of the large intestine, attended with bloody stools and fever.

Edema   An excess of fluid in the tissues.

Egg   Oleum ovorum or oil of hen eggs was a base in making up medicines, while the dried white was used as a dusting powder. The liquid white was used as an antidote in mercury poisoning.

Elder Flowers   Dried flowers of *Sambucus nigra*, used to make a tea for catarrh.

Electuary   Medicine that has been powdered and mixed with honey.

Elixir ad Longam Vitam   Tinctura aloes composita—a standby cathartic composed of aloes, gentian, rhubarb, zedoary, saffron, and alcohol.

Elixir of Vitriol   Aromatic sulfuric acid, a mixture of six parts of sulfuric acid to fifty-nine parts of alcohol, along with twenty parts of tincture of ginger and one of spirit of cinnamon. Tonic, refrigerant, astringent, useful in controlling diarrhea.

Elixir Proprietas   Tincture of aloes and myrrh, being ten parts of socotrine aloes in powder to five parts of saffron and one hundred parts of myrrh.

Embay   To anchor a vessel within a bay.

Emetic   Medicine that triggers vomiting.

Emollient   Soothing element in a lotion or unguent.

Epispastic   Plaster made of some blistering agent such as powdered cantharides.

Emplastra   Plasters; poultices applied on a cloth or leather.

Epsom Salts   Magnesium sulfate.

Ether   Ethyl oxide, prepared by the action of sulfuric acid on alcohol. Stimulant, carminative, useful in the treatment of asthma and angina. Æther purificatus was the version employed for general anesthesia.

Euphorbia   Resinous juice of *Euphorbia* species, a powerful irritant and vesicant.

Expectorant   Medicine that helps to shift mucus from the breathing passages.

Fast (whaling)   A "fast" boat is fastened to a live whale by a harpoon and a whaleline.

Fasten   To harpoon a whale successfully.

Febrifuge   Medicine that cools fevers, also known as antipyretic.

Ferni   Flour, ground meal.

Flaxseed   Linseed, the dried ripe seeds of *Linum* species. Demulcent, used for bronchitis, dysentery, and diarrhea. Also makes a soothing poultice.

Flense   Cut the blubber from a whale.

Flip   Beer that has been sweetened with sugar and molasses, strengthened with spirits, and heated with a hot poker.

Flukes   Horizontal tail of a whale.

Flurry   Whale's death throes.

Fomentation   Bathing with warm water, vinegar, or medicated lotions.

Forecastle   The sleeping quarters of the common seamen, in the bows of the ship.

Foremast   The mast closest to the bow of a ship.

Foresheet   A rope attached to a lower corner of the fore course.

Forward   Toward the bow of the ship.

Forward Cabin   Cabin in the after quarters of a whaleship that is forward of the captain's after cabin, and is often known as the saloon. Lit by a skylight, it is the messroom for the officers and captain, furnished with a large table built about the foot of the mizzen mast, a chair for the captain at the head, and benches along both sides. The doors to the pantry and the officers' staterooms lead off this cabin.

Frankincense   Resin of *Boswellia carteri*, an Arabian and African tree. Used in incense, and to make a tonic plaster.

Funnel   Chimney.

Futtock Shrouds   Ropes or rods that secure rigging of the topmast to the lower mast.

Galbanum   Gum of one of the *Ferula* species. See asafetida.

Galley   Cook room of a ship.

Gally   To alarm and frighten off a whale.

Gastrodynia   Pains in the stomach.

Ginger   Zingiber, the scraped dried root of *Zingiber officinale*. A kitchen spice; aromatic and carminative.

Glauber's Salts   Hydrated sodium sulfate, an aperient.

Glyster   Also known as a clyster. An enema.

Guaiacum   Resin obtained from the stem of *Guaiacum officinale*. Generally prescribed in combination with other medicines for chronic rheumatism, gout, and syphilis. The wood is known as lignum vitae.

Gum Arabic   Gum from various acacias, used in medicine and candy.

Gummes   Resins from various shrubs and trees.

Gunwale   The uppermost plank in the side of a whaleboat.

Haul   To pull. To haul on an oar is to row; to haul on a rope is to pull on it. When a yard was hauled, it was pulled around.

Heave   Active verb used frequently by seamen to indicate throwing objects away, as well as hauling on ropes. The past tense is "hove." A ship "hove-down" is hauled over on one side so that work can be carried out on the bottom of the hull.

Hemorrhoids   Varicose veins of the anus, commonly called piles.

Henbane   Leaves of *Hyoscyamus niger*. Sedative, used in insomnia when opium is not advisable. Employed to diminish pain and to prevent the griping of drastic purges, but to be used with great caution.

Hold   Cargo space of a ship, called "hole" in old whalers.

Honey   Known to Woodall as Mel depuratum, or oxymel. Honey melted in a water bath and strained while hot. Demulcent, laxative, and nutritive, relieves coughs.

Horse Piece   A large chunk of blubber cut from a blanket piece.

Horseradish   Woodall called this *Raphana sylvestris*, and King would have known it as *Cochlearia armoracia*, but it is known now as *Armoracia rusticana*. Tonic, diuretic, diaphoretic, can also be grated into a poultice for boils. A condiment with roast beef.

Hypnotic   Medicine that induces sleep, also known as a soporific.

Ipecac   Dried root of a plant variously called *Cephaelis ipecacuanha* or *Psychotria ipecacuanha*. Expectorant, diaphoretic, increases secretion of bile, slow-acting emetic. Used in croup, whooping cough, and bronchitis to expel phlegm. Prescribed for dysentery in conjunction with opium (Dover's powders). For bronchitis, often prescribed in combination with syrup of squills.

Jalap   Dried tubers of *Ipomoea purga*. Cathartic.

Jib   A triangular sail attached to the bowsprit.

Juniper   Woodall's "sabina," the leaves of *Juniperus sabina*. Stimulating, aperient, diuretic, a vermifuge.

Kaolin   Woodall's Bolis veris. Native aluminum silicate, forming a fine white clay. A base for pills, particularly of metallic salts. Also a treatment for diarrhea.

King's Evil   Scrofula (tuberculosis of the lymph nodes).

Kino   Juice taken from incisions in the trunk of *Pterocarpus marsupium*, evaporated to dryness. A powerful astringent, it is employed in cases of obstinate diarrhea.

Kumara   The sweet potato of New Zealand, a member of the Convolvulus family.

Larboard boat   Boat that hangs from davits on the port quarter.

Larboard   Old name for port side of a ship.

Lavender   The common garden herb, *Lavendula* species. The oil is an aromatic gastric stimulant and carminative, useful in flatulence and colic. When one part of oil of lavender is mixed with ten of alcohol, spirit of lavender is obtained, a drop of which is administered on a cube of sugar. Tinctura Lavandulæ Composita, compound tincture of lavender, is made up of oil of lavender, oil of rosemary, cinnamon bark, nutmeg, and alcohol.

Laxative   Medicine that assists intestinal evacuation, also known as a cathartic. There are three grades according to strength of action: aperient (gentlest), purgative, and drastic.

Lay   Whaleman's share of the profits of the voyage.

Ligature   Thread used to tie off blood vessels during surgery.

Line-Tub   A shallow tub containing a very neatly coiled whaleline, which is attached to the harpoon and should run out smoothly as the harpooned whale runs off or sounds.

Liniment   Medicine rubbed onto the skin to relieve sore muscles and joints.

Litharge   Lead monoxide; "white lead."

Lumbricus   Earthworm, for centuries an ingredient in medicine, such as in Woodall's Oleum Lumbricorum. The live earthworms were boiled in wine or vinegar to make a decoction.

Mainmast   Ship's principal mast, the center one in a three-masted ship.

Manna   Resin of the flowering ash, *Fraxinus* species. A mild laxative.

Manuka   The "tea tree" of Australia and New Zealand, noted for its masses of small white flowers and small leaves from which tea can be made; *Leptospermum* species.

Maranta   Arrowroot, a starch derived from the tubers of a tropical American and West Indies plant, *Maranta arundinacea*. As a demulcent, it is useful in the treatment of dysentery. The powder is mixed with a little cold milk, and then boiling milk added to make a glutinous porridge.

Materia Medica   Substances employed in the dispensing of medicine.

Melilot   Sweet or "plaster clover," *Melilotus officinalis*. Emollient, used in enemas and cataplasms.

Melissa   Lemon balm, *Melissa officinalis*, called thus because it attracts bees. Drunk as a tea, an ingredient in the famous Carmelite water prescribed for headaches, the flavoring agent in Benedictine liqueur. Excellent for garnishing fish. Tranquilizing, diaphoretic.

Mint   *Mentha* species. *M. spicata* is spearmint, *M. pulegium* is pennyroyal, *M. x piperita* is peppermint, of which the extract is menthol. All are spreading, very fragrant herbs. Soothing, diaphoretic, carminative, antiseptic. *M. spicata* makes mint sauce, and *M. pulegium* is an insect repellent. Victorians soaked strings in pennyroyal tea to be tied about their cats' and dogs' necks as a kind of flea collar.

Mistura   Mixture.

Mizzen   Aftermost mast of a three-masted ship.

Myrrh   Resin of *Balsamodendron myrrha*, also known as *Commiphora myrrha* or *C. abyssinica*.

Narcotic   Drug that affects the brain, either soothing or stimulating.

Nore   A sandbank in the Thames estuary recognized as an arrival point for ships coming in to London.

Nutmeg   Dried seed of *Myristica fragrans*. Aromatic and carminative, usually used to flavor medicines. Poisonous in excess.

Odontalgia   Toothache.

Olive Oil   Oil expressed from fruit of *Olea europea*. Laxative in itself, but mostly used as a lubricant in ointments, lotions, and enemas.

Opiate   Medicine that contains some form of opium; narcotic, soporific.

Opodeldoc   A liniment made of ten parts of soft soap to nine parts of camphor, two parts of oil of rosemary, one part of oil of thyme, and four parts of liquid ammonia, dissolved in a hundred parts of eighty-proof alcohol. A rubefacient counterirritant, useful in sprains, rheumatic pains, and joint stiffness.

Opthalmia   Inflamed eyes.

Orlop   Lowest deck of a large ship, immediately above the hold.

Papula   Pimple on the skin.

Paregoric   Compound tincture of camphor, containing opium, benzoic acid, camphor, oil of anise, and alcohol.

Pepper   Dried unripe fruit of black pepper, *Piper nigrum*. Carminative and a condiment, useful in hemorrhoids and urethritis. The alkaloid is piperine.

Pharmacopoeia   A book describing drugs, chemicals, and medicinal preparations, issued by an officially recognized authority (usually under the name of the city where it was published), and serving as a standard; updated annually.

Pill   Woodall's pilule, a convenient and portable form of medicine invented by the ancients. The medicine is molded into a small mass and held together with some excipient such as kaolin, glucose, egg white, or tragacanth gum. Then the pill is finished by being rolled in a powder or varnished.

Pitch   Pine tar, also known as naval tar or Stockholm tar. Taken internally or inhaled for bronchitis; makes an ointment for eczema.

Polypharmacology   The art of concocting complicated potions, often in a ritualistic procedure, such as in the manufacture of the various theriacs.

Polypodium   Peter Podgam fern, *Polypodium vulgare.* The grated root was an astringent purge.

Poop   On large ships, a deck above the quarterdeck.

Poppy   Oleum papaveris, or oil of poppies, was extracted from the nearly ripe dried fruits of the opium poppy. Similar in effect to opium, but very much weaker. Could be used as a soothing fomentation. Red poppy petals (of a different species) were used as a coloring agent.

Prau   More accurately spelled proa, but known to the South Seamen as prau or prow. An East Indies vessel that is long and narrow, usually with an outrigger, propelled by oars and a large lateen sail that is triangular or quadrilateral in shape. Very fast and thus admirably suited for piracy.

Press-Gang   A group of men, led by an officer, who forcibly compel men to join the navy.

Prolapse   A falling down of a part of the body from its normal position, especially the rectum.

Pyrethrum   Roots of Spanish pellitory, *Anacyclus pyrethrum,* chewed to mitigate toothache. (*Chrysanthemum cinerariaefolium,* commonly known as the painted daisy, is the source of the insecticide.)

Quarterdeck   The part of the deck between the mizzen mast and the stern from where the captain or officer in charge issues sailing directions and commands the ship.

Raise   To raise whales or raise land is to sight and announce them.

Rate   A seaman's rank. To disrate an officer is to demote him.

Recruit   To restore the stock of fresh water and provisions; can be used in the context of "recruiting" one's health or men for the crew.

Refrigerant   Drink that allays a feverish thirst.

Rhubarb   *Rheum officinale,* otherwise known as Chinese rhubarb. Grown in China and the Middle East; a laxative and stringent.

Right whale   Whale of the order Mysticeti or baleen whales, having baleen (whalebone) instead of teeth. Hunted in sub-Arctic and sub-Antarctic waters.

Rose   Used throughout history for perfuming and coloring medications. Slightly astringent, so makes a good gargle. Damascene roses were the most highly prized.

Rosemary   *Rosemarinus officinalis,* the familiar garden shrub. Tonic, stimulating, an excellent liniment and a very good antiseptic gargle. Also a flavoring herb for lamb and goat.

Saffron   Dried stigmas of the flowers of *Crocus sativus.* Used for color and flavor.

Sagapenum   Gum of one of the *Ferula* species (see Asafetida). Stimulant and expectorant.

Sage   *Salvia officinalis.* Aromatic, astringent, carminative, tonic. The leaves can be eaten, or made into a tea or added to wine.

Saint John's Wort   Herbal extract of *Hipericum perforatum,* often mixed with olive oil to produce a blood-red dye. Antibiotic; applied for relief of sprains and bruises and sciatica.

Salts of Lemon Citric acid. Refrigerant, relieves thirst in fevers. Useless in the treatment of scurvy, which is caused by a lack of ascorbic acid.

Sarsaparilla Dried root of *Smilax ornata*, one of the lily family. Alterative and tonic, prescribed for secondary syphilis.

Sassafras Dried root of *Sassafras officinale*. Aromatic, carminative, used in conjunction with other medicines.

Scammony Resin of *Convolvulus scammonia*. A brisk cathartic and anthelmintic.

Scrimshaw Folk art of the whalemen, achieved by etching pictures onto pieces of ivory or whalebone, or carving bone into curios.

Sedative Medicine that soothes by diminishing pain and relaxing the muscles.

Senna Dried leaflets of *Cassia acutifolia* or *Cassia augustifolia*. A purgative that is an efficient remedy for constipation.

Sheet (naut.) A rope attached to a lower corner (clew) of a sail, used to change the setting of the canvas and regulate its tension.

Shipkeeper The person who looks after a ship in the absence of the captain.

Simple Ingredient for medicine, usually herbal.

Sloe Fruit of blackthorn, a small wild plum, *Prunus sylvestris*. Prescribed for diarrhea, and "to comfort a weake stomake."

Snakeroot Dried roots of *Aristolochia serpentaria*, Virginian snakeroot. A stimulant for the stomach.

Soporific Medicine that induces sleep, also known as a hypnotic.

Spanker Boom Boom to which the lower edge of the spanker sail—the large fore-and-aft sail on the mizzen mast—is attached.

Spermaceti Sperm whale oil taken from the head, odorless, translucent, pearly and bland. A base in ointments, being emollient.

Sperm whale More correctly known as the spermaceti whale, *Physeter macrocephalis* or *P. catodon*. A toothed whale with a large cavity in the head containing fine spermaceti oil. Hunted in tropical and temperate waters.

Squill Dried bulb of the sea onion, *Scilla maritima*, otherwise known as *Urginea scilla*. Expectorant, diuretic, and a tonic for the heart, rather like digitalis.

Starboard Boat Boat that hangs from davits on the starboard quarter, traditionally the captain's.

Stays (naut.) Strong ropes that support a mast. Stays that run forward are forestays, and those that run sternward are backstays. A ship is in stays when her bow points to the eye (source) of the wind during the tacking procedure.

Stimulant Medicine that increases the function of a part.

Stomachic Medicine that strengthens the stomach, improving appetite and digestion.

Styptic   Substance that stops bleeding.

Styrax   Storax, the gum of liquidambar trees. Made into an antiseptic ointment with yellow wax and turpentine.

Succus   Juice extracted from fresh herbs. A method of preserving herb juices with alcohol was not introduced until 1835.

Sugar   Used to sweeten and preserve medicines.

Sugar of Lead   Lead acetate, an anti-inflammatory.

Sweet Oil   Olive oil.

Tack (verb)   To work the ship into a new course by turning her bow through the eye of the wind. When on the starboard tack, the wind comes from the starboard side. Also the name of the rope holding down the weather (windward) corner of a sail.

Tamarind   Pulp of *Tamarindus indica*, a West Indian tree. A refrigerant drink, slightly laxative.

Tartar Emetic   Tartarated antimony. Diaphoretic, expectorant, alterative, emetic, also a nervous depressant.

Tenaculuim   A fine hook used to pluck up arteries and so on during surgery.

Terebintha   Turpentine, extracted from various conifers. Antiseptic, expectorant, diuretic, anthelmintic. Used in liniments.

Thyme   *Thymus vulgaris*. Common thyme. Aromatic, analgesic, good for toothache, and an excellent gargle (is an ingredient in Listerine).

Tincture   A solution of medicine in alcohol.

Tonic   Medicine that imparts strength or tone to the parts of the body and their functions.

Topgallant Crosstrees   Horizontal wooden bars between the topmast and topgallant mast which provide a perch for the lookout.

Tragacanth   Gum of *Astralagus gummifer*. Demulcent, used as a pill excipient.

Trochiscus   Lozenges made of a base of acacia gum or rosewater with finely powdered sugar. Plural trochisci.

Trysail   A triangular or quadrilateral (fore-and-aft) sail.

Unguentum   Ointment. Plural unguenta.

Urethra   The duct leading from the bladder to the exterior; in males passing through the penis.

Urethritis   Inflammation of the urethra.

Verdigris   Various copper acetates, green in color, obtained by dipping strips of copper in wine lees, used to stimulate foul and indolent ulcers. Very poisonous but used as a food coloring until recent times.

Vermicide   Medication that kills intestinal worms.

Vermifuge   Expels worms from the gut.

Vesicant   A blistering agent.

Vitriol   Sulfuric acid, also known as coperas or copperas.

Waist Boat   Amidships boat on the port side.

Warp (naut.)   A light rope leading from a lance. It is used by the harpooner to snatch back the lance, ready for another thrust. As a verb, to work a ship out of an anchorage by taking an anchor out to its full extent in a boat, dropping it, and then "warping" or pulling the ship up to the anchor by working the windlass. A boat warp tethers a small boat to a mooring. Also the distortion of timbers due to weathering.

Whaleline   Rope leading from the line-tub to the harpoon.

Windlass   A mechanism in the bows of a ship that can be turned on a horizontal axis by men hauling down on handles, used to wind up the chain and weigh the anchor. On large men-of-war the capstan, which is worked on a vertical axis by men walking around it, performs the same function.

Yard   A spar that crosses a mast, from which a sail is slung.

BIBLIOGRAPHY

Adamson, Peter. *The Great Whale to Snare: The Whaling Trade of Hull.* Kingston Upon Hull: City of Kingston upon Hull Museums and Art Galleries, n.d.

Alsop, J. D. "Sea Surgeons, Health and England's Maritime Expansion: The West African Trade 1553–1660." *The Mariner's Mirror* 76:3. August 1990, 215–221.

Ambler, Eric. *The Ability to Kill.* New York: Curtis Publishing, 1956.

Anon. ("A Captain in the Royal Navy.") *Observations and Instructions for the Use of the Commissioned, the Junior and Other Officers of the Royal Navy....* London: P. Steel, 1804.

Ashley, Clifford W. *The Yankee Whaler.* Garden City, NY: Halcyon House, 1942. Reprint of 1926 edition.

Ashley, Raymond. "Scurvy—Scourge of Long Voyages at Sea." *No Quarter Given* 6:5. September 1999, 4–5.

Bateson, Charles. *The Convict Ships 1787–1868.* Wellington, NZ: A.H. & A.W. Reed, 1959.

Beale, Thomas. *The Natural History of the Sperm Whale....* London: Jan van Voorst, 1839. Repr. London: Holland Press, 1973.

Bennett, Frederick Debell. *Narrative of a Whaling Voyage Round the Globe....* London: Richard Bentley, 1840. Repr. New York: Da Capo Press, 1970.

Bockstoce, John R. *Whales, Ice, and Men: The History of Whaling in the Western Arctic.* Seattle: University of Washington Press, in association with the New Bedford Whaling Museum, 1986.

Booth, Martin. *Opium—A History.* London: Simon & Schuster, 1996.

Botkin, B. A. A. *A Treasury of New England Folklore.* New York: Brown, 1937.

Brewster, Mary. *"She Was a Sister Sailor": Mary Brewster's Whaling Journals 1845–1851.* Edited by Joan Druett. Mystic, CT: Mystic Seaport Museum, 1992.

Brown, Ivor. *A Book of England.* London: Collins, 1958.

Busch, Briton Cooper. *Whaling Will Never Do for Me: The American Whaleman in the Nineteenth Century.* Lexington, KY: University Press of Kentucky, 1994.

Camp, John. *The Healer's Art: The Doctor through History.* London: Frederick Muller, 1978.

Chase, Dr. *Doctor Chase's Receipt Book & Household Physician.* Detroit: F. B. Dickerson, 1887.

Cobbett, William. *Rural Rides.* London, 1830.

Colby, Barnard L. *For Oil and Buggy Whips: Whaling Captains of New London County, Connecticut.* Mystic, CT: Mystic Seaport Museum, 1990.

Coulter, John. *Adventures in the Pacific.* . . . Dublin: William Curry Jr. & Co., 1845.

———. *Adventures on the Western Coast of South America.* . . . London: Longman, Brown, Green and Longmans, 1847.

Dalton, William (edited and annotated by Niel Gunson). *The Dalton Journal: Two Whaling Voyages to the South Seas 1823–1829.* Canberra: National Library of Australia, 1990. Original in the collection of the National Library of Australia.

Daniel, Mike. "The French Pox," and "Blackbeard's Blockade of Charleston: Or How Syphilis Might Have Brought About the End of the Golden Age of Piracy." *No Quarter Given* 6:5. September 1999, 10–11.

Davis, William M. *Nimrod of the Sea, or, The American Whaleman.* New York: Harper & Bros., 1874.

Denman, Thomas. "Memoir of my own Life, written in 1779," and "Continuaton" of that memoir by B. (Denman's son-in-law, Matthew Baillie). Pages lvi–lxxix of *An Introduction to the Practice of Midwifery.* London: E. Cox, 1832. Seventh edition. This fascinating memoir is an account of Denman's service with the British Navy from 1755 to 1777 and the story of his private practice in London. It formed the basis of a series of journals kept by "John Knyveton" that were "transcribed" and "edited" by Ernest A. Gray, and published in three volumes (q.v.). While fictional, the journals are a tribute both to Denman's interesting career and Gray's imagination and sense of eighteenth century style.

Directory to Lewes [Sussex]. 1812.

Dover, Thomas. *The Ancient Physician's Legacy to his Country.* London, 1732.

Dow, George Francis. *Whaleships and Whaling: A Pictorial History.* Salem, MA: Marine Research Society, 1925.

Druett, Joan. "Rough Medicine: Doctoring the Whalemen." *The Dukes County Intelligencer* 30:2. Nov. 1988, 3–15.

———. "Vineyarders Catch the 1849 Gold Bug." *The Dukes County Intelligencer* 31:1. August 1989, 3–19.

———. *Exotic Intruders: The Introduction of Plants and Animals into New Zealand.* Auckland, NZ: 1983.

———. *Petticoat Whalers: Whaling Wives at Sea 1820–1920.* Auckland, NZ: William Collins, 1991.

Ellman, Edward Boys. *Recollections of a Sussex Parson.* London: Skeffington & Son, 1912.

Estes, J. Worth. "Stephen Maturin and Naval Medicine in the Age of Sail." *A Sea of Words: A Lexicon and Companion for Patrick O'Brian's Seafaring Tales.* Edited by Dean King with John B. Hattendorf and J. Worth Estes. New York: Henry Holt, 1995, 37–56.

———. *Dictionary of Protopharmacology: Therapeutic Practices, 1700–1850.* Canton, MA: Science History Publications, 1990.

———. *Naval Surgeon: Life and Death at Sea in the Age of Sail.* Canton, MA: Science History Publications, 1998.

Fernández-Armesto, Felipe. *Columbus and the Conquest of the Impossible.* New York: Saturday Review Press, 1974.

Forster, Honore. "British Whaling Surgeons in the South Seas, 1823–1843." *The Mariner's Mirror* 74:4. November 1988, 401–15.

———. *The South Sea Whaler: An Annotated Bibliography of Published Historical, Literary and Art Material Relating to Whaling in the Pacific Ocean in the Nineteenth Century.* Sharon, MA: The Kendall Whaling Museum with Edward J. Lefkowicz Inc. of Fairhaven, MA, 1985.

———. *More South Sea Whaling: A Supplement to The South Sea Whaler....* Canberra: Division of Pacific and Asian History, Research School of Pacific Studies, The Australian National University, 1991.

———. "Melville and the Whaling Doctors." *Melville Society Extracts* 85. May 1991, 6–9.

———, ed. *The Cruise of the "Gypsy"—The Journal of John Wilson, Surgeon on a Whaling Voyage to the Pacific Ocean 1839–1843.* Fairfield, WA: Ye Galleon Press, 1991.

———. "The Mariana Islands, 1830–1831: From the Journal of John Lyell on the Whaleship *Ranger*." *ISLA: A Journal of Micronesian Studies* 1:2. Dry Season, 1992, 355–87.

Gordon, Eleanora C. "Sailors' Physicians: Medical Guides for Merchant Ships and Whalers, 1774–1864." *Journal of the History of Medicine and Allied Sciences* 48. April 1993, 139–156.

Gordon, Richard. *The Alarming History of Medicine.* London: Sinclair-Stevenson, 1993.

Gray, Ernest A. *The Diary of a Surgeon in the Years 1751–1752 By John Knyveton, Licentiate of the Society of Apothecaries; Doctor of Medicine of the University of Aberdeen; Teacher of Midwifery to & Man Midwife in Infirmary Hall; Surgeon's Mate, H.M.S.* Lancaster. *Edited & Transcribed by Ernest Gray.* New York: D. Appleton-Century, 1937. Fiction, but based on the memoir of Thomas Denman, MD (q.v.).

———. *Surgeon's Mate, the Diary of John Knyveton, Surgeon in the British Fleet during the Seven Years War 1756–1762, edited and transcribed by Ernest Gray.* London: Robert Hale, 1942. See above.

Greer, Richard A. "Honolulu in 1847." *Hawaiian Journal of History* 4. 1970, 59–95.

Gunson, Niel, ed. *The Dalton Journal—Two Whaling Voyages to the South Seas 1823–1829.* Canberra: National Library of Australia, 1990.

Guttridge, Leonard, with J. D. Smith. *The Commodores: The Drama of a Navy Under Sail.* London: Peter Davies, 1970.

Hegarty, Reginald. *The Rope's End.* Boston: Houghton-Mifflin, 1965.

Hochwald, Susan Kirp. "What Was Good for What Ailed You: Curatives and Remedies in the 1800s." *Historic Nantucket,* Fall 1998, 15–19.

Hohman, E. P. *The American Whaleman.* New York: Longmans, Green, & Co., 1928.

Jameson, John Franklin. *Privateering and Piracy in the Colonial Period, Illustrative Documents.* New York: Macmillan, 1923.

Janos, Elisabeth. *Country Folk Medicine: Tales of Skunk Oil, Sassafras Tea, and Other Old-Time Remedies.* New York: Galahad Books, 1995.

Jones, A. G. E. *Ships Employed in the South Seas Trade 1775–1861 (Parts I and II) and Register General of Shipping and Seamen Transcripts of Registers of Shipping 1787–1862 (Part III).* Canberra: Roebuck Series No. 36, 1986.

———. Volume 2. *Ships Employed in the South Seas Trade 1775–1859 (Part I), Admiralty Protections from Impressment 1777–1811 (Part II), Aspects of the South Seas Trade (Part III).* Canberra: Roebuck Series No. 46, n.d.

Keevil, J. J., with Christopher Lloyd and Jack L. S. Coulter. *Medicine and the Navy: 1200–1900.* Four volumes. Edinburgh: E. & S. Livingston, 1957–1963.

Kowalchik, Claire, and William H. Hylton, eds. *Rodale's Illustrated Encyclopedia of Herbs.* Emmaus, PA: Rodale Press, 1987.

Lipman, Arthur, with George E. Osborne. "Medicine and Pharmacy Aboard New England Whaleships, I: The Captain, an Apothecary-surgeon at sea." *Pharmacy in History* II. Nov. 1969, 119–131.

Martin, Kenneth R. *Delaware Goes Whaling 1833–1845.* Greenville, DE: The Hagley Museum, 1974.

Mayhew, Henry. *Mayhew's London: Being Selections from "London*

Labour and the London Poor" by Henry Mayhew [first published in *1851*]. Edited by Peter Quennell. London: Spring Books, n.d.

Mitchell, Ron, with David Gould. *East Grinstead—Then & Now*. Midhurst, Sussex: Middleton Press, 1985.

Morton, Harry. *The Wind Commands: Sailors and Sailing Ships in the Pacific*. Vancouver: University of British Columbia, 1975.

Murray, Dian H. "Chinese Pirates." *Pirates: Terror on the High Seas— from the Caribbean to the South China Sea*. Edited by David Cordingly. North Dighton, MA: JG Press, 1998.

Nicholson, Ian Hawkins. *Shipping Arrivals and Departures, Sydney, Volume 2, 1826–1840*. Canberra: Roebuck Series No. 23, 1977.

Oehler, Helen Irving. "Nantucket to the Golden Gate in 1849, From Letters in the Winslow Collection Transcribed, with Foreword." *California Historical Society Quarterly* 29. March 1950, 1–18.

Parish, Rev. W. D. *A Dictionary of the Sussex Dialect and Collection of Provincialisms in use in the County of Sussex*. Foreword by Francis W. Steer. Augmented and expanded by Helena Hall. Bexhill-on-Sea, Sussex: Gardner's, 1957. First published 1875.

Perkins, Edward T. *Na motu, or, Reef-Rovings in the South Seas*. . . . New York: Pudney & Russell, J. H. Colton & Co., 1854. (Probably fiction.)

Pyle, Dorothy. "The Intriguing Seaman's Hospital." *Hawaiian Journal of History* 8. 1974, 121–135.

Richardson, J. R. *The Local Historian's Encyclopaedia*. Lewes, Sussex, 1974.

Riggs, Dionis Coffin. *From Off-Island*. New York: Whittlesey, 1940.

Ross, W. Gillies. *Arctic Whalers, Icy Seas: Narratives of the Davis Strait Whale Fishery*. Toronto: Irwin Publishing, 1985.

Schmitt, Frederick P. *Mark Well the Whale!—Long Island Ships to Distant Seas*. Cold Spring Harbor, NY: Whaling Museum Society, 1986.

Selinger, Gail. "Dr. John Tweedy's Bill of Medicines, Newport, Novr. 8th, 1743, for the Privateer Sleep *Revenge* gathered before her next voyage." *No Quarter Given* 6:5. September 1999, 6.

Sherman, Stuart C. *Whaling Logbooks and Journals 1613–1927: An Inventory of Manuscript Records in Public Collections*. Originally compiled by Stuart Sherman, revised and edited by Judith M. Downey and Virginia M. Adams. New York: Garland Publishing, 1986.

Smith, Charles Edward. *From the Deep of the Sea*. Diary of surgeon on *Diana* of Hull. Edinburgh: Paul Harris, 1977.

Smith, Richard Dean. "The Herb-Doctor and Mineral-Doctor in *The Confidence Man*." *Melville Society Extracts* 85, May 1991, 9–11.

Smollett, Tobias. *The Adventures of Roderick Random*. Edited, introduced, and annotated by Paul-Gabriel Boucé. New York: Oxford University Press, 1981.

Spence, Bill. *Harpooned: The Story of Whaling*. New York: Crescent Books, 1980.

Squire, Peter Wyatt. *Squire's Companion to the Latest Edition of the British Pharmacopoeia*. (18th edition.) London: J. & A. Churchill, 1908.

Stackpole, Edouard. *The Sea-Hunters: The New England Whalemen During Two Centuries, 1635–1835*. New York: Lippincott, 1953.

Starbuck, Alexander. *History of the American Whale Fishery*. Secaucus, NJ: Castle Books, 1989. Facsimile of the 1876 edition.

Sussex Record Society. *The Town Book of Lewes 1702–1837*. Lewes, Barbican House: Sussex Record Society, volume 69, n.d. [1972].

Thrower, Dr. W. R. *Life at Sea in the Age of Sail*. London: Phillimore, 1972.

Tomes, William H. *The Whaleman's Adventures in the Sandwich Islands and California*. Boston: Lee & Shepard, 1876.

Troup, James A., ed. *The Ice-Bound Whalers: The Story of the* Dee *and the* Grenville Bay*, 1836–37*. Stromness: The Orkney Press, in association with Stromness Museum, 1987.

Turner, E. S. *Call the Doctor: A Social History of Medical Men*. London: Michael Joseph, 1958.

Turner, Eunice. "Naval Medical Service, 1793–1815." *The Mariner's Mirror* 46, June 1960, 119–33.

Tyrwhitt-Brooks, J., MD. *Four Months Among the Gold-finders in Alta California*. London: David Bogue, 1849.

Vogel, Karl. "Medicine at Sea in the Days of Sail." *Milestones in Medicine*. New York: Appleton-Century, 1938.

Wace, Nigel, with Mrs. Bessie Lovett. *Yankee Maritime Activities and the Early History of Australia*. Canberra: Research School of Pacific Studies, The Australian National University, 1973.

Watt, James. "Surgeons of the *Mary Rose*: The Practice of Surgery in Tudor England." *The Mariner's Mirror* 69:1. February 1983, 5–10.

Weinred, Ben, with Christopher Hibbert. *The London Encyclopaedia*. London: Macmillan, 1983.

West, Janet, with R. H. Barnes. "Scrimshaw by William Lewis Roderick: A Whale Bone Plaque Dated 1858 showing the Barque *Adventure* of London Whaling off Flores and Pulau Komba in the Indian Ocean." *The Mariner's Mirror* 76:2, May 1990, 135–48.

Whitebrook, Robert Ballard. *Coastal Exploration of Washington*. Palo Alto, CA: Pacific Books, 1959.

Wilbur, C. Keith. *Revolutionary Medicine 1700–1800*. Chester, CT: The Globe Pequot Press, 1980.

Wilson, John. *The Cruise of the "Gipsy": The Journal of John Wilson, Surgeon on a Whaling Voyage to the Pacific Ocean 1839–1843*. Edited by

Honore Forster. Fairfield, WA: Ye Galleon Press, 1990. Original in the collection of the Royal Geographical Society, London.

Woodall, John. *The Surgions Mate* Facsimile of the book published in 1617, introduced and with an appendix by John Kirkup. Bath, England: Kingsmead Press, 1978.

UNPUBLISHED RESOURCE MATERIAL

Almy, Almira. Journal kept on *Cape Horn Pigeon* of Dartmouth, MA, 1854–1855. Nicholson Whaling Room, Providence Public Library.

Anon., logbook kept on *Perry* of Edgartown, MA, 1877. The Kendall Whaling Museum, Sharon, MA.

Anon., logbook kept on *Vesper* of New London, 1857. Old Dartmouth Historical Society–New Bedford Whaling Museum.

Brown, Dr. James. Journal kept on *Japan* of London, 15 December 1834 to 5 July 1837. Old Dartmouth Historical Society–New Bedford Whaling Museum.

Chase, Capt. Josiah, logbook kept on *Hunter* of New Bedford, 1868. The Kendall Whaling Museum, Sharon, MA.

Chatwin, Dale. "The *Vigilant* Journal: A British Whaling Ship Voyage in Indonesian Waters and the Pacific, 1831–1833." Thesis, Australian National University, 1990.

Deblois, Captain John. Correspondence. Newport Historical Society.

Fisher, Captain Elisha. Journal kept on *Trident* of New Bedford, 1862–1863. G. W. Blunt White Library, Mystic Seaport Museum.

Fysh, Eldred E. Journal kept on *Coronet* of London, May 30, 1837, to April 1839. Nantucket Historical Association.

Gibbs, Almira. Journal kept on *Nantucket* of Nantucket, 1855–1859. Nantucket Atheneum.

Hackler, Rhoda Elizabeth. "Our Men in the Pacific: A Chronicle of United States Consular Officers at Seven Ports in the Pacific Islands and Australasia During the Nineteenth Century." Doctoral thesis, University of Hawaii, 1978.

Harlow, John J. Journal kept on *Zone* of Fairhaven, MA, 1858. Nantucket Historical Association.

Haviland, J. E. Journal kept on *Baltic* of New Bedford, 1856–1858. Nicholson Whaling Room, Providence Public Library.

Hodgkinson, Dr. Samuel. Journal kept on *General Scott* of Fairhaven, April to June, 1843. Hocken Library, Dunedin, New Zealand, MS–0756–2.

Hooper, William. Letters. University of Hawaii.

Hunt, Caleb. Journal kept on *S. R. Sopler* of Provincetown, MA, 1865. The Kendall Whaling Museum.

King, Dr. John B. Journal kept on *Aurora* of Nantucket, 1837–1840. Nantucket Historical Association.

Lahaina Restoration Foundation. "Chronological Table," and "Notes."

Lipman, Arthur. "Medicine and Pharmacy Aboard New England Whaling Vessels: II. Drugs Used: Their Indications, Applications, Sources and Costs." Manuscript, New Bedford Free Public Library.

Lipman, Arthur, with George E. Osborne. "Medicine and Pharmacy Aboard New England Whaling Vessels." Manuscript, New Bedford Free Public Library.

Noddy, Dr. Tom. Journal kept on *Java* of New Bedford, November 30, 1854, to October 31, 1855. Old Dartmouth Historical Society–New Bedford Whaling Museum.

Owen, Dr. Robert Smith. Journal kept on *Warrens* of London, April 5, 1837, to February 12, 1840. The Kendall Whaling Museum.

Sampson, John. Journal kept on *Parnasso* of New Bedford, 1821–1823. Old Dartmouth Historical Society–New Bedford Whaling Museum.

Smart, G. M. "The Town [East Grinstead] in 1823." East Grinstead Society.

Stickney, Mary. Journal kept on *Cicero* of New Bedford, 1880. Old Dartmouth Historical Society–Bedford Whaling Museum.

Swift, Capt. John. Logbook kept on Good *Return* of New Bedford, 1844–1847. Old Dartmouth Historical Society–New Bedford Whaling Museum.

Taber, Sarah. Journal kept on *Copia* of New Bedford, 1848–1851 (item on captain killed by hand falling on him). Mariner's Museum, Newport News, VA.

Underwood, Eliza. Journal kept on *Kingsdown* of London, 1830–1831. Dixson Library, State Library of New South Wales.

Waldron, Elizabeth. Journal kept on *Bowditch* of Warren, Rhode Island, September 18, 1853 (Capt. Brown crushed with a slab of blubber). New Bedford Free Public Library.

INDEX